MAKING
READING
MATTER

MAKING READING MATTER

SHARON M. SNYDERS, Ph.D.
Ivy Tech Community College

PEARSON

Boston Columbus Indianapolis New York San Francisco Upper Saddle River
Amsterdam Cape Town Dubai London Madrid Milan Munich Paris Montreal Toronto
Delhi Mexico City Sao Paulo Sydney Hong Kong Seoul Singapore Taipei Tokyo

Editor-in-Chief: Eric Stano
Senior Acquisitions Editor: Nancy Blaine
Development Editor: Paul Sarkis
Assistant Editor: Amanda Dykstra
Editorial Assistant: Jamie Fortner
Senior Marketing Manager: Kurt Massey
Executive Digital Producer: Stefanie A. Snajder
Digital Project Manager: Janell Lantana
Senior Digital Editor: Robert St. Laurent
Project Manager: Anne Ricigliano
Project Coordination, Text Design, Art Rendering and Electronic Page Makeup: Cenveo Publisher Services
Text Permissions: Jenn Kennett, Creative Compliance
Photo Permissions: Kerri Wilson, PreMediaGlobal
Senior Cover Design Manager: Nancy Danahy
Cover Designer: Kay Petronio
Cover Photos: yuyangc/Shutterstock and Gl0ck/Shutterstock
Procurement Specialist: Mary Ann Gloriande
Printer and Binder: Quad/Graphics-Taunton
Cover Printer: Lehigh-Phoenix Color/Hagerstown

Credits and acknowledgments borrowed from other sources and reproduced, with permission, in this textbook appear on the appropriate page within text and on pages 421–425.

Lexile® is a trademark of MetaMetrics, Inc., and is registered in the United States and abroad.

1 2 3 4 5 6 7 8 9 10—QGT—14 13 12 11

www.pearsonhighered.com

ISBN-13: 978-0-13-242341-0 Student Edition
ISBN-10:   0-13-242341-3 Student Edition

ISBN-13: 978-0-13-242342-7   AIE
ISBN-10:   0-13-242342-1   AIE

DEDICATION

To my daughter Skye and my husband Mark.
Also to my students who make teaching and learning a joy!

Thanks for encouraging and blessing me every day!

—Sharon M. Snyders

Brief Contents

Detailed Contents

4 Supporting Details   145

7 Advanced Patterns of Organization 286

THEME Life and Job Skills

SPOTLIGHT ON LEARNING STYLES—LISTEN 287

Paragraphs Developed with Classification 287

Paragraphs Developed with Compare/Contrast 291

Paragraphs Developed with Cause/Effect 296

Paragraphs Developed with a Combination of Patterns 299

LEARNING STYLE ACTIVITIES 312

How to Live: Follow Your Heart, Risk Be Damned from www.cbsnews.com

A Note To Students

Welcome to a new way to read! You probably already know that reading is critical to your college life and success. When we need information or inspiration, we might look to sources such as books, magazines, newspapers, or the Internet for answers or ideas. We seek solutions from reliable sources when we care about issues. When we are interested, we read more, and when we read more, we improve our skills and become more confident and competent at reading.

Busy people are not usually willing to spend (or waste) time reading just anything. There is too much out there to read and not enough time to read it all. When we are gathering information, we may become overwhelmed with the amount of information available. We need to choose to read sources that are useful, relevant, and real. It is my hope that *Making Reading Matter* helps you reach your goals and dreams.

I wish you the best!

Sharon Snyders

Preface

I was inspired to write this textbook when I looked at my students' faces and heard their complaints about how meaningless the material was in the reading textbooks I was assigning. When I heard them talk about how they just didn't like to read or express how hard it was, I knew there had to be a better way. Many of my students told me they had never read a complete book and rarely read anything at all! It was heartbreaking to see students who had decided they would never be someone who was good at reading. My students came from different life circumstances and were dealing with many difficult and sometimes dangerous issues in their lives. I knew that if I could just find a way to get them reading, they might find answers, inspiration, and hope to change their lives.

Unique Features of This Text

Making Reading Matter is different from other reading textbooks because it includes three key features to keep students interested and help them to learn: relevant content, diverse sources, and engaging activities designed expressly for different learning styles.

This book includes the familiar structures of a reading textbook that we need for academic skills development: building vocabulary with word parts and in context, finding the main ideas and supporting details, finding implied main ideas, recognizing patterns of organization, detecting facts and opinions, and recognizing inferences.

While this book includes coverage of—and practice with—the necessary reading skills, it also includes content selected to be relevant to students. Unlike other books, many of which include unrelated excerpts from different disciplines, each chapter of *Making Reading Matter* has engaging material from diverse sources—magazines, the Internet, literature, textbooks, and other media—all of which relate to a central theme. The themes were chosen to help engage students in the process of reading, and they include topics such as life relationships, money management, and health and wellness.

Each chapter in *Making Reading Matter* also includes coverage and activities for students with different learning styles so that *all* students will improve their reading skills. At the beginning of every chapter there is a *Spotlight on Learning* box. This section highlights different learning styles and gives examples of ways the learning styles are used. Individual chapters also include collaborative projects, hands-on activities, personal reflections, and ways to use the Web to enhance reading. Activities related to each lesson are grouped together within each chapter. Multilingual learners will also find *English 2.0* boxes in each chapter designed to help students understand idioms.

Each student will have the opportunity to access and understand his or her own learning style by answering some questions in the *Get Ready to Learn* introduction of this textbook or by going to an Internet Web site. Students will also learn an effective reading strategy, *SQ3R* (presented in context in Chapter 3, "Main Ideas"), and some note-taking strategies that will help them succeed in this course as well as in other college courses.

Making Reading Matter incorporates many activities that reinforce knowledge so students can build confidence and competence with a particular skill. In addition, some activities involve new information using the latest technology and others may encourage students to get involved in current social issues.

Integrated throughout the book, students will also find the *Spotlight on Success Plan:*

Spotlight on Success Plan

PRACTICE THE NEW SKILL (three practice questions)
REVIEW WHAT YOU LEARNED (five review questions)
MASTER THE LESSON (ten section mastery questions)

The *Spotlight on Success Plan* works like this:

When a concept is first introduced, students are given an example and then three quick practice exercises. When students immediately practice the new skill, they build competence and confidence. After several concepts have been learned, students are then given a five-question review. The reviews may be more challenging as they cover more than one concept. Since the students have confidently been practicing each concept as it is presented throughout the chapter, the review will reinforce their learning. At the end of a chapter, but before the longer reading selections are presented, each chapter has two ten-question mastery tests. The mastery tests are more challenging and comprehensive for the skills presented in the chapter.

Students who have used the *Spotlight on Success Plan* have indicated they are comfortable when they know what to expect in each chapter. They can rely on the rhythm of building up to the more difficult material. They like the quick exercises when they are first learning and are more willing to tackle the challenges as the chapter progresses.

Instructors can adapt the *Spotlight on Success Plan* to fit the needs of students. When students need immediate practice to learn a new skill, they can turn to the "Practice the New Skill" exercises following the topic. If students understand the concept with just the example in class or by doing one of the three practice exercises, instructors can either skip the other exercises or assign them as homework.

The "Review What You Learned" exercises can be used as quick quizzes in class or as an out-of-class assignment. The exercises in Review are more challenging than those in Practice. Assessing the student at his level will help the instructor know if more instruction and/or practice are needed.

The "Master the Lesson" assessment is more challenging than the Practice and Review. Instructors may choose to assign one of the Mastery tests as homework or as an in-class quiz. If more practice is needed, the second Mastery test can be done.

As mentioned earlier, each chapter also includes five in-depth readings related to the chapter theme, so students can pull together the skills and practice using them on more challenging texts. The five readings at the end of each chapter come from (1) the Internet, (2) textbooks, (3) literature, (4) magazines/periodicals, and (5) visual images.

Making Reading Matter was written to give students real choices about what they read. Each chapter contains more readings than most students and professors will cover in a week or two of class. Most of the readings are only excerpts of longer, richer, and more in-depth material. All of the material has been cited to give students the reference if they'd like to read more. I carefully chose materials for this book hoping they will spark curiosity and encourage students to read more. The intent of this book is to present opportunities to become a better reader while using practical, useful, thought-provoking, entertaining, and uplifting material. It is my greatest hope as a teacher and author that students will improve their skills, confidence, and enjoyment of reading through *Making Reading Matter*.

Organization

Each chapter presents reading skills and concepts while adhering to a theme. We start Chapter 1, Vocabulary—Context Clues, with the theme of

"Exploring College." This offers tips about getting used to college and, at the same time, teaches vocabulary through context clues.

In Chapter 2, Vocabulary—Word Parts, students continue to build their vocabulary with prefixes, roots, and suffixes. The examples and exercises in this chapter are related to the theme of "Staying Healthy."

Chapter 3, Main Ideas, helps students to focus on an author's main point in paragraphs related to the theme of "Creating Better Relationships." This chapter includes readings about accepting others who are different from us and improving the relationships important in our lives. After developing the skills of finding the topic and the main idea, students can practice their skills with several longer readings at the end of the chapter. This chapter also introduces students to the SQ3R strategy for reading.

In Chapter 4, the text will guide students to better understand supporting details. This chapter uses reading material related to the theme of "Using Your Time Wisely." Material in this chapter is related to managing time at school, at work, and in personal life.

Once students have mastered finding the main idea and supporting details, they learn how to find implied main ideas in text in Chapter 5. This chapter uses the theme of "Having Fun" to develop more challenging reading skills.

In Chapters 6 and 7, students will learn to determine an author's patterns of organization. Paying attention to an author's organizational pattern helps students to read more effectively and efficiently. In Chapter 6, the readings relate to the theme of "Money Matters," and in Chapter 7, the readings relate to the theme of "Job and Life Skills."

Chapter 8 helps students begin to develop the skills of separating facts from opinions. Using the theme of "Staying Current," exercises and activities are used to develop students' ability to distinguish opinions from facts, while also exposing them to issues related to politics, populations, and poverty.

Once students can tell the difference between facts and opinions, they learn to make Inferences. Chapter 9 helps students to read between the lines and begin to draw important conclusions in reading. In this chapter, the theme "What Are My Dreams?" offers true stories and articles about people who have achieved their personal, academic, and career goals.

With the help of *Making Reading Matter*, my hope is that students will develop the ability to examine written materials, explore diverse sources, and determine their usefulness for real decisions that need to be made in life.

Supplements to Accompany
Making Reading Matter

Instructor's Manual and Test Bank (ISBN 013242343X). The Instructor's Manual features lecture hints, in-class activities, handouts, and quizzes to accompany each chapter, as well as sample course outlines and other helpful resources for structuring and managing a developmental reading course. The Test Bank consists of two multiple-choice tests per chapter. The Instructor's Manual and Test Bank is available both in print and for download from Pearson's Instructor Resource Center (www.pearsonhighered.com/irc). Written by Mary Jeffery.

Pearson MyTest Test Bank (ISBN 0205900623). Pearson MyTest is a powerful assessment generation program that helps instructors easily create and print quizzes, study guides, and exams. Select questions are drawn from the Instructor's Manual and Test Bank to accompany *Making Reading Matter* and from other developmental reading test banks. Unique questions may be added. Save the finished test as a Word document or PDF to export it to WebCT or BlackBoard. Available at www.pearsonmytest.com.

PowerPoint Presentation (ISBN 0205210759). PowerPoint presentations to accompany each chapter consist of classroom-ready lecture outline slides, lecture tips and classroom activities, and review questions. Available for download from Pearson's Instructor Resource Center. Written by Mary Jeffery.

Answer Key (ISBN 0205116566). The Answer Key contains the solutions to the exercises in the student edition of the text. Available for download from Pearson's Instructor Resource Center.

Annotated Instructor's Edition (ISBN 0132423421). An annotated instructor's edition is available for this text. It provides answers to the activities and exercises in the text printed on the write-on lines that follow each exercise.

Acknowledgments

Thank you to the following reviewers who took their time to read various versions of the manuscript and provide valuable suggestions to improve this series.

Karin Alderfer, *Miami Dade College*

Angela Barber, *Pearl River Community College*

Kathy Barker, *Grays Harbor College*

Marie Barnes, *Wayne Community College*

Gary Bergstorm, *College of the Desert*

Meredith Bohne, *Quinsigamond Community College*

Denise Clay, *Fullerton College*

Beth Conomos, *Erie Community College*

Mike Costello, *New Mexico College*

Julia Erben, *Gulf Coast Community College*

Dr. Xiwu Feng, *LaGuardia Community College*

Teresa Fugate, *Lindsey Wilson College*

Carol Hagan, *Jefferson College*

Kayla Gardner Harding, *Tulsa Community College*

Elaine Herrick, *Temple College*

Dr. Mary Huffer, *Lake Sumter Community College*

Debbie Lee, *Nash Community College*

Diana Mareth, *Del Mar College*

Peter M. Marcoux, *El Camino College*

Linda Mininger, *Harrisburg Area Community College*

Julianne Myers, *Vincennes University*

Cindy Ortega, *Phoenix College*

Cynthia Ross, *State College of Florida*

Miriam Simon, *Montgomery College*

Diane Schellak, *Burlington County College*

Majorie Sussman, *Miami Dade College*

Michelle Van de Sande, *Arapahoe Community College*

Sonja Yturralde, *Imperial Valley College*

I appreciate your honest constructive criticism as well as your encouragement throughout the developmental process. Hearing what you and your students need kept me motivated to work hard to improve the books!

In addition, I want to thank Nancy Blaine and her assistant, Jamie Fortner, from Pearson for their immeasurable work on this book. I thank my editor, Paul Sarkis, for his ideas and support along the way as the text was being developed. Thank you to Pearson's Production, Marketing, Permissions, and Supplements departments for all their hard work to take care of the details. I also want to thank Pearson's sales teams, especially Ted Krischak, for encouraging me and working so hard to make sure everyone gets the books and materials they need for successful learning.

Sincere thanks to my colleagues at Ivy Tech Community College, Purdue University, the Indiana Association for Developmental Educators (INADE), the National Association for Developmental Educators (NADE), and the College Reading and Learning Association (CRLA) for their great discussions and ideas, for sending me articles and books their students like, for trying out many of my exercises and readings with their own students, and for giving me honest feedback over the past several years.

Thanks to my students for letting me know what they like and don't like and for telling me when the exercises are engaging and when I need to change them. I also thank my students for being excited to try new activities and ways of learning—you continue to make teaching and writing a joy!

Deepest thanks to my family, neighbors, and friends, who often heard much more about the book than they probably need or wanted to know. Special thanks to our dear friends Pastor Stacy and Kim Littlefield and my wonderful sisters, Lorrie Tracy, Donna Nevin, Debbi Pelligrini, and Marybeth Chappell who have read to me and shared inspirational words all my life—thanks for being so encouraging and supportive. Thanks as well to Doug and Kristy Griffin for your constant and meaningful encouragement.

Thanks so much to my very loving daughter Skye and husband Mark for all the times you patiently listened as I brainstormed or shared material and for the many creative ideas you shared!

Finally, I want to thank the readers, non-readers, and soon-to-be-discovered readers, who have inspired me and kept me motivated during the times I didn't think I could do all the work required to bring this book to life. I know what knowledge and joy are in store for you as you discover your abilities! My hope is for every person to experience liberation through reading and understanding any type of material life presents. Thanks for giving me this opportunity to share the empowerment and joy of reading with you!

—Sharon M. Snyders

Introduction: Get Ready to Learn

Spotlight on Learning Styles

One of the best things you can do for yourself and for your success as a student is to discover your learning preference. The VARK Questionnaire is one of many different assessment tools available. You may take the questionnaire online by logging onto the website www.vark-learn.com and by following the directions.

Now that you know your learning preferences, you can choose strategies and techniques that will work best for you. Throughout *Making Reading Matter* there are several activities to accompany each skill. Consider trying the activities which best match your learning style preference.

In *Making Reading Matter* we will be referring to the different learning styles as

Look (seeing)

Listen (hearing)

Write (using written words)

Do (hands-on, experiencing)

Think about how you can use your strengths and preferences to maximize your learning.

Reading Techniques (SQ3R)

SQ3R is simply an organized strategy for reading. The letters in the acronym represent the steps in the strategy: S is for Survey; Q is for Question; and 3R is for Read, Recite, and Review. It may seem strange at first, but once you've practiced it a few times, SQ3R will become a useful technique for you to use when you read. You'll be able to stay focused on the material and retain the important information.

Survey	Skim over the material. Read the title, subtitle, subheadings, first and last paragraphs, pictures, charts, and graphics. Note italics and bold print.
Question	Ask yourself questions before you read. What do you want to know? Turn headings and subheadings into questions and/or read questions if provided.
Read	Read the material in manageable chunks. This may be one or two paragraphs at a time or under one subheading at a time.
Recite	Recite the answer to each question in your own words. This is a good time to write notes as you read each section. Repeat the question-read-recite cycle.
Review	Look over your notes at the end of the chapter, article, or material. Review what you learned and write a summary in your own words.

The SQ3R strategy is discussed in detail in Chapter 3. You will have the opportunity to learn about it more in depth and practice using it in a structured way.

Note-taking Strategies

Active Reading

Before you do anything else—get out a pencil and maybe highlighters. Now, as you read, write things down.

(Circle ideas) you want to remember.

Jot down notes in the margin of the text *NOTES, NOTES, NOTES*

Underline important concepts.

Write abbreviations for important definitions (def.) and examples (ex.).

If you like color, and are a visual learner, use highlighters.

Have paper nearby so you can write additional notes as you read.

Also, as you use the SQ3R strategy, you are doing more than letting your eyes move across the paper from left to right. You are now thinking about the text before you read, while you are reading, and when you are finished. You are asking questions and finding answers. You are processing what you read more than once, which will lead to better comprehension and deeper understanding of the material.

1 Vocabulary – Context Clues

LEARNING OUTCOMES

LO1 Use shortcuts and time-savers while you read.

LO2 Use clues to guess the meaning of unknown words.

THEME – Exploring College

SPOTLIGHT ON LEARNING STYLES 🔊)) L<small>ISTEN</small>

Have you ever been talking with someone and then heard a word or expression you didn't know? So, what do you do if you don't want to ask? You listen to the conversation for clues about what it means. One time I was talking to a co-worker about a student who was very annoying and disrespectful in a class toward the professor and the other students. My co-worker said, "I know what you mean; she has a major *tude*." I had never heard that expression *tude*. But I kept listening. She continued, "The student has a *chip on her shoulder* and she seems to be daring someone to knock it off as soon as she walks in the room." I had heard of the term *chip on her shoulder* and knew it meant someone who has a bad attitude and holds grudges, often inviting confrontations. My co-worker added, "That student will only make it in school if she learns how to keep her attitude out of the classroom. She needs to get some help with her anger issues and learn how to act in college." I thought about what I heard and used my listening learning style to figure out that *tude* means *attitude* and in this situation, a *negative attitude*.

Attending college means dealing with change in your life.

- You may have just graduated, or you may be returning to school after taking several years off.
- You may be raising a family, or you could be living with your parents, roommates, or on your own.
- You may live five minutes from your campus, or you could have a long commute.
- You may have worked for years and just been laid off by your company.
- You may have had a medical or personal situation and needed to find a new career.
- You may be returning from serving in the military.
- You may be looking to make a change in occupation so you can do something different.
- You may be tired of living paycheck to paycheck and want something better for yourself and your family.
- You may not know what you want to do, but you think that getting a college degree is a good way to start.

No matter what your background or your situation is, every student has this in common: Succeeding in college requires taking the unique skills you've already developed in your life and applying those skills to new situations. Many things may seem strange, frustrating, or maybe even overwhelming when you first start college. But, you will do fine if you keep a positive attitude and try to apply your previous knowledge to your new situation. An open mind will help you to learn new strategies, skills, and ideas, and to adjust to these new expectations.

You have the opportunity today to move forward and create the life you desire. You will select your major and many of the courses you wish to take. You will also choose where and how you will spend your energy and your time. And even when the to-do list is getting longer, you still have a choice! Managing your time and using it wisely may be the most important skill you develop as you adjust to the demands of college.

Shortcuts, Time-savers, and Educated Guessing

Reading college level textbooks, professional magazines, and research articles may take up much of your time while you are in college. Learning new

> **LO1**
> Use shortcuts and time-savers while you read.

vocabulary for specific majors may also require more effort as you move forward in your studies.

Reading without knowing vocabulary words can be frustrating. You can be going along at a good pace and then get stuck. When you are unsure what the author means, you have to figure out what to do. What are your choices?

- Ask someone what the word means, or maybe skip over the word.
- Get out a dictionary or look up the word online.

But these alternatives can feel irritating or discouraging, too. You may even want to quit reading.

One strategy for learning vocabulary is to use clues from the sentence or surrounding paragraph to figure out the meaning of the words you don't know. It is just like what you probably already do when you listen to people talk and are unsure of a word or phrase. Paying attention to the clues surrounding a word is a skill that really works. This chapter helps you to build on what you already know about looking for clues and helps you refine it to use with reading for college.

Using Vocabulary in Context (What clues can help me figure out the word?)

Context clues give the reader some hints about the meaning of the unknown word using the surrounding text (or context). You probably have already successfully used this technique throughout your life as you came upon unfamiliar words. The strategy requires paying attention to the surrounding text for hints about the unknown word.

> **LO2**
> Use clues to guess the meaning of unknown words.

For example, if you were asked to state the meaning of *colossal,* it might be difficult to figure it out without some background knowledge. But, the better the context clues found in the text, the easier time you will have guessing the meaning.

Try to guess the meaning of the word *colossal* with the clues given in the sentences below.

I received a colossal assignment. _____

The meaning of *colossal* isn't clear yet since several different words could describe an assignment. For example, it could mean easy, complicated, big, or small.

I know I'll have trouble getting the colossal assignment done by the due

date. _____

With the extra clues, you know that *colossal* has something to do with not being able to get the assignment done on time. You know it doesn't mean an easy or simple assignment.

The assignment was so colossal, I had to break it down into smaller parts

and try to get one step done at a time. _____

The extra clues of breaking it down into smaller parts helps you guess that *colossal* means huge or complicated.

*The assignment was the largest I had ever seen. It was **colossal!**_____*

Now you've got it! The more clues you read, the easier it became to correctly guess the meaning was "huge." The clue *largest* finally gave it away.

As you read through the strategies and work through the practice exercises in this chapter, you will improve your ability to learn new words by paying attention to the clues in the sentences and using them to make educated guesses about their meanings. One suggestion is to highlight the context clues in the sentences to help you determine the meanings.

Four Types of Context Clues

1. Synonyms and Definitions
2. Antonyms
3. Examples
4. Experience, Prior Knowledge, and Perception

 Synonyms and Definitions

Synonym clues are words that mean the same as the unknown word. Authors sometimes give the definition of a word right in the sentence. The meaning of the new word is easier to guess if you use the punctuation, such as commas or dashes, to help identify the definition. Textbook authors often use this technique to help students learn new words.

A synonym clue may also be in the sentence before or after the sentence with the unknown word.

EXAMPLE ──

Directions: Circle the word or phrase that best matches the italicized word. Use the highlighted context clues to help find the meaning.

1. Being *attentive* in class is useful. Concentrating on what the professor says will help you get the most from a class.

   a. energetic   c. sympathetic
   b. focused   d. realistic

2. Most instructors will hand out a *syllabus*, or course outline, the first week of class.

   a. reading list   c. course outline
   b. sign-up sheet   d. attendance sheet

In question 1, *attentive* means the same as concentrating on what the professor says. Therefore, the correct answer is (b) focused. In question 2, the meaning of *syllabus* is (c) course outline. It is defined right after the word in the sentence and is set apart with commas.

PRACTICE THE NEW SKILL

Directions: Circle the word or phrase that best matches the italicized word. Highlight the context clues in each sentence.

1. Jen had to deal with many *obstacles* to succeed in college. She dealt with several issues that seemed to get in her way.

    a. things that are annoying   **c.** things that are critical

    b. things that get in the way   **d.** things that are interesting

2. Many students have mixed feelings, or are *ambivalent*, about starting college.

    a. nervous   **c.** confident

    b. unsure   **d.** angry

3. Terry now considered his high school work *insufficient*. The work he did was not enough to prepare him for the demands of college level classes.

    a. not secure   **c.** not enough

    b. not impressive   **d.** not fun

Antonyms

Antonym clues are words that mean the opposite of the unknown word. In this case you will need to look for clues that contrast with the unknown word. One hint is to look for signal words such as *in contrast to, as opposed to, while, on the other hand, but, on the contrary,* or *rather than.*

EXAMPLE

Directions: Circle the word or phrase that best matches the italicized word. Use the highlighted context clues to help find the meaning.

1. Professors do not expect students to have *self-confidence* in the subject they are learning. *On the contrary,* they expect students to feel the need for assistance in what they are learning.

    a. don't feel the need for assistance

    b. feel the need for assistance

    c. feel the need for reminders

    d. don't feel the need for reminders

2. Students who ask for help at the learning center *prior* to an assign-ment's due date tend to do well as opposed to those who wait until after they receive a poor grade to ask for help.

   a. during   **c.** before

   b. after   **d.** at the same time

In question 1, *self-confidence* means (a) don't feel the need for assis-tance. You can see that the second sentence is the opposite of the first sentence because of the clue "on the contrary." In question 2, the meaning of *prior* is (c) before. The clue is the phrase "as opposed to" showing the opposite meaning of *prior* is "after."

PRACTICE THE NEW SKILL

Directions: Circle the word or phrase that best matches the italicized word. Highlight the context clues in each sentence.

1. When thinking about choosing a major, don't *overlook* your college's career center. On the contrary, pay attention to the center's self-assessment inventories.

   a. ignore   **c.** obtain

   b. overestimate   **d.** visit

2. It is easier to stay alert in class if you sit up straight rather than *slouch* in your seat.

   a. sit up straight   **c.** sleep

   b. bend downward   **d.** daydream

3. Knowing your *aptitudes* can help you select a career; however, knowing what areas are not your talents can also help you evaluate possible career choices.

   a. attitude   **c.** experience

   b. friends   **d.** talents

 ## Examples

Authors also may give examples of a concept to help the reader understand the meaning of a word. When looking for examples it is important to think about what the author is trying to explain and maybe make a picture or a movie in your mind.

EXAMPLE

Directions: Circle the word or phrase that best matches the italicized word. Use the highlighted context clues to help find the meaning.

1. *Prioritizing* your responsibilities is like doing your homework before you go out with your friends.

   a. simplifying jobs

   b. making things equal

   c. avoiding tasks

   d. choosing the most important activity first

2. Talking to classmates and people in the student lounge are two ways to *socialize*.

   a. meet people

   c. be political

   b. study

   d. contribute

In question 1, the sentence shows that one way to prioritize responsibilities is to do your homework before you go out with your friends. This is the same as (d), choosing the most important activity first. In question 2, two examples of ways to socialize are included—talking to classmates and people in the student lounge. These are examples of ways to (a) meet people.

PRACTICE THE NEW SKILL

Directions: Circle the word that best matches the italicized word. Highlight the context clues in each sentence.

1. Keeping a good attitude, managing your time, and eliminating distractions will all *contribute* to your success in college.

   a. hurt

   c. avoid

   b. add

   d. mock

2. *Academic* success includes completing assignments and getting good grades.

   a. school

   c. social

   b. athletic

   d. financial

3. Eliminating personal *distractions* such as television, Internet, and cell phone interruptions are important if you want to concentrate on school work.

   a. needs

   b. disappointments

   c. disruptions

   d. misunderstandings

 ### Experience, Prior Knowledge, and Perception

You may also use your own experiences to help you learn new words. Think about situations at work, home, or activities in your life. You might also think about stories you've heard or read about and people you've known. It may be useful to create an image in your mind as you read the sentences. Then try to replace the unknown word with a word that makes sense. You may need to use the rest of the text to figure out the meaning of the unknown word. Sometimes simply reading further into the paragraph will reveal the clues you need.

EXAMPLE

Directions: Circle the word or phrase that best matches the italicized word. Use the highlighted context clues to help find the meaning.

1. The first week of school was so *intimidating*. Jeff was afraid he would get lost on the campus, be late to his classes, or forget his books.

   a. inviting

   b. scary

   c. fun

   d. social

2. Discovering your *learning style* will help you study more effectively. Do you learn best when you work with your hands or when you read and reflect? Or, do you learn best when you see and draw ideas or when you listen and talk over ideas with other people? If you use the method that works best for you it will be easier to stay focused and to remember what you are studying.

   a. habits for learning

   b. way you learn best

   c. place you learn best

   d. weaknesses

In question 1, getting lost, being late to class, or forgetting your books may be scary. Therefore, the best match for the word *intimidating* is (b). In question 2, as you read through all the sentences, it becomes clear that *learning style* means (b), the way you learn best.

PRACTICE *THE NEW SKILL*

Directions: Circle the word that best matches the italicized word. Highlight the context clues in each sentence.

1. Students must complete the *requirements* of the assignment to earn a good grade. If the professor expects a minimum of two double-spaced pages, the student will not earn an "A" if she turns in only a page and a half.

   a. homework   **c.** margins

   b. citations   **d.** expectations

2. Krystal worked very hard studying for the midterm. When she saw her grade was an "A" she was *elated*—she even jumped up and down and cheered!

   a. overjoyed   **c.** jealous

   b. joking   **d.** disappointed

3. People often have to overcome *barriers* in their lives before they succeed in college. Financial situations, poor academic preparation, job responsibilities, and low self-image are just a few examples of things that may prevent students from doing well in school.

   a. successes   **c.** friends

   b. challenges   **d.** fences

Putting Context Clues all Together

When we read, it helps if we pay attention to all the clues given in the text. Look at the following example to see how several context clues lead to the meaning of an unknown word.

EXAMPLE

Directions: Examine how the word ***perseverance*** is used in the paragraph to see if there are any context clues to the meaning.

Susan knew that she would need a great deal of ***perseverance*** to get through the most difficult classes in college. She would need to keep trying no matter how long it took to understand the concepts.

Think about what each of the highlighted phrases means or what clues it gives you.

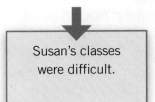

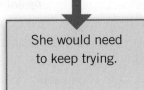

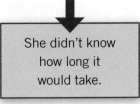

Together, these facts let you predict (or infer) that ***perseverance***

means _____

Answer: *Perseverance* means determination, to keep trying.

PRACTICE THE NEW SKILL

Directions: Examine how the word or phrase is used in the sentence or paragraph to see if there are any context clues to the meaning.

1. ***academic integrity***

   "Having *academic integrity* means valuing education and learning over grades. It is following a code of moral values, prizing honesty and fairness in all aspects of academic life—classes, assignments, tests, papers, projects, and relationships with students and faculty."

   Source: Excerpt from *Keys to Success: Building Analytical, Creative, and Practical Skills,* 6th Edition, p. 15 by Carol Carter, Joyce Bishop, Sarah Kravits, Judy Block. Copyright © 2009 by Carol Carter, Joyce Bishop, Sarah Kravits, Judy Block. Printed and Electronically reproduced by permission of Pearson Education, Inc., Upper Saddle River, New Jersey.

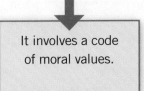

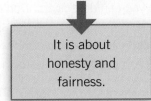

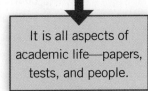

Together, these facts let you infer that *academic integrity* means _____

_____

_____

2. *violated*

Unfortunately, the principles of academic integrity are frequently ***violated*** on college campuses. In a recent survey, three of four college students admitted to cheating at least once during their undergraduate careers. Violations of academic integrity—turning in previously submitted work, using unauthorized devices during an exam, providing unethical aid to another student, or downloading passages or whole papers from the Internet—aren't worth the price. Consequences of violations vary from school to school and include participation in academic integrity seminars, grade reductions or course failure, suspension, or expulsion.

Source: Excerpt from *Keys to Success: Building Analytical, Creative, and Practical Skills,* 6th Edition, p. 16 by Carol Carter, Joyce Bishop, Sarah Kravits, Judy Block. Copyright © 2009 by Carol Carter, Joyce Bishop, Sarah Kravits, Judy Block. Printed and Electronically reproduced by permission of Pearson Education, Inc., Upper Saddle River, New Jersey.

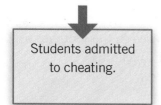

Students admitted to cheating.

Examples of violations listed.

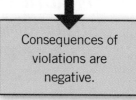

Consequences of violations are negative.

Using context clues, you can infer ***violated*** means _____

3. *accomplish*

Take a moment to *acknowledge* what you ***accomplish***, whether it is a good grade, a job offer, or any personal victory. Let your success fuel your confidence that you can do it again. Don't forget to reward yourself when you succeed. Take the kind of break you like best—see a movie, socialize with some friends, read a book for fun, declare a no-work day. Enjoy what college has to offer outside the classroom.

Source: Excerpt from *Keys to Success: Building Analytical, Creative, and Practical Skills,* 6th Edition, p. 17 by Carol Carter, Joyce Bishop, Sarah Kravits, Judy Block. Copyright © 2009 by Carol Carter, Joyce Bishop, Sarah Kravits, Judy Block. Printed and Electronically reproduced by permission of Pearson Education, Inc., Upper Saddle River, New Jersey.

Acknowledge—recognize

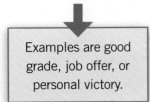

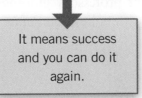

Using context clues, you can infer *accomplish* means _____

REVIEW WHAT YOU LEARNED

Vocabulary in Context

Directions: Circle the word or phrase that best matches the correct meaning of the italicized word. Highlight the context clues in the sentence.

1. An *apathetic* student will not do well in school. The student who is uncaring will eventually fail.

   a. uncaring

   b. angry

   c. caring

   d. happy

2. Scott was *wary* of some of his old friends' habits. He was cautious because of their lack of self discipline.

   a. cautious

   b. confident

   c. wishful

   d. overwhelmed

3. The professor told us we would need to use a *particular* dictionary for the class. She wanted everyone to be using the same definitions from the same source when we learned new words.

   a. expensive

   b. large

   c. specific

   d. modern

4. Building *rapport* with your instructors can be done by asking questions during class or visiting with them during their office hours.

   a. a relationship

   b. bridges

   c. respect

   d. an idea

5. Knowing your professors' grading *criteria* will help you meet their expectations throughout the semester.

    a. applications

    b. requirements

    c. considerations

    d. transcripts

REVIEW WHAT YOU LEARNED

Vocabulary in Context

Directions: Circle the word or phrase that matches the correct meaning of the italicized word. Highlight the context clues in each sentence.

1. In college you will need to be *diligent*, or hard working, to succeed.

    a. dedicated

    b. hard working

    c. careful with money

    d. succeed

2. College is exciting because you set your own career goals and then the program of study and specific courses that will best prepare you for your *vocation*.

    a. vacation

    b. career or job

    c. audition

    d. portfolio

3. It may take a few weeks to become *accustomed* to being a college student. Once you are adjusted to the new routine it will be easier.

    a. skeptical

    b. easier

    c. eager

    d. adjusted

4. Maria will do well in our class since she is *receptive* to new ideas, unlike Kelsey, who thinks she knows it all.

    a. open

    b. adjusted

    c. opposed

    d. hostile

5. It is *imperative* that he find a parking spot if he expects to get to class on time.

    a. demanding

    b. unlikely

    c. important

    d. irrelevant

/MASTER THE LESSON/

Vocabulary in Context

Directions: Read the passage below. Use context clues and the dictionary to find the meaning of the bold words.

1   Don't worry. Making an ***ally*** of a professor is not a difficult task. Professors enjoy interacting with their students; it is often the only feedback they get on how well they are doing their job. To create a meaningful connection, you should begin with regular attendance at office hours. Some students worry that they don't have any specific problems to discuss. The secret is to be ***observant.*** There are many more opportunities to speak with a professor than you might realize at first. When you are working on a paper, you can see the professor to talk about possible topics, then again to get feedback on the idea you selected, and then again to check the structure of your argument once you begin writing. When an exam is approaching, you can ask for ***clarification*** on particularly difficult material covered in class. And if you are in a technical class, the door is always open to discuss homework problems or concepts that you can't quite grasp.

2   If these efforts result in a strong *rapport*, allow your conversations to shift gradually from specific class-related issues to academic advice in general. Keep this ***dialogue*** open even after the semester ends, making sure to keep in touch with the professor on a regular basis. Swing by his or her office every once in a while to give an update on how things are going. If the professor offers other courses relevant to your interests, make a point of taking them. By demonstrating such a concentrated effort to learn from the wisdom of your target professor, over time, he or she will develop a *vested* interest in your success.

3   This approach is not **feckless brown-nosing**, so ignore those who suggest otherwise. Befriending a professor is about fulfilling the perfectly natural desire to have a more experienced person guide you through a complicated and exciting period of your life. It's a ***mutually*** beneficial relationship that provides the professor with a sense of impact and fulfillment, and provides you with a variety of wonderful new opportunities and *counsel*. Leave the ***shiny red apple***

Rapport—relationship, bond, connection
Vested—committed
Counsel—advice, guidance, direction

15

at home—a serious professional relationship is a sign of a serious commitment to your academic career.

Source: Newport, Cal. (2005). *How to Win at College: Surprising Secrets for Success from the Country's Top Students.* New York: Broadway Books, Random House, p. 22.

ENGLISH 2.0

feckless brown-nosing means: ineffective (feckless) words and/or actions that will boost another person's ego to gain favor

shiny red apple means: something a child would give to a teacher to gain favor

---

1. *ally*

Making an *ally* of a professor is not a difficult task. Professors enjoy interacting with their students; it is often the only feedback they get on how well they are doing their job. To create a meaningful connection, you should begin with regular attendance at office hours.

Professors enjoy interacting with their students.

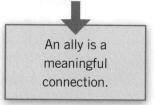

An ally is a meaningful connection.

Using context clues, you can infer *ally* means _____.

2. *observant*

The secret is to be *observant*. There are many more opportunities to speak with a professor than you might realize at first. When you are working on a paper, you can see the professor to talk about possible topics, then again to get feedback on the idea you selected, and then again to check the structure of your argument once you begin writing.

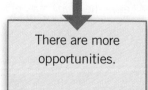

There are more opportunities.

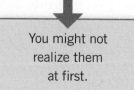

You might not realize them at first.

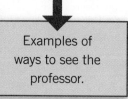

Examples of ways to see the professor.

Using context clues, you can infer **_observant_** means _____

3. *clarification*

When an exam is approaching, you can ask for **_clarification_** on particularly difficult material covered in class. And if you are in a technical class, the door is always open to discuss homework problems or concepts that you can't quite grasp.

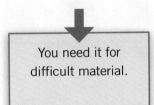

You need it for difficult material.

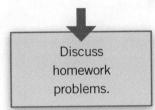

Discuss homework problems.

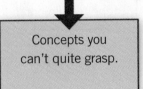

Concepts you can't quite grasp.

Using context clues, you can infer **_clarification_** means _____

4. *dialogue*

If these efforts result in a strong *rapport*, allow your conversations to shift gradually from specific class-related issues to academic advice in general. Keep this **_dialogue_** open even after the semester ends, making sure to keep in touch with the professor on a regular basis. Swing by his or her office every once in a while to give an update on how things are going.

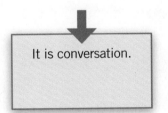

It is conversation.

It means to keep in touch.

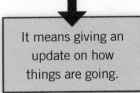

It means giving an update on how things are going.

Using context clues, you can infer **_dialogue_** means _____

5. *mutually*

This approach is not feckless brown-nosing, so ignore those who suggest otherwise. Befriending a professor is about fulfilling the perfectly natural desire to have a more experienced person guide you through a complicated and exciting period of your life. It's a *mutually* beneficial relationship that provides the professor with a sense of impact and fulfillment, and provides you with a variety of wonderful new opportunities and *counsel*. Leave the shiny red apple at home—a serious professional relationship is a sign of a serious commitment to your academic career.

It provides the professor with impact and fullfillment.	It provides you with opportunities and counsel.	It is a beneficial relationship.

Using context clues, you can infer *mutually* means _____

MASTER THE LESSON

Vocabulary in Context

Directions: Read the passage below. Use context clues and the dictionary to find the meaning of the bold words.

Mark Jones: SCANA Senior Customer Service Trainer; Columbia, SC

1   Basically, I had to make a hard, ***life-altering*** decision. I did not want to live my life in debt as my father had, so I made up my mind that I would have to take a few steps back to eventually go forward. I began to look for a job that offered educational benefits. I scanned the phone book for hospitals, utility companies, banks, and government agencies that offered this benefit. Every Monday night, their job lines would be updated and I would call, fill out an application, and wait. Nothing!

2   Finally, I learned how to properly fill out an application. I would call the job lines many times and write down every word in their advertisements. Then, I would craft my application and letter based on *their needs,* not *my experiences.* I had to learn to apply for a job as if I already had it. After two years and many attempts to ***secure*** a ***suitable*** position, a utility company hired me—AND they had educational benefits. Finally, I could go back to school and get another car! I began working toward my degree and after six long, hard years, I graduated with a Bachelor of Science in business management. It was not easy, as I am sure you know. I had to take some courses online, and I was in class every Friday night for years and years.

3   During my time in college, I worked my way up in the company and today, 17 years later, I am a senior trainer for SCANA, an $11 billion Fortune 500 utility holding company founded in 1846. I design training programs and development materials for new hires, system enhancements, and employee upgrades.

4   I look back on my childhood and early adulthood and I am proud of the fact that I did not let my past or my family ***dictate*** my future. I survived. I refused to ***succumb*** to their life. I knew that I had to have my own life with my own fate. You can have this too. Never let your past or your family tell you what you're capable of doing. Take chances. Take risks. And, if you have to take a step backward to go forward, never be ashamed to do that, too.

Source: Excerpt from *Cornerstone: Creating Success Through Positive Change,* 6th Edition, pp. 362–363 by Robert M. Sherfield and Patricia G. Moody. Copyright © 2011 by Robert M. Sherfield and Patricia G. Moody. Printed and Electronically reproduced by permission of Pearson Education, Inc., Upper Saddle River, New Jersey.

1. *life-altering*

Basically, I had to make a hard, ***life-altering*** decision. I did not want to live my life in debt as my father had, so I made up my mind that I would have to take a few steps back to eventually go forward.

  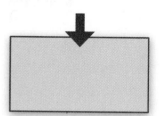

Using context clues, you can infer ***life-altering*** means _____.

2. *secure*

I had to learn to apply for a job as if I already had it. After two years and many attempts to ***secure*** a suitable position, a utility company hired me—AND they had educational benefits.

 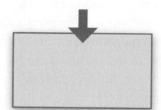 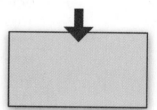

Using context clues, you can infer ***secure*** means _____.

3. *suitable*

After two years and many attempts to secure a ***suitable*** position, a utility company hired me—AND they had educational benefits. Finally, I could go back to school and get another car!

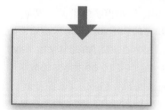  

Using context clues, you can infer ***suitable*** means _____.

4. *dictate*

I look back on my childhood and early adulthood and I am proud of the fact that I did not let my past or my family **dictate** my future. I survived. I refused to succumb to their life. I knew that I had to have my own life with my own fate. You can have this too. Never let your past or your family tell you what you're capable of doing.

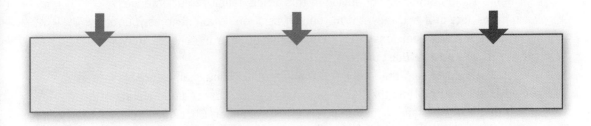

Using context clues, you can infer **dictate** means _____.

5. *succumb*

I look back on my childhood and early adulthood and I am proud of the fact that I did not let my past or my family dictate my future. I survived. I refused to **succumb** to their life. I knew that I had to have my own life with my own fate. You can have this too. Never let your past or your family tell you what you're capable of doing.

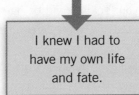

I survived.

I knew I had to have my own life and fate.

Never let your past or family limit you.

Using context clues, you can infer **succumb** means _____.

LEARNING STYLE ACTIVITIES

*L*ook, *L*isten, *W*rite, *D*o

Choosing a College Major:
How to Chart Your Ideal Path

1   The most important piece of advice in this article follows this sentence, so please make note of it and repeat it to yourself as often as you need as you read this article and make decisions regarding choosing a major in college. Are you ready for it? The advice: **Don't panic.**

2   I know it's easier said than done, but I can't tell you how many students I have advised since the time that I have been a professor that seem in a state of panic if they are uncertain of their major, let alone a career. Choosing a major, thinking about a career, getting an education—these are the things college is all about. Yes, there are some students who arrive on campus and know exactly their major and career ambitions, but the majority of students do not, thus there is no need to rush into a decision about your major as soon as you step on campus.

3   And guess what? A majority of students in all colleges and universities change their major at least once in their college careers; and many change their major several times over the course of their college career.

4   This article is all about giving you some pointers and direction—some steps for you to take—in your journey toward discovering that ideal career path for you. But it is a journey, so make sure you spend some time thinking about it before making a decision. And don't be discouraged if you still don't have a major the first time you take this journey ... your goal should be narrowing your focus from all possible majors to a few areas that you can then explore in greater depth.

5   Please also keep in mind that many schools have double majors, some triple majors, and most minors as well as majors. Way back when I was an undergraduate at Syracuse University, I was a dual major in marketing and magazine journalism. Today I am a college professor and Webmaster of a top career resources Website . . . which brings me to the last piece of general advice before you begin your journey: your major in college is important for your first job after graduation, but studies show that most people will change careers— yes, careers—about four or five times over the course of their lives—and no major exists that can prepare you for that!

6   The **first** stop on your journey should be an examination or self-assessment of your interests. What types of things excite you? What types of jobs or careers appeal to you? If you are not sure, start the process at Quintessential Careers:

Career Assessment. Also, many, if not all, college career centers have a variety of self-tests you can take to help you answer some of these questions.

7   The **second** stop on your journey is an examination of your abilities. What are your strengths? What are your weaknesses? What kind of skills do you have? You can begin this self-examination by looking at the courses you took in high school. What were your best subjects? Is there a pattern there? What kinds of extracurricular activities did you participate in while in high school? What kinds of things did you learn from part-time or summer jobs? While you can only do part of it now, you may want to skim through our article, Using a SWOT Analysis in Your Career Planning.

8   The **third** stop on your journey involves examining what you value in work. Examples of values include: helping society, working under pressure, group affili- ation, stability, security, status, pacing, working alone or with groups, having a positive impact on others, and many others. Again, a visit to your college's career center should help. You can also check out our Workplace Values Assessment for Job-Seekers, which examines what you value in your job, your career, and your work.

9   The **fourth** stop on your journey is career exploration. The University of Cali- fornia at Berkeley offers Career Exploration Links—Occupations, which allows you to explore a general list of occupations or search for a specific occupation and provides links to resources that give you lots of information about the occupation(s) you choose. There are many schools that offer similar "what can I do with a major in . . . ?" fact sheets or Websites, but one of my favorites is at Ashland University. You can also learn more about various occupations, includ- ing future trends, by searching the Bureau of Labor Statistics' Occupational Outlook Handbook. You can find all these resources—and more—at Quintessen- tial Careers: Career Exploration Tools.

10   The **fifth** stop on your journey is the reality check. You need to honestly evaluate your options. Do you really value physicians and have an interest in being a doctor, but have little skills in science? Does your occupation require an advanced degree, but your future commitments preclude graduate study? Do you have a strong interest in the arts, but your family is convinced you will become a CPA like your father? There are often ways to get around some of the obstacles during the reality check, but it is still important to face these obstacles and be realistic about whether you can get around them.

11   The **sixth** and final stop on your journey is the task of narrowing your choices and focusing on choosing a major. Based on all your research and self-assess- ment of the first five stops on your journey, you should now have a better idea

of the careers/majors you are not interested in pursuing as well as a handful of potential careers/majors that do interest you. What are the typical majors found at a comprehensive university? Visit Quintessential Careers: College Majors for a listing of the typical college majors.

Use our Choosing a College Major Worksheet to assist you in your quest.

12   What are some other resources for helping you get more information about a major and/or a career?

Take advantage of:

- Your **college's course catalog**—you'll be amazed at the wealth of information you can find here . . . from required courses to specialized majors and tracks.
- Your professors, including your academic adviser—talk with your professors, whether you have taken a class with them or not . . . many of them have worked in the field in which they teach and all are experts about careers and career opportunities.
- Your **classmates**, especially upperclassmen—these are the folk who are deep into their major, perhaps already having had an internship or gone through job interviews . . . use them as a resource to gather more information.
- Your **college's alumni**—unless your college was just founded, your school probably has a deep and varied group of alums, many of whom like to talk with current students . . . so use them as a resource to gather more information about careers.
- Your **family and friends**—there's a wealth of information right at your fingertips. Next time you go home or call home, ask your family about majors and careers.
- Your **college's career center**—almost always under-appreciated, these folk have such a wealth of information at their fingertips that it is a shame more students don't take advantage of them . . . and not just in your senior year—start visiting in your first year because most have resources for choosing a major and a career, as well as internship and job placement information. Read more about this option by reading our article, *It's Never Too Early—or Too Late—to Visit Your College Career Office.*

13   There are also a number of books that you may find useful, including:

- *The Complete Idiot's Guide to Choosing a College Major*, by Randall S. Hansen – my book. (Alpha).

- *College Majors Handbook with Real Career Paths and Payoffs: The Actual Jobs, Earnings, and Trends for Graduates of 60 College Majors*, by Neeta P. Fogg, Paul Harrington, Thomas Harrington (Jist).
- *The College Board Book of Majors* (College Board).
- *How to Choose a College Major*, by Linda Landis Andrews (VGM Career Horizons).
- *Major in Success: Make College Easier, Beat the System, and Get a Very Cool Job*, Patrick Combs (Ten Speed Press).

Questions about some of the terminology used in this article? Get more information (definitions and links) on key college, career, and job-search terms by going to our Job-Seeker's Glossary of Job-Hunting Terms.

Dr. Randall S. Hansen is founder of Quintessential Careers, one of the oldest and most comprehensive career development sites on the Web, as well CEO of EmpoweringSites.com. He is also founder of MyCollegeSuccessStory.com and EnhanceMyVocabulary.com. He is publisher of Quintessential Careers Press, including the Quintessential Careers electronic newsletter, QuintZine. Dr. Hansen is also a published author, with several books, chapters in books, and hundreds of articles. He's often quoted in the media and conducts empowering workshops around the country. Finally, Dr. Hansen is also an educator, having taught at the college level for more than 15 years. Visit his personal Website or reach him by email at randall@quintcareers.com.

Source: Retrieved from http://www.quintcareers.com/choosing_major.html

👁 *L*OOK   Go to your college career center and look at the posters and magazines on display. Then go to the Web sites mentioned in this article and see what ideas are out there to help you with your career planning. Also, create a picture or concept map showing the six stops in your career exploration journey (as described in the article). You may draw your picture any way that makes sense to you.

🔊 *L*ISTEN   After reading through the advice in the article, think of people you might talk with to learn more about careers that interest you. Your college's career center may be a good starting point. Make an appointment with a career counselor or career advisor to discuss ways you can explore potential majors. Also, in your own words, describe to a friend the 6 stops in your career journey (using the article as a guide).

✏ *W*RITE   Go to the resources mentioned in the article and read more about career planning. Check out some of the books mentioned. They may be available at your campus or public library and can be read for free! Also, go to your college's career center and read about careers that interest you. Write out an action plan of things you can do to further explore career paths. Finally, write an outline of the 6 stops in your journey listed in the article.

👆 *Do*   Try out some of the suggestions in the article. One way is by going to the article's Web site. Then click on the links for more details about ideas that are interesting to you. Also, go through the 6 stops in the article and apply them to your own career choice. Find a way to share your 6 stops with a friend.

Reading Practice

The next section of the chapter will help you build your vocabulary skills while you read a variety of materials from diverse sources. All five of the readings address topics about exploring college.

The first reading is *High School Versus College Life: A Freshman Year Guide to Different Student Academic Expectations* from an Internet Web site called *Suite 101*.

The second reading is from a section titled *Attitude* from "Understanding Your College" from the textbook, *The Community College Experience: Plus*.

The third reading selection is called "College Talk" from the book, *Chicken Soup for the College Soul: Inspiring and Humorous Stories About College*.

The fourth reading selection is "Leadership for the 21*st* Century: Eleven High-Profile Women Share Their Trials and Triumphs. Leading the Way" from *Newsweek* magazine. Gwen Sykes, Chief Financial Officer, NASA, is featured in this part of the article.

The final reading is a visual image of diversity.

Internet   READING 1

High School Versus College Life: A Freshman Year Guide to Different Student Academic Expectations

1   *Are you freaking out about going to college? Yes, college is more difficult than high school. To help you out, here are some of the differences you can expect.*

2   Eek! You're going to college! It's exciting, but you're probably a little nervous about freshman year, right? You know how your high school teachers have been telling you that college is going to be much more difficult than high school? Well, they're right.

3   Scared? Part of the scary part is that you don't know what to expect **academically.** People keep telling you your school work is going to be tough, but you don't know exactly what that means. So how *is* college different than high school?

4   Here's the big difference: in college, *you are **responsible** for your own education*. In high school, teachers made sure that you were on track. In college, you are on your own. Here are some ways that college is different than high school.

- **You don't have to go to class.** That's awesome, right? Not really. To many students, skipping class is too big a temptation to **resist**. Here's the scoop: if you don't go to class all or most of the time, you'll do poorly.

ENGLISH 2.0

On track means: working toward your goals, similar to "on the path of success." Hint: think of a race track or a train track and how the car or the train needs to stay on the track to be successful.

Scoop means: the main information you need like a summary or the most important point. Hint: think of needing just a scoop of peanuts or ice cream from a larger container and not the whole thing.

- **You need to manage your time.** In high school, your teacher will tell you to read pages 35–48 for class tomorrow and to start working on your paper. In college, the professor hands you a **syllabus**. It tells you when readings need to be done and when assignments are due. You need to take the syllabi from all of your classes and figure out how to best divide up your time.

- **You need to study more.** Professors expect you to study 2–3 hours outside of class for every hour spent in class. In college, studying *has* to be a major part of your life.

- **The reading load is heavier and tougher.** Expect many more pages and many more big words. And *don't* expect the professor to go over all the readings in class. The readings may **overlap** with the lecture, but not always, so you have to do the reading and learn it on your own. And yes, it *will* be on the test.

- **Taking notes is more difficult.** In high school, your teacher will probably give you an outline of his or her lecture and tell you what points will be on the test. In college, the professor often just talks. It's your responsibility to write everything down and know what is important.

- **You won't be reminded about deadlines and tests.** It's your responsibility to know your deadlines. Read your syllabus frequently.

- **There are no A's for effort.** In high school, teachers sometimes give students credit if they try and don't do well at something. In college, you can study your tail off and get a D on the test. The only thing that matters is the end result, not the effort.

- **Your parents won't be able to help much.** By law (in the U.S.), professors *cannot* discuss your school work with your parents. The school considers you an adult, and sharing your personal information with other adults is illegal. Your parents may be able to give you **guidance** about classes and your social life, and if you're lucky, they'll help you out financially. For the most part, though, you're on your own.

- **Help is available, but you have to seek it out.** People will be happy to help you, but you need to seek out their **assistance.** Don't be afraid to ask for help from your professors and TAs, and seek additional help from academic advisors, the campus study skills center, and the writing lab.

- **You need to balance work and play.** Your social life has to come second to your school work, and your parents and teachers won't be around to make sure that happens.

- **Discipline problems will not be tolerated.** Students are expected to act like adults in class. Students who do not can be removed from class or from campus.

- **You choose most of your classes and your major.** In high school, many or most of your classes were chosen for you. In college, you get to choose your major and your plan of study. This can be **intimidating,** but also rewarding.

5   Sound painful? At times, it will be, especially at first. First semester freshman year is about learning how to be a college student. If you work **diligently** and hold yourself up to high expectations, the work will seem easier with time.

Source: Suite 101, Naomi Rockler-Gladen, Apr 23, 2007; http://collegeuniversity.suite101 .com/article.cfm/high_school_versus_college

Vocabulary

Directions: Use the context clues to help you identify the correct meaning of the words below. Circle the word that best matches the meaning of the word as it is used in the reading above.

1. **academically** (see paragraph 3)
    a. socially
    b. related to athletics
    c. related to school
    d. historically

2. **responsible** (see paragraph 4)
    a. accountable
    b. encouraged
    c. acceptable
    d. limited

3. **resist** (see paragraph 4, list)
    a. accomplish
    b. oppose
    c. insist
    d. treat

4. **syllabus** (see paragraph 4, list)
    a. outline of requirements
    b. list of readings
    c. attendance sheet
    d. financial aid notice

5. **overlap** (see paragraph 4, list)

   a. before

   b. after

   c. at the same time

   d. not required

6. **guidance** (see paragraph 4, list)

   a. advice

   b. money

   c. books

   d. promise

7. **assistance** (see paragraph 4, list)

   a. help

   b. consideration

   c. approval

   d. favors

8. **tolerated** (see paragraph 4, list)

   a. respected

   b. divided

   c. allowed

   d. appreciated

9. **intimidating** (see paragraph 4, list)

   a. interesting

   b. scary

   c. imitating

   d. accepted

10. **diligently** (see paragraph 5)

    a. little

    b. carefully

    c. easily

    d. later

Critical Thinking/Writing/Discussing

To visualize the differences between high school and college more clearly, draw a vertical line down the middle of a piece of paper. Label one column "high school" and the other "college." List the author's ideas in the correct columns on your paper. Think about what you've already noticed since you've been in college. Add more differences to your lists and share them with other students.

READING 2

Attitude

1   A good attitude will take you far in the journey to achieve your goals. Sometimes it will be hard to maintain a positive outlook because you feel **overwhelmed**
with the challenges of college, work, and family, but if you can maintain a good
attitude, your chances of success are greater. Good attitudes are **infectious,**
and you will soon find that your professors and classmates will reflect the good
attitude you have.

2   The other side of a positive attitude is a negative one, and at some point in
your college career, you will feel as though the world is out to **undermine** your success. You may feel overwhelmed with the responsibilities of going to school and
working, or you may feel frustrated that you have not progressed in your classes
the way you hoped. There are numerous reasons that you may, temporarily at least,
have a **pessimistic** outlook on your college education or your life. Bringing a bad
mood into the classroom, however, can make your attitude worse and your outlook
gloomier. Even though you may feel **anonymous** most of the time, instructors do
notice when students are **disgruntled** and unwilling to learn. Although instructors
may not know why a student is upset, they are still **affected** by the student's bad
attitude. At the very least, they may see negativity as a sign of immaturity.

3   Common "bad attitude" mistakes that students make include

- acting as if they know more than the professor.
- rolling their eyes or shaking their heads when an instructor is presenting materials or making an assignment.
- making negative comments out loud about the class, the instructor, or other
students.
- **resisting** or refusing to do an assignment.
- slouching down in the seat, looking bored.
- getting angry about a low grade.
- walking out of class because of anger or boredom.

Presenting a good attitude in class is easier than you think. In fact, it just takes a
little attention to the messages you send with your face, body, and language. Tips
for presenting a good attitude include

- coming to class prepared with the **appropriate** books and materials.
- paying attention.

- demonstrating an effort to master the material and to complete assignments.
- providing positive or **constructive** feedback in class or privately.
- smiling and being friendly!

4   The belief that instructors only like students who make A's or students who **gush** with compliments about the course is false. The truth is that professors like students who show a genuine interest and demonstrate effort in the course, regardless of the grades they earn. It is the student with the good attitude, then, who gets the most from the instructor because he or she realizes that a student with a good attitude is someone who is willing to learn.

Source: Excerpt from *The Community College Experience: Plus Edition,* 1st Edition, pp. 8–9 by Amy Baldwin. Copyright © 2007 by Amy Baldwin. Printed and Electronically reproduced by permission of Pearson Education, Inc., Upper Saddle River, New Jersey.

Vocabulary

Directions: Use the context clues to help you identify the correct meaning of the words below. Circle the word that best matches the meaning of the word as it is used in the reading above.

1. *overwhelmed*

Sometimes it will be hard to maintain a positive outlook because you feel ***overwhelmed*** with the challenges of college, work, and family, but if you can maintain a good attitude, your chances of success are greater. (see paragraph 1)

It will be hard to maintain a positive attitude.	Challenges of college, work, and family	A good attitude will help your success.

Together, these facts let you infer that ***overwhelmed*** means

a. overpowered.   c. excited.

b. confident.   d. overdue.

2. *infectious*

Good attitudes are ***infectious***, and you will soon find that your professors and classmates will reflect the good attitude you have. (see paragraph 1)

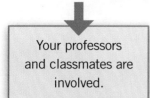

Your professors and classmates are involved.

They reflect something.

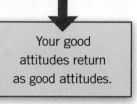

Your good attitudes return as good attitudes.

Together, these facts let you infer that *infectious* means

   a. diseased.   c. preventable.

   b. spreading from one to another.   d. ill.

3. undermine (see paragraph 2)

   a. encourage   c. discover

   b. lose   d. damage

4. pessimistic (see paragraph 2)

   a. joyful   c. giving the best

   b. expecting the worst   d. realistic

5. gloomier (see paragraph 2)

   a. harder   c. sadder

   b. higher   d. happier

6. anonymous (see paragraph 2)

   a. fearful   c. kind

   b. unknown   d. tired

7. disgruntled (see paragraph 2)

   a. unhappy   c. energetic

   b. slow   d. noisy

8. affected (see paragraph 2)

   a. diseased   c. contagious

   b. procrastinated   d. influenced

9. resisting (see paragraph 3)

   a. losing   c. ignoring

   b. attracting   d. refusing

10. **appropriate** (see paragraph 3)

    a. correct   c. used

    b. cheapest   d. partial

11. **constructive** (see paragraph 3)

    a. strong   c. helpful

    b. negative   d. weak

12. **gush** (see paragraph 4)

    a. fall behind   c. pour

    b. brag loudly   d. fight

Critical Thinking/Writing/Discussing

Discuss why attendance is important to success in college. Besides information and assignments, what can students miss when they do not attend class regularly?

Literature

READING 3

College Talk

1   It seemed to come on like the flu. Suddenly, out of nowhere, everyone was talking, about college. Lunchtime discussions changed from who's dating whom into who's going to what college and who did or did not get accepted. And just like the flu leaves its **victims** feeling awful and helpless, such was the case for this new fascinating subject and me.

2   I don't clearly remember the actual conversations. I do, however, remember why I wasn't interested in all this "college talk." We didn't have enough money for me to go to a real college. I would begin my college years at a *junior college*. This was the final word and I had accepted it. I didn't even mind terribly. I just wished everyone would stop talking about this university and that *Ivy League* school.

3   The truth is I was jealous. I had worked so hard to get good grades in school and for what? Each time I found out someone else I knew had just been accepted to the college of their dreams I would turn a deeper shade of green. I didn't like feeling this way, but I couldn't help it. It felt like they were going to jump ahead of me. They were going to have the big life experiences that turn a teenager into an adult and I was going to get left behind.

4   My boyfriend was very sweet and barely mentioned it every time an envelope arrived for him with a "Congratulations, you've been accepted to yet another college of your choice!" I knew about them only because his parents lacked the **sensitivity** with which he was so blessed. He always **shrugged** it off and would tell me, "You would have had the same response. Watch, you'll get a full **scholarship** to the college of your choice in two years and you can laugh at us all for foolishly killing ourselves to arrive at the same place." He had a point. I just thought it was awfully sweet of him to make sure I saw it this way.

5   My friends and I kept in touch those first few months and, more often than not, I was the one offering words of support and understanding. They spoke of roommates from hell, classes they couldn't get into, and the ones they did being so big they couldn't even see their professor. Not only could I see mine, but one of my favorites invited us to his house on a lake. We would go there for class and stay hours afterwards talking and sharing our **theories** on human behavior. It was because of this class that I decided to major in **psychology.**

6   Needless to say, my **tortured** thoughts of being left behind while they went out and gathered life experiences in huge doses changed to thoughts of counting my blessings. I was getting a fine serving of life experience. I was letting go of friends and my first true love. I was moving into a humble **abode** that for the first time in my life I could call my own and I was taking a full load of classes by choice, not **requirement.**

7   As time passed and I grew more and more comfortable with my **circumstances,** I was also able to understand something I hadn't when I was angry and **envious.** Real life will be filled with moments of friends making more or loved ones being promoted first. When these things happen, I know I will be prepared. I have already had a taste of this experience and I passed the test quite nicely.

Source: Canfield, J, Hansen, M., Kirberger, K, & Clark, D. (1999). *Chicken Soup for the College Soul: Inspiring and Humorous Stories About College.* Deerfield Beach, FL: Health Communications. Story by Kimberly Kirberger; from the "Transition" chapter, pp. 41–42.

Junior college—a school teaching the first two years of college
Ivy League—an association of colleges in the Northeastern United States

Vocabulary

Directions: Use the context clues to help you identify the correct meaning of the words below. Circle the word that best matches the meaning of the word as it is used in the reading above.

1. **victims** (see paragraph 1)
   a. ones harmed
   b. comedians
   c. scholars
   d. criminals

2. **sensitivity** (see paragraph 4)
   a. touch
   b. sight
   c. consideration
   d. sound

3. **shrugged** (see paragraph 4)
   a. laughed
   b. lessened the importance of
   c. exaggerated the importance of
   d. yelled

4. **scholarship** (see paragraph 4)
   a. admission
   b. SAT score
   c. loan of financial aid
   d. grant of financial aid

5. **theories** (see paragraph 5)
   a. beliefs that guide actions
   b. fears that guide actions
   c. experiences
   d. restrictions

6. **psychology** (see paragraph 5)
   a. study of plants
   b. study of behavior
   c. study of maps
   d. study of life

7. **tortured** (see paragraph 6)
   a. painful
   b. joyful
   c. silly
   d. tattoo

8. **abode** (see paragraph 6)
   a. hotel
   b. home
   c. guest house
   d. vacation

9. **requirement** (see paragraph 6)

    a. choice
        c. elimination

    b. option
        d. something that is necessary

10. **circumstances** (see paragraph 7)

    a. situation
        c. feelings

    b. circles
        d. fears

11. **envious** (see paragraph 7)

    a. laughing
        c. sleepy

    b. jealous
        d. energetic

Magazine/Periodical   **READING 4**

Leadership for the 21st Century: Gwen Sykes, Chief Financial Officer, NASA

1   "I was a *military brat*, born at *West Point*. When I was 5, Dad got stationed in Alaska. Growing up in a large state with a small population encouraged me to develop a **self-reliant,** can-do attitude. I often tell people about the summer I spent

in Nome when I was a teenager. Outside of Alaska, people talk about Nome once a year, during the *Iditarod*. The other 11 months of the year, nobody says anything about Nome because there's nothing there. That summer, I remember there was one grocery store, one landing strip, one church, an assortment of houses, and that was it. I found a small group of kids my age and we would go to the beach, where the walruses would be sunning themselves. So we took it upon ourselves to do a little bit of walrus rolling for entertainment. A group of us would just run out on the beach and pick a **particular** walrus sunning and kind of roll him and listen to him whine as he rolled. It's kind of **akin** to cow tipping that folks do in the Midwest. I tell folks that if I can roll a walrus, I guess there's nothing I can't do.

2   After I graduated from high school, I decided to find out what the rest of the world was about, so I went to Catholic University here in Washington, D.C. That was a very significant **transition** for me, coming from the great state of Alaska. I remember telling my mom that I couldn't understand how these trees grow with cement around them. There was a lot of city learning that I had to do. In Alaska, most of the people I knew were military or Alaskan natives or what we call the environmental folks. Here in Washington, you get people from all over the world. I was kind of like a kid in a candy store during my college years.

3   I majored in accounting. That was an interest I developed working for my father, who had his own company in Alaska. He brought me to work, put me on the payroll and told me what my hourly salary was. I had done all my figuring for the first two weeks and I knew I was getting something like $200. And when he handed me that check and it was only $150, I said, "Where's my $50?" He said I hadn't **calculated** for *FICA* and other assorted Uncle Sam-type taxes. So that was my first **foray** into taxes. And I really wanted to know who these guys were and how come they were taking my money.

4   I wasn't always good in math. I've had opportunities where I go out and speak to a lot of the schools. At one, I had a young lady come up to me and ask, "Do I have to be good in math to be like you?" She had the mike close to her mouth and she didn't provide me with any eye contact, which gave me the **indication** that she probably wasn't doing that well in math. But she was truly a child who was **inspired** on some level by me. I answered honestly, and I told her I got a D in algebra. Boy, did the teachers **balk** at that one. But we have to share with our children that there are times of failure. I said to her, "Yes, I got a D in algebra. But my parents saw that I had a challenge. They stepped up to the plate and helped me.

West Point—the site of the U.S. Military Academy
Military brat—child of a member of the armed services
Iditarod—sled dog race in Alaska
FICA—Federal Insurance Contributions Act, an amount deducted from a person's paycheck and paid to the federal government for Social Security

And I have **overcome** the challenge that there's just nothing that I can't do. I had to study hard, but I was able to do it." I think that we need to tell children that there are going to be times when you stumble, times when you fail. It's how you pick yourself up that counts.

5   I'm often asked what it's like to work in such a **male-dominated** environment. I don't think or see the world as a man's environment, a woman's environment, a black environment, a white environment, Hispanic environment. I just see the world. When I walk into a meeting and there's a **crucial** challenge at the table, we're all there to come up with a plan so we can move forward. I'm not really paying attention to how many are men, how many are women and what the **ethnicity** of the individuals at the table are. I'm there making sure that we have the right people at the table to make the right decision.

6   I have been married once but am currently divorced. Women of my generation understand that we really can't have it all. We can have some things that are important to us. But we can't have it all. You're only one person. So you have to make choices and be comfortable with those choices. In order for marriage to work, you have to find someone who understands your motivation and your **drive** and will work with you rather than against you. I do believe that at some point in my journey, I will have that. So please, Mom, don't give up. I haven't. Someday my prince will come. And he'll be running alongside me, OK?

Vocabulary

Directions: Use the context clues to help you identify the correct meaning of the words below. Circle the word that best matches the meaning of the word as it is used in the reading above.

1. **self-reliant** (see paragraph 1)

    a. self-confident   c. cautious

    b. reliable   d. fearful

2. **particular** (see paragraph 1)

    a. patient   c. specific

    b. huge   d. gray

3. **akin** (see paragraph 1)

   a. cousin

   b. similar

   c. unlike

   d. unrelated

4. **transition** (see paragraph 2)

   a. disappointment

   b. vehicle

   c. familiarity

   d. change

5. **calculated** (see paragraph 3)

   a. forgotten

   b. computed

   c. guessed

   d. tried

6. **foray** (see paragraph 3)

   a. attempt

   b. requirement

   c. avoidance

   d. mistake

7. **indication** (see paragraph 4)

   a. condition

   b. separation

   c. trust

   d. sign

8. **inspired** (see paragraph 4)

   a. reminded

   b. motivated

   c. hired

   d. sweated

9. **balk** (see paragraph 4)

   a. stop

   b. cry

   c. yell

   d. yawn

10. **overcome** (see paragraph 4)

    a. visited

    b. given up

    c. overwhelm

    d. conquered

11. **male-dominated** (see paragraph 5)

    a. controlled by men

    b. controlled by women

    c. postal service

    d. letters

12. **crucial** (see paragraph 5)

    a. boring

    b. interesting

    c. important

    d. unimportant

13. ethnicity (see paragraph 5)

    a. background or related group **c.** foods you like

    b. knowing right from wrong   **d.** effectiveness

14. drive (see paragraph 6)

    a. military offensive   **c.** force to fly

    b. desire to do   **d.** gear

Critical Thinking/Writing/Discussing

Discuss some challenges you are facing now in school. What specific actions can you take to help overcome your obstacles and move closer to your dreams?

Visual Image   READING 5

A diverse group of college students

In college you will explore diverse topics and cultures and meet many different people. Study the images and apply your skill of using context clues to "read" the picture. Pay close attention to the details to determine the meaning of the word *diversity*. Define *diversity* and discuss the types of diversity represented.

2 Vocabulary – Word Parts

THEME – Staying Healthy

SPOTLIGHT ON LEARNING STYLES Do

I love it when I see a new word and recognize a part of it. It's like a little puzzle I get to solve. My mind automatically tries to connect the new word to something else I already know. My daughter in high school asked me once to help her understand *geometry*. Well, it had been about 30 years since I looked at a geometry book, but I did offer her this, "*Geo* means earth and *metry* means to measure, so geometry means measuring the earth." She was not impressed with my assistance and said the word parts were not what she needed to get her math homework done. I tried. . . .☺

Recognizing Word Parts (Where have I heard this before?)

You probably already know thousands of words. Many of these words are built with the same word parts. When you think about the word parts you already know and see them in an unknown word, it will help you guess the meaning of the new word.

> **LO1**
> Use word parts to understand the meaning of words.

In college you will hear and read many new vocabulary words in different subjects. In your personal life you may also come across unfamiliar words as you try to make healthy choices for yourself and your family.

A good way to improve your understanding as you read, and therefore to make better decisions, is to use what you already know and work from there. Building on the word parts you know and memorizing more

- will help build your vocabulary quickly and
- lead to better comprehension.

Let's see how the word parts work together to form words. First, think about a familiar word such as *thermometer*.

- It is made up of two parts: *therm* and *meter*.
- When you see the word *thermometer* you might think about other words with *therm* such as
  - *Thermos*
  - *thermal* underwear
  - or *thermostat*.

- What do those words have in common?
  - A *thermo*meter measures the temperature.
  - A *thermo*s controls the heat of a liquid.
  - *Therm*al underwear keeps you warm while you're sledding.
  - A *thermo*stat controls the temperature in your house.

So, perhaps, the word part *therm* has something to do with temperature or heat.

- You might also think about words with *meter* such as the metric measurements:
  - *meter*
  - *centimeter*
  - *millimeter*
  - *kilometer*, etc.
- If you know that *thermometer* measures temperature, and *therm* is temperature, then *meter* must mean to measure.

So, if you see the word, <u>micro</u>meter

- you can think about how *meter* means *measure* and
- then see if the word part *micro* looks familiar.

You might ask yourself where else you've seen the word part *micro*.

- How about *microscope, micro-organism, microwave ovens,* or *micro machines?*
- Then ask what these words have in common.
  - A *microscope* zooms in to view very small particles.
  - *Micro organisms* are very small life forms or organisms.
  - *Microwave* ovens use small waves to conduct heat.
  - *Micro machines* are tiny toys.

Going back to *micrometer,* you just put *micro* (meaning "very small") with *meter* (meaning "measure"), and you will understand that a *micrometer* measures very small items with precision.

Word parts may be more easily remembered if you study them in related groups. Similar to remembering names, dates, or directions, it may help to see a pattern between words. Like learning the alphabet or your basic math facts, memorizing word parts can serve as an important foundation

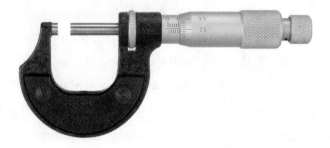

for building the rest of your vocabulary. Once you've learned to recognize the patterns and memorized the unfamiliar word parts, you should notice a definite improvement in your word knowledge.

Prefixes, Roots, and Suffixes

Words in the English language are primarily made up of Latin and Greek word parts. The root of the word will reveal the basic meaning. Prefixes then may be added to the beginning of the word and suffixes may be added to the end of the word to change the meanings. In the next few pages of this chapter, you will have the opportunity to learn many word parts and to use them to improve your reading. The lists of prefixes, roots, and suffixes below include word parts you may use to build your vocabulary. The examples, practice, and longer readings in this chapter are related to staying healthy.

Prefixes

A *prefix* is a word part located at the beginning of a word. A prefix changes the meaning of the word, and it cannot stand alone. For example, the prefix *multi* is used in the word *multivitamin*. You already know what a vitamin is. But why are some called *multivitamins?* Think about what you are getting when you take a multivitamin—several different vitamins you need to be healthy, such as vitamin A, vitamin B6, vitamin B12, vitamin C, etc. So, without even looking it up, you already know that *multi* means many.

    Helpful hints to learn prefixes:

- Group them into related categories.
- Connect the word parts you are learning in this course to words you've heard before or in your other college classes. For example, the

following list of prefixes representing numbers may be used in your math classes. You may also recognize them in familiar words.

Prefixes Representing Quantities

Prefix	Meaning	Example	Definition
semi	half, partly	semicircle	half circle
mono	one	monotone	one tone
uni	one	unit	a measure of one
multi	more than one	multiply	more than one addition
poly	many	polygon	many sides
du, duo	two	duet	two singing together

EXAMPLE

Directions: Fill in the blank with either the prefix or the meaning from the list above.

_____ precious = <u>less than or partly</u> precious gem

If you wrote *semi* in the blank above, you are correct.

PRACTICE THE NEW SKILL

Directions: Fill in the blank with either the prefix or the meaning from the list above.

1. <u>poly</u>graph = an instrument that records _____ changes in the body such as blood pressure, respiration, etc.; it is often used as a lie detector

2. <u>mono</u>nucleosis = an infectious disease with an abnormal increase in the number of white blood cells with _____ nucleus in the bloodstream

3. _____form = wearing <u>one</u> style of clothing or being the same (such as what police officers wear)

Prefixes Representing Quantities (continued)

Prefix	Meaning	Example	Definition
bi	two	bisect	cut in two
tri	three	triangle	three angles
dec	ten	decade	ten years
cent	hundred or 1/100	century	one hundred years
kil	thousand	kilogram	one thousand grams
mil	thousand or 1/1000	millimeter	1/1000 of a meter

PRACTICE THE NEW SKILL

Directions: Fill in the blank with either the prefix or the meaning from the list above.

1. <u>bi</u>ceps = _____ muscles that work together in the front of you upper arm

2. _____ mester = one <u>third</u> of a time period

3. _____ imeter = <u>1/100</u> of a meter

Prefixes Representing Time

Prefix	Meaning	Example	Definition
post	after	postpone	delay until later
pre	before	prenatal	before the baby is born
re	again or back	reapply	apply again
retro	past	retroactive	applicable to the past (laws, pay)

PRACTICE THE NEW SKILL

Directions: Fill in the blank with either the prefix or the meaning from the list above.

1. <u>pre</u>mature = _____ maturity, as in a baby born before the due date

   2. <u>retro</u>fit = fit with parts not available in the _____

   3. _____ align = align <u>again</u> (as in the spine when visiting a
   chiropractor)

Prefixes Showing Direction/Relationship

Prefix	Meaning	Example	Definition
ab, a	away from	asymmetrical	not symmetrical
co	jointly, together	codefendant	joint defendant
circum	around	circumference	distance around a circle
de	down	decline	bend or slant down

PRACTICE THE NEW SKILL

Directions: Fill in the blank with either the prefix or the meaning from
the list above.

   1. _____ operate = work <u>together</u> toward a common goal

   2. <u>circum</u>stance = situation _____ an event

   3. _____ generate = going in a <u>downward</u> direction (as in
   conditions getting worse)

Prefixes Showing Direction/Relationship (continued)

Prefix	Meaning	Example	Definition
e, es, ex, exo	out	exterior	outside
inter	between, among	interstate	between different states
intra	within	intravenous	within a vein
per	thoroughly, through	perspire	excrete through the skin
pro	for, forward	promote	to move forward

PRACTICE THE NEW SKILL

Directions: Fill in the blank with either the prefix or the meaning from the list above.

1. <u>per</u>meate = to go _____ the pores

2. _____ ocular = <u>within</u> the eye

3. _____ pose = to put <u>forward</u> for consideration

Prefixes Showing Direction/Relationship (continued)

Prefix	Meaning	Example	Definition
sub	below or under	subcontractor	under the contractor
sym, syn	together	symbiosis	living together of organisms
super	above or higher	supernatural	above normal or natural, larger
trans	across	transmit	send across

PRACTICE THE NEW SKILL

Directions: Fill in the blank with either the prefix or the meaning from the list above.

1. <u>sub</u>total = _____ the total, less than the total

2. <u>syn</u>ergy = _____ action or operation (as of muscles, drugs, etc.)

3. _____ fusion = transferring blood from one person <u>across</u> to another

Prefixes Meaning *Not*

Prefix	Meaning	Example	Definition
a, an	not or without	asymmetrical	not symmetrical
anti	opposite or against	antibiotic	against germs
dis	not or opposite	disinfect	not infect

il (before l)	not	illiterate	not literate
im (before b, p, m)	not	immature	not mature
in	not	insecure	not secure
ir (before r)	not	irresponsible	not responsible
mis	wrong	misplace	wrong place
non	not	non-profit	not for profit
un	not	unpredictable	not predictable

PRACTICE THE NEW SKILL

Directions: Fill in the blank with either the prefix or the meaning from the list above.

1. <u>mis</u>understanding = _____ understanding

2. <u>ir</u>replaceable = _____ replaceable

3. _____logical = <u>not</u> logical

4. _____possible = <u>not</u> possible

5. _____smoking = <u>against</u> smoking

REVIEW WHAT YOU LEARNED

Vocabulary in Word Parts—Prefixes

Directions: Fill in the blank with the prefix.

1. _____gram = a <u>thousand</u> grams

2. _____generate = to create or generate <u>again</u>

3. _____generate = going in a <u>downward</u> direction (as in conditions getting worse)

4. _____active = to move <u>forward</u> in your actions

5. _____operative exam = exam <u>after</u> the operation

REVIEW WHAT YOU LEARNED

Vocabulary in Word Parts—Prefixes

Directions: Fill in the blank with the meaning.

1. <u>re</u>set = set _____

2. <u>im</u>mature = _____ mature

3. <u>mis</u>interpretation = _____ interpretation or understanding

4. <u>pre</u>natal vitamins = vitamins you take _____ the baby is born

5. <u>tri</u>ceps = _____ muscles that work together in the back of the upper arm

Roots

A root is the base of a word or the place a word's meaning originates. Greek and Latin language roots make up much of the English language. Becoming familiar with several roots will help you expand your vocabulary. When you come across a new word, you can think about what looks familiar and then make an educated guess about the meaning of the word.

Roots Representing Feelings or Emotions

Root	Meaning	Example	Definition
cred	believe	incredible	not believable
path	feeling or suffering	empathy	understanding of another
patho	disease	pathologist	one who studies diseases
phobia	fear	claustrophobia	fear of being in closed spaces

PRACTICE THE NEW SKILL

Directions: Fill in the blank with either the prefix or the meaning from the list above.

1. <u>patho</u>gen = an agent that causes _____ such as bacteria or fungus

2. _____ible = believeable

3. phobo<u>phobia</u> = _____ of phobias

Roots Representing Motion or Action

Root	Meaning	Example	Definition
duc, duct	to lead	educate	to lead to knowledge
fac	to do or make	manufacture	to make
port	to carry	portable	able to move or carry
spec	to look	speculate	to look into the future
tract	to pull	tractor	machine for pulling
tort	to twist	contort	to twist out of shape
vers, vert	to turn	reverse	turn backwards

PRACTICE THE NEW SKILL

Directions: Create words by putting word parts together. Use both prefixes and roots.

Example: <u>revert</u> = <u>to turn back to a former position or state</u>

1. _____ _____ = _____

2. _____ _____ = _____

3. _____ _____ = _____

Roots Representing Communication

Root	Meaning	Example	Definition
audi	to hear	audiologist	doctor who treats hearing problems
dic, dict	to speak or tell	dictate	to say or read aloud
graph, gram	write, record	graphology	study of handwriting

Roots Representing Communication (*Continued*)

miss, mitt	to send	remit	to send again
phono	sound	phonograph	record the sound
scrib, script	to write	prescription	to write before
voc, voke	to call or voice	vocation	one's calling or ministry

PRACTICE *THE NEW SKILL*

Directions: Create words by putting word parts together. Use both prefixes and roots.

Example: <u>prescribe</u> = <u>to write before</u> (as in the doctor writing before the pharmacist)

1. _____ _____ = _____
2. _____ _____ = _____
3. _____ _____ = _____

Other Roots

Root	Meaning	Example	Definition
cardio	heart	cardiologist	person who studies the heart
cide	to kill	pesticide	kill an insect (pest)
fer	to bear	transfer	to bear across
luc, lum	to shine or light	illuminate	put light on
logy, ology	study of	psychology	study of behavior or mind
psych	mind	psychologist	person who studies the mind
spir	breathe	perspiration	breathe out through the skin
tele	distance	telephone	sounds across distance
vita, viv	life	vital signs	signs of life (i.e., pulse)

PRACTICE THE NEW SKILL

Directions: Create words by putting word parts together. Use both prefixes and roots.

Example: <u>telephone</u> = <u>hear across a distance</u>

1. _____ _____ = _____

2. _____ _____ = _____

3. _____ _____ = _____

REVIEW WHAT YOU LEARNED

Vocabulary in Word Parts—Roots

Directions: Fill in the blank with the meaning that matches the root.

1. homo<u>cide</u> = _____ of a person

2. il<u>lum</u>inate = to put _____ on the situation or to make more clear

3. dis<u>tort</u>ed = physically _____ out of shape

4. de<u>scribe</u> = tell or depict in _____ or spoken words

5. <u>vit</u>amin = pills or liquids you take to improve your _____

REVIEW WHAT YOU LEARNED

Vocabulary in Word Parts—Roots

Directions: Complete the chart below. Write the meaning of each word part and the meaning of the word.

WORD/MEANING	PART/MEANING	PART/MEANING
prescribe =	**pre** =	**scribe** =

Use the word in a sentence.

_____

_____

Suffixes

Suffixes are word parts found at the end of words. A suffix changes the meaning of the word by changing the form of the word but still keeping the basic meaning (or root) the same.

Suffixes That Form Nouns

ance	resist	resistance
ant	stimulate	stimulant
cy	advocate	advocacy
ence	differ	difference
ion	impose	imposition
ism	patriot	patriotism
ity, ty	mature	maturity
ment	move	movement
ness	well	wellness

PRACTICE THE NEW SKILL

Directions: Add the appropriate suffix in the blank space.

1. The results of the tests were important. The import _____ was clear to the family.

2. He was a cynic about the new rules. His cynic _____ created trouble for him.

3. She was so happy when she was singing. Her happi _____ was contagious to those around her.

Suffixes That Form Nouns Related to a Person

ee	refer	referee
er	teach	teacher
or	act	actor
ian	library	librarian
ist	art	artist

/ *PRACTICE* THE NEW SKILL /

Directions: Add the appropriate suffix in the blank space.

1. She practiced nursing. She was a nurse practition _____.

2. He was being trained on the job. He was a train _____.

3. Laughter is good for us, but you need to find a comedy that makes *you* laugh. Choose your favorite comed _____.

Suffixes That Form Verbs

ate	anticipation	anticipate
ize	character	characterize
ify	simple	simplify
al	deny	denial

/ *PRACTICE* THE NEW SKILL /

Directions: Add the appropriate suffix in the blank space.

1. We are hoping for good participation for the walk. The more people who particip _____, the more money will be raised for the cause.

2. Some people like to exercise to jazz music. They say they're going to "Jazzerc _____."

3. I prefer to drink clean and pure water. I try to pur _____ my water before I drink it.

Suffixes That Form			Adjectives	Adverbs (add "ly")
able	capable of	respect	respectable	respectably
ible	capable of	rely	reliable	reliably
ful	full of	success	successful	successfully
ous	full of	courage	courageous	courageously
less	without	hope	hopeless	hopelessly

PRACTICE THE NEW SKILL

1. The sleep-deprived person forgot many things. He was more forget _____.

2. I enjoy watching the sunset as I walk the dog. The evening is enjoy _____.

3. She had hope that her new sleep CD would help her fall asleep. She was hope _____.

REVIEW WHAT YOU LEARNED

Vocabulary in Word Parts—Suffixes

Directions: Read the passage below. Note the highlighted words.

Does Chewing Gum Improve Memory?

Researchers investigate whether chewing gum improves the brain's memory-forming ability.

Since 2002, when English **researchers** published a paper on the topic, a dozen studies have followed on the topic of gum chewing and **cognition**. The **evidence** is not sufficient to support the claim that chewing gum improves working memory (**information** needed **temporarily**, such as phone numbers) or episodic memory (initial and delayed recall of information such as words). Further muddying the waters, some of the research was funded by companies that sell gum and stand to profit from pro-gum findings.

Source: Retrieved from http://health.msn.com/health-topics Web site / Harvard Health Publications, Harvard Medical School.

Circle the suffix in each of the words below.

1. researchers
2. cognition
3. evidence

4. information
5. temporarily

REVIEW WHAT YOU LEARNED

Vocabulary in Word Parts—Suffixes

Directions: Read the passage below and note the highlighted words.

How Safe Are Cell Phones? It makes sense to modify how you use them.

First came warning labels on cigarettes. Then nutritional information on packaged food. Could the next step be a **radiation** notice on your cell phone?

In a much-quoted 2006 study, Swedish **scientists** found "substantially increased risks" of cancer for both short- and long-term users of mobiles. And a November 2009 article in the *Journal of Clinical Oncology*—reviewing 23 of the most **rigorous** earlier studies—found "**possible evidence** linking mobile-phone use to an increased risk of tumors."

Source: Retrieved from http://health.msn.com/health-topics Web site,
Dr. Ranit Mishori, PARADE

Circle the suffix in each of the words below.

1. radiation
2. scientists
3. rigorous

4. possible
5. evidence

"BRB" (Be Right Back) Vocabulary Skills

LO2
Apply new vocabulary
strategies to your reading.

When you are reading and come across a new word, you might need to take some time to figure it out. The *"BRB"* or *Be Right Back* skills let you get away from the reading passage for a short time, and then return to it as soon as possible. Just like when talking, texting, or chatting on Facebook, you might have to leave a conversation for a little while, but you plan to *be right back.*

Your new vocabulary skills of using words parts and context clues are very useful as you encounter unknown words. There will be times, however, when you will need to consult an outside source, such as the dictionary, to determine the correct meaning of a word. Readers who know when to use one or more of the three methods (word parts, context clues, and dictionary) to decide the meaning of unknown words will have better results in less time. The sooner you can figure out the word meaning and get back to the reading, the easier it will be to comprehend the text.

"BRB" Using Word Parts, Context Clues, and the Dictionary

If you see a word such as **predictable**, first you might recognize a word part or two and it may give you an idea about the meaning. Sometimes you can figure out words without using your list of memorized word parts. You can use words you already know to decode the new word.

Next, look how the word is used in the sentence or paragraph to see if there are any context clues to the meaning.

My dog watched me every morning as I put my socks and shoes on. As soon as I picked up the house keys, he came to the door. He knew I was ready to take him on his walk again. My behavior was *predictable*.

I did the same thing every morning.

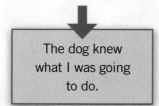

The dog knew what I was going to do.

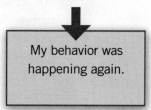

My behavior was happening again.

Together, these facts let you predict (or infer) that *predictable* means a behavior that can be guessed before it happens.

Now look up the word *predictable* in the dictionary or on an Internet site such as www.dictionary.com or www.merriam-webster.com, just to be sure. If you use a dictionary Web site, type your word into the search box. Online dictionaries also offer you the option of hearing the word pronounced when you click on a megaphone symbol after the word. Here is the result from www.dictionary.com:

---

pre·dict (each hyphen indicates a syllable or sound separation)

prɪˈdɪkt [pri-**dikt**] (The pronunciation guide shows how the word sounds; the first syllable - "pre" sounds like "pri"; the bold print on the second syllable shows that the emphasis for the sound is on the second syllable — "dict" sounds like "dikt").

–verb (used with object)
1. to declare or tell in advance; prophesy; foretell: *to predict the weather; to predict the fall of a civilization.*

–verb (used without object)
2. to foretell the future; make a prediction.

Origin:
1540–50; < L *praedictus*, ptp. of *praedīcere* to foretell, equiv. to *prae-* pre- + *dic-*, var. s. of *dīcere* to say + *-tus* ptp. suffix; see dictum

—Related forms
pre·dict·a·ble, *adjective*
pre·dict·a·bil·i·ty, *noun*
pre·dict·a·bly, *adverb*
mis·pre·dict, *verb*
non·pre·dict·a·ble, *adjective*
un·pre·dict·ed, *adjective*
un·pre·dict·ing, *adjective*

Second entry:

pre·dict 🔊 [prĭ-dĭkt'] (The pronunciation guide for the second entry is quite different. It uses symbols you will probably also see at the bottom of the page or in a guide in a printed dictionary. In this style, the syllable that is emphasized when you say the word has a diacritical mark (') at the end. Just like in the first dictionary.com entry, the pronunciation guide puts the stress on the second syllable).

v.   **pre·dict·ed, pre·dict·ing, pre·dicts**

v.   *tr.*
To state, tell about, or make known in advance, especially on the basis of special knowledge.
v.   *intr.*
To foretell something; prophesy.

[Latin praedīcere, praedict- : prae-, *pre-* + dīcere, *to say*; see deik- in Indo-European roots.]
pre·dict'a·bil'i·ty *n.*, **pre·dict'a·ble** *adj.*, **pre·dict'a·bly** *adv.*, **pre·dic'tive** *adj.*, **pre·dic'tive·ly** *adv.*, **pre·dic'tive·ness** *n.*, **pre·dic'tor** *n.*

Synonyms: These verbs mean to tell about something in advance of its occurrence by means of special knowledge or inference: *predict an eclipse; couldn't call the outcome of the game; forecasting the weather; foretold events that would happen.*

The dictionary confirms what we already discovered—*predict* means to foretell the future. Therefore, *predictable* means something that can be foretold or told in advance.

When you go to a dictionary source, as in the example above, there may be multiple meanings for a word. Then you must use context clues to help you decide which meaning makes the most sense. For example, in the sentence, "My behavior was *predictable*," both meanings in the first www.dictionary .com entry makes sense; however, the second entry best matches the way the word is used in a sentence.

The dictionary also gives the origin of the word or word parts. **Predictable** has Latin and Indo-European origins. The study of word origins is called *etymology*. Reading the origins of words in a dictionary is a great way to expand your vocabulary and could be a fun way to spend a rainy day if the electricity goes off.

PRACTICE THE NEW SKILL

Directions: Use the word part chart, the context clues chart, and the dictionary entries to infer the correct meaning of each word.

1. *subscription*

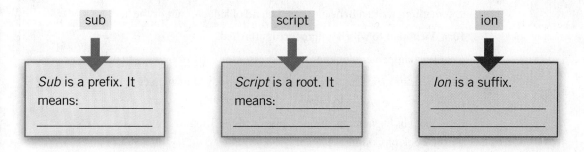

sub	script	ion
Sub is a prefix. It means: _____ _____	*Script* is a root. It means: _____	*Ion* is a suffix. _____ _____

Directions: Using the context clues in the sentence, infer the meaning of *subscription.*

Before I could receive my health magazine each month, I had to prepay for my ***subscription***. I paid for 12 monthly issues.

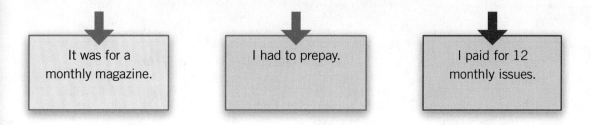

It was for a monthly magazine.	I had to prepay.	I paid for 12 monthly issues.

Using the facts from the sentence, what can you infer is the meaning of *subscription*? _____

According to www.dictionary.com:

---

sub·scrip·tion

səb'skrıp ʃən [*suh* b-**skrip**-sh*uh* n]

–noun

1. a sum of money given or pledged as a contribution, payment, investment, etc.

2. the right to receive a periodical for a sum paid, usually for an agreed number of issues.

3. an arrangement for presenting a series of concerts, plays, etc., that one may attend by the payment of a membership fee: *to purchase a 10-concert subscription.*

4. *Chiefly British.* the dues paid by a member of a club, society, etc.

5. a fund raised through sums of money subscribed.

6. a sum subscribed.

7. the act of appending one's <u>Signature</u> or mark, as to a document.

8. a signature or mark thus appended.

9. something written beneath or at the end of a document or the like.

10. a document to which a signature is attached.

11. assent, agreement, or approval expressed verbally or by signing one's <u>name</u>.

12. *Ecclesiastical.* assent to or acceptance of a body of principles or doctrines, the purpose of which is to establish uniformity.

13. *Church of England.* formal acceptance of the Thirty-nine Articles of 1563 and the Book of Common <u>prayer</u>.

Using words parts, context clues, and the dictionary, what is the best meaning for **subscription**? _____

2. *sympathize*

sym	path	ize
Sym is a prefix. It means: _____ _____	*Path* is a root. It means: _____ _____	*Ize* is a suffix. _____ _____

Directions: Using the context clues in the sentence, infer the meaning of ***sympathize.***

I ***sympathize*** with you about your sadness. I know it must be hard not to be able to follow your normal routine.

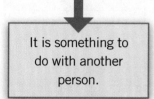

It is something to do with another person.

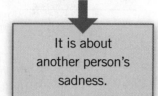

It is about another person's sadness.

She knows it must be hard for the other person.

Using the facts from the sentence, what can you infer is the meaning of ***sympathize***? _____

According to www.dictionary.com

sym·pa·thize

ˈsɪm pə͵ θaɪz [**sim**-p*uh*-thahyz]

–verb (used without object),-**thized, -thiz·ing.**

1. to be in sympathy or agreement of feeling; share in a feeling (often fol. by *with*).
2. to feel a compassionate sympathy, as for suffering or trouble (often fol. by *with*).
3. to express sympathy or condole (often fol. by *with*).
4. to be in approving accord, as with a person or cause: *to sympathize with a person's aims.*
5. to agree, correspond, or accord.

Using words parts, context clues, and the dictionary, what is the best meaning for ***sympathize***? _____

3. *incredible*

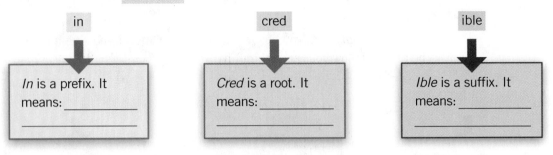

In is a prefix. It means: _____ _____

Cred is a root. It means: _____ _____

Ible is a suffix. It means: _____ _____

That 5K run for the zoo was ***incredible***! I could not believe hundreds of people showed up at 7 a.m. on a Saturday morning to run around the zoo!

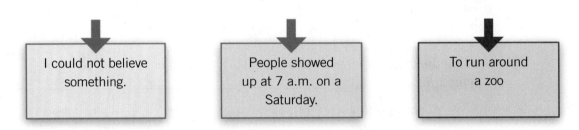

I could not believe something.

People showed up at 7 a.m. on a Saturday.

To run around a zoo

Using the facts from the sentence, what can you infer is the meaning of ***incredible***? _____

According to www.dictionary.com

> **in-cred-i-ble**
>
> [in-**kred**-*uh-buh* l]
>
> *–adjective*
>
> 1. so extraordinary as to seem impossible: *incredible speed.*
>
> 2. not credible; hard to believe; unbelievable: *The plot of the book is incredible.*
>
> **—Synonyms**
>
> 2. farfetched, astonishing, preposterous.

Using words parts, context clues, and the dictionary, what is the best meaning for ***incredible*** _____

/ MASTER THE LESSON /

Vocabulary

Directions: As you read the article below, highlight words with prefixes, roots, and suffixes you recognize.

How To Lose Weight

About.com Health's Disease and Condition content is reviewed by our Medical Review Board

So, let's say you stepped on the bathroom scale this morning and you realized your weight had crept up to a number you really weren't comfortable seeing. Your clothes are too tight, you're feeling sluggish and you're afraid your health might suffer, so it's time to lose weight.

Dieting to lose weight isn't fun and there aren't any short cuts. You need to eat less. It can be tedious, progress is slow and you might feel deprived without your favorite high-calorie goodies to get you through another day. And most people who try to lose weight either don't lose any, or lose some weight and gain it all back later. Sounds depressing, doesn't it?

But all hope is not lost. In order to lose weight successfully, you need to have a plan.

You already know your weight (or if you don't—go hop on a scale). See just how overweight or obese you are by calculating your BMI. How much weight should you lose? That really varies from person to person, but you can aim for about 10% of your current weight to start. Once a week, get back on the scale and recalculate your BMI so you can keep track of your progress. If you have any health concerns, you should speak to your doctor before starting a weight loss program.

Now, to lose weight you need to eat less or move around more. Better yet, do both. Exercise will help you lose weight and improve your health. You don't need to do anything fancy, just getting out for an hour of walking five days each week will help you trim those extra pounds. However some people prefer the intensity of weight training or like to schedule exercise classes at a health club. Just choose what works to keep motivated.

So back to your diet. Taking care of your nutritional needs is important so make it a priority in your life. First you need to know how many calories to take in every day. Use a calorie calculator to help you figure this out. You'll need to eat fewer calories than you are currently eating every day to lose weight, but please don't go under 1,200 calories per day without speaking to your doctor.

You need to keep track of those calories you take in (and the calories you burn during exercise). You can use a food diary to keep track of all the foods you eat, or join Calorie Count, which has a huge database of foods to make diet record-keeping easy.

But there's more to dieting than just cutting calories. You need to eat healthy foods and in the correct amounts so that you get enough carbohydrates, protein and fats, plus lots of vitamins, minerals, and fiber, while avoiding excess saturated fats, trans fats and sodium. The best way to do this is to plan your meals ahead of time, every day.

To build a meal plan, you need to understand how much food you are actually eating. Many of us tend to underestimate the actual volume of food we eat during the day, so it's best to measure all your servings, at least for awhile until you become more skilled in estimating portion sizes by sight alone. Invest in a digital kitchen scale and use measuring cups and spoons and measure everything.

So what foods go into your meal plan? Become familiar with the food pyramid so you know how many of the different food groups you need. Aim for:

- 5 to 11 servings of grain (half should be whole-grain)
- 2 to 3 servings dairy or calcium containing foods
- 1 to 2 servings of protein sources such as meat, eggs, poultry, fish or legumes
- 5 to 9 servings of fruits and vegetables every day

Limit the amounts of extra fats and sugar found in condiments, dressings and sauces.

Strive to fill your daily meal plan with a variety of healthy foods and leave room for a small treat so you'll feel less deprived. And remember that beverage calories count too. You can sit down with paper and pen to make up your meal plan or use Calorie Count to build a meal plan. To use Calorie Count to build a meal plan, log in, choose your foods and mix, match, add and subtract items for one day until you find a meal plan you like. Make your meal plans for a few days at a time so you can go to the store and buy all the foods you need. A meal plan can actually help you save grocery money when you eliminate impulsive purchases from the snack aisle.

To get you started, I'll give you an example of a daily meal plan. It provides about 1,800 calories for the whole day, with plenty of fiber and the nutrients. If you wish to whittle away some more calories, you can omit the glass of wine, dark chocolate, honey, mayonnaise, oil and vinegar dressing, and the butter to save about 450 calories. You also may look for reduced calorie varieties of your favorite condiments and dressings and use non-nutritive sweeteners to tame your sweet-tooth. What you don't want to do is cut back on the healthy fruits, vegetables, and whole grains because they're packed with nutrients and fiber.

Breakfast

- 3/4 cup oatmeal
- 1 tablespoon honey
- 1/2 cup non-fat milk
- 1/4 cup blueberries
- 6 ounces orange juice
- 1 cup black coffee

Mid Morning Snack

- 1 apple
- 12 almonds
- sparkling water with lemon

Lunch

- Sandwich with 3 ounces tuna, a thick tomato slice, 1 tablespoon mayonnaise and lettuce on two slices whole wheat bread
- 1 cup raw baby carrots
- Sparkling water or diet soft drink

Afternoon Snack

- 1 cup plain non-fat yogurt

- 1/4 cup crunchy whole grain cereal
- 1 tablespoon honey

Dinner

- Salad with 1 cup raw spinach, 1 ounce cheddar cheese, 1/2 cup cherry tomatoes and 1 tablespoon oil and vinegar dressing
- 3 ounce steak
- 1/2 cup mashed potatoes with one pat butter
- 1 cup green beans
- 4 ounces red wine

Evening Snack

- 1 1/2 ounces dark chocolate

Does this meal plan look like it can keep you feeling satisfied all day? If not, you can alter your meal plan to include more nutrient dense, low calorie foods like green and leafy vegetables. If your meal plan leaves you feeling hungry every day, maybe you are cutting your calories back too severely. Remember that it's okay to lose weight slowly.

Be sure to allow yourself room for one treat every day (about 100 calories) and you can experiment with non-nutritive sweeteners to fight sugar cravings. And drink plenty of water—zero calories and you can flavor it with a slice of lemon or lime, or choose sparkling water if you like the fizz.

Source: http://nutrition.about.com/od/diets/a/mealplan.htm. By Shereen Jegtvig, About.com Guide. *Updated October 11, 2011*

Directions: Choose 5 of the words you highlighted in the article then complete the chart listing the word parts, and their meanings.

WORD MEANING	PREFIX MEANING	MEANING	SUFFIX AND MEANING
antioxidants	*Anti* means *against*		

MASTER *THE LESSON*

Vocabulary

Directions: Complete the chart below. Write the word meaning, and the meaning of each prefix, root, and suffix.

WORD MEANING	PREFIX MEANING	ROOT MEANING	SUFFIX MEANING
cardiologist	*cardi* means	*olog* means	*-ist* means
regenerate	*re* means	*gen* means	*-ate* means

Directions: Use each of the words in a sentence.

Cardiologist _____

_____

_____

Regenerate _____

_____

_____

MASTER THE LESSON

Vocabulary

Directions: Fill in the blank with the meaning that matches the under-lined word part.

1. <u>circum</u>vent = go _____ the issue or situation (like when avoiding)

2. <u>ex</u>it = to go _____

3. <u>super</u>natural = _____ the normal or natural

4. <u>ir</u>responsible = _____ responsible

5. <u>mal</u>nutrition = _____ nutrition (underfed or lack of healthy food)

Directions: Fill in the blank with the word part that matches the under-lined meaning.

6. _____smoking = <u>against</u> smoking

7. _____polar = having <u>two</u> opposite extremes

8. _____adjust = to adjust <u>again</u>

9. _____lateral = <u>one</u> sided

10. disrespect_____ = not <u>full</u> of respect

LEARNING STYLE ACTIVITIES

*L*ook, *L*isten, *W*rite, *D*o

Change Your Exercise Vocabulary

Wednesday May 19, 2010

If you struggle to find the motivation to exercise, maybe changing your vocabulary can help. Yes, grammar lessons may seem silly in the *throes* of exercise disinterest, but there are some common phrases that slip into the mind at such times. Maybe getting rid of them will change how you approach your workouts:

- **As Soon As:** This phrase makes you feel like you're planning a future workout without actually having to commit to it. We might say, "As soon as my life isn't so crazy, I'll finally start working out." This can morph into any number of as-soon-as-es: As soon as my kids graduate from college or as soon as my bangs grow out or as soon as there is worldwide peace, I'll get to my work-out. Getting rid of the excuses can help you focus on what you want, rather than what's standing in your way.

- **Should:** Anything that starts with, "I really should . . ." is usually a phrase said out of guilt and often involves tasks that we either need to permanently take off our to-do list ("I really should try bungee jumping") or do immediately ("I really should get out and take a walk while the weather is nice."). Replacing the word 'should' with will (or will not) instantly changes your commitment level.

- **I'm too (insert feeling here):** Many of us use this phrase all the time, especially when it comes to exercise. Too tired, too bored, too stressed, too busy, too confused, too hot . . . whatever it is, there's always a reason to skip exercise. Taking the 'too' out of it forces you to focus on the problem and do something about it. For example, if you're tired, ask yourself if you're physically tired or mentally tired from a long work day. If it's mental fatigue, exercise can actually increase energy levels, so you can actually solve the problem with the very thing you're trying to avoid. You're welcome.

What's your vocabulary when it comes to exercise? Are negative thinking patterns getting in the way of your workouts? Leave a comment and tell us how, and what, you think about exercise.

Throes—struggles

Comments

May 19, 2010 at 9:01 am

1. **Kevin S. says:**

   I am always looking for a reason, or an excuse not to work out. As I get older, the motivation is started to decrease. I have never gotten back to where I was before "the accident" and probably never will. I never want to give it up altogether.

May 19, 2010 at 12:31 pm

2. **Becki says:**

   I've found the best thing for me to do is to stop the internal discussion. I cut off the "I'm too busy/tired/etc." excuses in my head and use the Nike mantra "just do it"—end of (internal) discussion. If you let yourself go down that road of excuses, you are likely going to cave in and avoid the exercise.

May 19, 2010 at 12:41 pm

3. **Brad says:**

   Make all the geek fun you want to, however, Jedi Master Yoda from Star Wars hits the proverbial nail on the head with, "There is no 'try', only 'do' or 'do not'!"

   When I'm entertaining ideas of not exercising, I just think of how bad it sucks to be in the hospital. Use it or lose it!

   Source: Retrieved from http://exercise.about.com Web site.

ENGLISH 2.0

Go down that road of excuses means: decide to tell yourself excuses

Cave in means: give in

Hits the proverbial nail on the head means: to mean the right thing at the right time

---

Directions: Choose one of the Learning Style Activities to complete alone or with other students.

👁 *Look*   As you read the article from the Web site, highlight the three major common phrases (see the bold print subheadings). Then highlight what each of the ideas means from the text. Draw a cartoon of someone using one of the phrases or of one of the people who made a comment on the blog. Your drawing can be a positive or a negative example.

🔊 *L*ISTEN   As you read the Web site article, say each of the three major common phrases out loud when you read them. Also say the negative examples listed in the article under each subheading. Then say some of the positive phrases you could use to help yourself make a commitment to exercising. Finally, read the blog comments and then write what you would say if you added a posting to the blog.

✎ *W*RITE   Write the three key ideas from the Web site article. Use the bold print subheadings in the article to help you focus on them. Then write examples of each of the major phrases listed. Read the blog comments and then write your own response to the article.

👆 *D*o   As you read the Web site article, think of your own experience using each of the major phrases (see the bold print subheadings). If you have not personally used them, think of a time you may have heard someone else use the phrases in person or in an advertisement. Finally, read the blogs and then write your own opinion from your experiences.

Reading Practice

The next section of the chapter will help you build your vocabulary skills while you read materials from diverse sources. All five of the readings address topics about staying healthy.

The first reading is "Tips for Healthy, Thrifty Meals" from an Internet Web site, http://publications.usa.gov.

The second reading, "Managing Stress," is from the textbook, *The Community College Experience Plus*.

The third reading is a funny story called, "Exercise and Other Dirty Words" from a book titled, *Porch Talk: Stories of Decency, Common Sense, and Other Endangered Species* by Philip Gulley.

The fourth reading selection is titled, "Your Own Brain Can Sabotage Success," from the Associated Press.

The final visual image is a *Rhymes with Orange* cartoon. The topic of the cartoon is using fish oil.

Internet   **READING 1**

Directions: As you read the article, highlight words with prefixes, roots, and suffixes you recognize.

Tips for Healthy, Thrifty Meals

WHY PLAN MEALS?

To help you and your family be healthier. When you plan meals, you can make sure you include enough foods from each food group. Pay special attention to serving enough vegetables and fruits in family meals.

To help you balance meals. When you are serving a food with a lot of fat or salt, you can plan lowfat or low-salt foods to go with it. For example, ham is high in salt. If you have ham for dinner, you also can serve a salad or a vegetable that doesn't need salt.

To save money. If you plan before you go food shopping, you will know what you have on hand and what you need. Also, shopping from a list helps you avoid expensive "impulse" purchases.

To save time and effort. When you plan meals, you have foods on hand and make fewer trips to the grocery store. Planning also helps you make good use of leftovers. This can cut your cooking time and food costs.

TIPS FOR PLANNING

Build the main part of your meal around rice, noodles, or other grains. Use small amounts of meat, poultry, fish, or eggs. For example, make a casserole by mixing rice, vegetables, and chicken.

Add variety to family meals. In addition to cooking family favorites, try new, low-cost recipes or food combinations. For example, if you usually serve mashed potatoes, try baked crispy potatoes or potato salad for a change.

Make meals easier to prepare by trying new ways to cook foods. For example, try using a slow cooker or crock-pot to cook stews or soups. They cook foods without constant watching.

Use planned leftovers to save both time and money. For example, prepare a beef pot roast, serve half of it, and freeze the remaining half to use later. You also can freeze extra cooked meats and vegetables for soups or stews.

Do "batch cooking" when your food budget and time allow. For example, cook a large batch of baked meatballs or turkey chili, divide it into family-size portions, and freeze some for meals later in the month.

Plan snacks that give your family the nutrients they need. For example, buy fresh fruits in season like apples or peaches. Dried fruits like raisins or prunes, raw vegetables, crackers, and whole wheat bread are also good ideas for snacks.

TIPS FOR SHOPPING

Before you go shopping

- Make a list of all the foods you need. Do this in your kitchen so you can check what you have on hand.
- Look for specials in the newspaper ads for the stores where you shop.
- Look for coupons for foods you plan to buy. But remember, coupons save money only if you need the product. Also, check if other brands are on sale, too. They may cost even less than the one with a coupon.

While you shop

- When your food budget allows, buy extra low-cost, nutritious foods like potatoes and frozen orange juice concentrate. These foods keep well.
- Compare the cost of convenience foods with the same foods made from scratch. "Convenience foods" are products like fancy baked goods, frozen meals, and vegetables with seasonings and sauces. Most of these cost more than similar foods prepared at home. Also, you can use less fat, sugar, and salt in food you make at home.
- Try store brands. They usually cost less than name brands, but they taste as good and generally have the same nutritional value.
- Take time to compare fresh, frozen, and canned foods to see which is cheapest. Buy what's on special and what's in season.
- Prevent food waste. Buy only the amount that your family will eat before the food spoils.

Source: http://publications.usa.gov/USAPubs.php?PubID=1317 "Recipes and Tips for Healthy, Thrifty Meals" United States Department of Agriculture Center for Nutrition Policy and Promotion

Questions

Directions: Use context clues to help you find the meaning of the high-lighted word.

1. *impulse*

   To save money. If you plan before you go food shopping, you will know what you have on hand and what you need. Also, shopping from a list helps you avoid expensive "*impulse*" purchases.

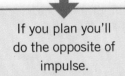

If you plan you'll do the opposite of impulse.

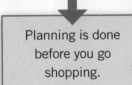

Planning is done before you go shopping.

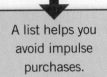

A list helps you avoid impulse purchases.

   Together, these facts help you figure out that *impulse* means _____.

2. *poultry*

   Build the main part of your meal around rice, noodles, or other grains. Use small amounts of meat, *poultry*, fish, or eggs. For example, make a casserole by mixing rice, vegetables, and chicken.

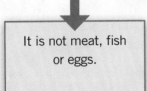

It is not meat, fish or eggs.

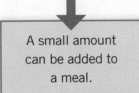

A small amount can be added to a meal.

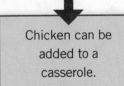

Chicken can be added to a casserole.

   Together, these facts help you figure out that *poultry* means _____.

3. *crock-pot*

   Make meals easier to prepare by trying new ways to cook foods. For example, try using a slow cooker or *crock-pot* to cook stews or soups. They cook foods without constant watching.

Meals will be easier to prepare.

Slow cooker

Food cooks without constant watching.

Together, these facts help you figure out that ***crock-pot*** means _____.

4. *batch cooking*

Do ***"batch cooking"*** when your food budget and time allow. For example, cook a large batch of baked meatballs or turkey chili, divide it into family-size portions, and freeze some for meals later in the month.

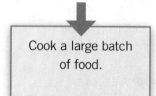
Cook a large batch of food.

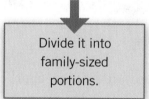
Divide it into family-sized portions.

Freeze some for meals later in the month.

Together, these facts help you figure out that ***batch cooking*** means

_____.

5. *concentrate*

When your food budget allows, buy extra low-cost, nutritious foods like potatoes and frozen orange juice ***concentrate***. These foods keep well.

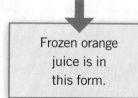
Frozen orange juice is in this form.

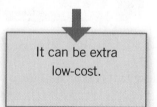
It can be extra low-cost.

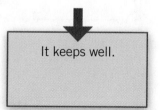
It keeps well.

Together, these facts help you figure out that ***concentrate*** means

_____.

6. *convenience*

Compare the cost of ***convenience*** foods with the same foods made from scratch. "Convenience foods" are products like fancy baked goods, frozen meals, and vegetables with seasonings and sauces. Most of these cost more than similar foods prepared at home. Also, you can use less fat, sugar, and salt in food you make at home.

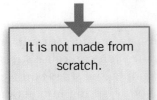

It is not made from scratch.

fancy baked goods, frozen meals, etc.

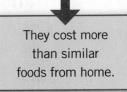

They cost more than similar foods from home.

Together, these facts help you figure out that ***convenience*** means

_____ .

7. *spoils*

Prevent food waste. Buy only the amount that your family will eat before the food ***spoils***.

Prevent.

Food waste

Buy only the amount you need.

Together, these facts help you figure out that ***spoils*** means

_____ .

Critical Thinking/Application

Discuss in a well-developed paragraph one or more tips from the article you could use. Give specific examples from your life of how you could apply the suggestions.

_____

Textbook **READING 2**

Directions: As you read the section of the textbook below, highlight words that have prefixes, roots, and suffixes you recognize. Then complete the Activity, "Assessing Your Stressors."

Managing Stress

Stress is a physical and psychological response to outside stimuli. In other words, just about anything that stimulates you can cause stress. Not all stress, however, is bad for you. For example, the stress you feel when you see someone get seriously hurt enables you to spring into action to help. For some students, the stress of an upcoming exam gives them the energy and focus to study. Without feeling a little stressed, these students might not feel the need to study at all.

Not everyone, however, handles stress the same way, and what is a stressful situation for you may not be for someone else. How we handle stress depends on our genetic makeup, past experiences, and the stress-reducing techniques we know and practice. There are ways to reduce stress or change our reaction, both physically and psychologically. First, though, it is important to be able to identify causes of stress. This list is not exhaustive, but it can start you thinking about different ways you experience stress.

POSSIBLE CAUSES OF STRESS

- Self-doubt
- Fear of failure or the unknown
- Speaking in public
- Uncomfortable situations
- Pressure to succeed (from yourself or others)
- Lack of support—financial, physical, or psychological
- The demands of a job such as a promotion/demotion, deadlines, and evaluations
- Life experiences such as the death of a loved one, having a child, getting married, and moving
- Too many activities and not enough time to complete them
- Congested traffic
- Waiting in lines

Stress Patterns

Each of us has certain triggers, such as the ones listed previously, that stress us. Usually, however, the same situation doesn't stress us the same way each time we are in it. Take, for example, waiting in line at the bank. One day, you might be extremely angry about waiting 15 minutes in line to cash a check because you are late for a job interview. The next time, though, you are in the same line waiting the same amount of time, you may be calm and relaxed because you are enjoying a little quiet time to think while your mother waits in the car. Thus, it is not necessarily the situation or action that causes negative stress, but more likely other factors that are involved.

When you suffer from lack of sleep, you may be more likely to react negatively to people and situations that usually do not bother you. When you feel unsure of your ability to be successful in college, you may take constructive criticism as a personal attack. Being aware of times and situations that cause you the most stress is one step to managing your stress better. For example, if you realize that you are sensitive to others' feedback because you feel insecure, then you may be less likely to react negatively. Complete the activity below.

ACTIVITY *Assessing Your Stressors*

Identify which situations are stressful and which are not. Consider other situations, or people, that cause you to react negatively and add them to this list. The goal is to recognize a pattern of stress and then work to overcome it. When you can tell your professor or coworker that you experience negative stress when assigned a big project, then they can help you create a plan to complete it.

SITUATION	STRESSES ME	DOES NOT STRESS ME
Starting a big project		
Paying bills		
Being in a messy environment		
Receiving graded papers and exams		
Not getting enough sleep		
Taking a personal or professional risk		
Getting out of bed		
Not getting feedback on my work		
Being distracted by other people		
Thinking about the future		
Taking tests		

Source: Excerpt "Managing Stress" and "Activity Assessing Your Stressors" from *The Community College Experience: Plus Edition*, 1st Edition, pp. 78–80 by Amy Baldwin. Copyright © 2007 by Amy Baldwin. Printed and Electronically reproduced by permission of Pearson Education, Inc., Upper Saddle River, New Jersey.

Questions

Directions: Choose 5 of the words you highlighted and complete the chart below.

WORD AND MEANING	PREFIX AND MEANING	ROOT AND MEANING	SUFFIX AND MEANING
Psychological means related to the study of the mind	*psych* means mind	*olog* means study of	*al* means related to

Literature **READING 3**

Exercise and Other Dirty Words

1   Several years ago, my wife began subscribing to a magazine that routinely contained offensive, distasteful language. Copies of the magazine were soon strewn about the house—next to her chair, on the kitchen table, atop the nightstand next to our bed.

2   My polite requests that they be discarded fell on deaf ears.

3   "What's wrong with my magazines?" she asked.

4   I told her I found the language in them repulsive.

5   "What language?" she asked.

6   "All those dirty words."

7   "What dirty words? I don't know what you're talking about."

8   It was just as I had feared. Constant exposure to foul language had desensitized her. I picked up a magazine and thumbed through it. It didn't take long to spy an offending word. "Right there," I said, pointing.

9   "Exercise is not a dirty word," she said.

10   "Then how about that one," I asked, jabbing at the word *calisthenics*. There were other words in her magazine too disgusting to mention.

11   Despite my protests, she continued to leave the magazines in plain sight, even circling articles and leaving them where I couldn't help but notice.

12   It's been said that you don't know a person until you marry her. That is certainly true in my case. My wife was a sweet, reasonable person when I married her, but in the past ten years or so, she's become a fanatic. She exercises constantly, walking four miles each day. Once, I accompanied her, on a pleasant summer evening after the heat had broken. Within a few blocks, it was clear we had different expectations. I was under the impression we were taking a stroll, while she believed we were on the *Bataan Death March*.

13   "Walk faster," she barked.

14   "What's the hurry?" I asked. "Can't we just enjoy ourselves?"

15   Several of our neighbors were out working in their yards. I slowed down to visit with them.

16   "Just wave and keep on walking," she hissed. "Do not stop."

17   I began to fear for my safety. She appeared to want to strike me in the kneecap, crippling me, leaving me along the road to die. I saw her glancing about for a stout stick with which to clout me.

Calisthenics—exercises
Bataan Death March—A forced, grueling 60-mile march of U.S. and Filipino prisoners of war during WWII that resulted in many deaths.

18   That night, while lying in bed, after she'd fallen asleep, I suggested, softly, that we not take any more walks together. It was all for naught. When I awoke the next morning, there was a box of granola on the kitchen table.

19   "Where are my Cocoa Krispies?" I asked.

20   "In the trash. From now on, it's healthy food and exercise for you. Eat up. You're going to need your strength."

21   We walked three miles that day. It was absolutely dreadful. I broke at the two-mile marker, pleading with her to turn back, get the car, and drive me home.

22   "Absolutely not."

23   We were out front of Ron Randolph's home. "How about I see if Ron can drive me home?"

24   "Stop your whining."

25   I walked again the next day, and the day after that.

26   That was five years ago, and I've walked three miles a day ever since, for a total of three thousand and eighty-five miles, roughly the distance from my front door to the country of Panama.

27   The weather is beautiful down here, and until my wife comes to her senses, I have no intention of going home.

Source: Gulley, P. (2007). *Porch Talk: Stories of Decency, Common Sense, and Other Endangered Species.* New York: Harper Collins, pp. 73–76.

ENGLISH 2.0

Fell on deaf ears means: were not heard or were ignored.

Questions

1. Throughout most of the article, the author describes exercise as a *dirty word*. List all the words he uses in the reading that support this idea.

_____

_____

_____

_____

_____

_____

2. When the author says magazines were *strewn* about the house, what does he mean? Highlight the context clues to help figure out the meaning in the paragraph below.

> Copies of the magazine were soon *strewn* about the house—next to her chair, on the kitchen table, atop the nightstand next to our bed.

Strewn means: _____

3. The author describes his wife as a *fanatic*. Highlight the clues to help find the meaning in the paragraph below.

> It's been said that you don't know a person until you marry her. That is certainly true in my case. My wife was a sweet, reasonable person when I married her, but in the past ten years or so, she's become a *fanatic*. She exercises constantly, walking four miles each day.

Fanatic means: _____

4. What does the author say his wife wants to do when he says she will *clout* him with a stick? Highlight the clues to help find the meaning in the paragraph below.

> I began to fear for my safety. She appeared to want to strike me in the kneecap, crippling me, leaving me along the road to die. I saw her glancing about for a stout stick with which to *clout* me.

Clout means: _____

5. What does the author mean when he says his suggestion to his wife was *all for naught*? Highlight the clues to help find the meaning in the paragraph below.

> That night, while lying in bed, after she'd fallen asleep, I suggested, softly, that we not take any more walks together. It was *all for naught*. When I awoke the next morning, there was a box of granola on the kitchen table.
>
> "Where are my Cocoa Krispies?" I asked.
>
> "In the trash. From now on, it's healthy food and exercise for you. Eat up. You're going to need your strength."

All for naught means: _____

Magazine/Periodical   **READING 4**

Your Own Brain Can Sabotage Success

1   WASHINGTON—Uh-oh, the new year's just begun and already you're finding it hard to keep those resolutions to junk the junk food, get off the couch or kick smoking.

2   There's a biological reason a lot of our bad habits are so hard to break—they get wired into our brains.

That's not an excuse to give up.

3   Understanding how unhealthy behaviors become ingrained has scientists learning some tricks that may help good habits replace the bad.

4   "Why are bad habits stronger? You're fighting against the power of an immediate reward," said Dr. Nora Volkow, director of the National Institute on Drug Abuse and an authority on the brain's pleasure pathway.

5   It's the fudge vs. broccoli choice: Chocolate's yum factor tends to beat out the knowledge that sticking with veggies brings an eventual reward of lost pounds.

6   "We all as creatures are hard-wired that way, to give greater value to an immediate reward as opposed to something that's delayed," Volkow said.

7   Just how that bit of happiness turns into a habit involves a pleasure-sensing chemical named dopamine. It conditions the brain to want that reward again and again—reinforcing the connection each time—especially when it gets the right cue from your environment.

8   People tend to overestimate their ability to resist temptations around them, thus undermining attempts to shed bad habits, said experimental psychologist Loran Nordgren, an assistant professor at Northwestern University's Kellogg School of Management.

9   "People have this self-control hubris, this belief they can handle more than they can," said Nordgren, who studies the tug-of-war between willpower and temptation.

10   In one experiment, he measured whether heavy smokers could watch a film that romanticizes the habit—called "Coffee and Cigarettes"—without taking a puff. Upping the ante, they'd be paid according to their level of temptation: Could they hold an unlit cigarette while watching? Keep the pack on the table? Or did they need to leave the pack in another room?

11   Smokers who'd predicted they could resist a lot of temptation tended to hold the unlit cigarette—and were more likely to light up than those who knew better than to hang onto the pack, said Nordgren. He now is beginning to study how recovering drug addicts deal with real-world temptations.

12   But temptation can be more insidious than how close at hand the cigarettes are.

13   Always snack in front of your favorite TV show? A dopamine-rich part of the brain named the striatum memorizes rituals and routines that are linked to getting a particular reward, explains NIDA's Volkow. Eventually, those environmental cues trigger the striatum to make some behaviors almost automatic.

Source: Neergaard, Lauran. (January 4, 2011). *Journal & Courier, p. A4.*

Directions: As you read the article, highlight or underline words that have word parts (prefixes, roots, and/or suffixes). Also highlight words you don't know.

Use the BRB (Be Right Back) technique to figure out the meaning of the words. Remember to use word parts and context clues, and, if needed, look them up in a dictionary.

1. *biological*

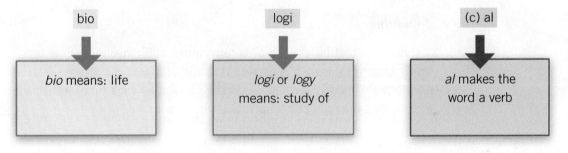

bio	logi	(c) al
bio means: life	*logi* or *logy* means: study of	*al* makes the word a verb

Biological means: _____

2–3. *unhealthy* and *ingrained*

Understanding how ***unhealthy*** behaviors become ingrained has scientists learning some tricks that may help good habits replace the bad.

un	health	y
un is a prefix. It means: not	*health* literally means "health, free of disease."	*y* makes the word an adjective.

There's a biological reason a lot of our bad habits are so hard to break—they get wired into our brains. That's not an excuse to give up. Understanding how **_unhealthy_** behaviors become **_ingrained_** has scientists learning some tricks that may help good habits replace the bad.

Bad habits are so
hard to break.

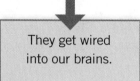

They get wired
into our brains.

Help good habits
replace the bad

Unhealthy means: _____

Ingrained means: _____

4. _dopamine_

Just how that bit of happiness turns into a habit involves a pleasure-sensing chemical named **_dopamine._** It conditions the brain to want that reward again and again—reinforcing the connection each time—especially when it gets the right cue from your environment.

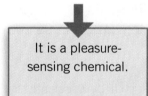

It is a pleasure-
sensing chemical.

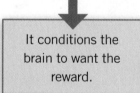

It conditions the
brain to want the
reward.

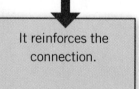

It reinforces the
connection.

Dopamine means: _____

_____

5. _predicted_

Smokers who'd **_predicted_** they could resist a lot of temptation tended to hold the unlit cigarette—and were more likely to light up than those who knew better than to hang onto the pack, said Nordgren.

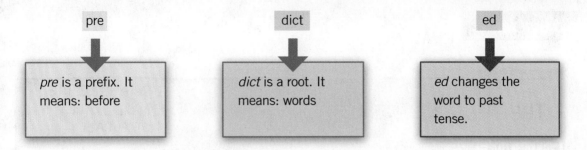

| pre | dict | ed |

pre is a prefix. It means: before

dict is a root. It means: words

ed changes the word to past tense.

Predicted means: _____

Directions: Look at the words below. Rewrite each word, with the suffix on a separate blank.

Example: connection: _____connect_____ + _____-ion_____

6. temptation: _____ + _____

7. experimental: _____ + _____

8. romanticizes: _____ + _____

9. memorizes: _____ + _____

10. environmental: _____ + _____

Visual Image   ## READING 5

Rhymes with Orange

Note: *Aurally* means "through hearing and listening." *Source: Journal & Courier* (2010, March 10), p. D5.

Directions: Use your knowledge of word parts and context clues to understand the meaning in this cartoon.

1. What does the doctor mean when he says, "I said take the fish oil ***orally***"?

_____

2. What did the patient do when he took the fish oil ***aurally*** instead?

_____

3. In the picture on the left side under the cartoon title, *The Follow-Up*, what do you notice in the patient's ear? _____

The cartoonist uses the picture and the words to give two meanings for the phrase *"I'm sorry . . . I didn't catch that".*) What two different meanings could there be?

4. _____

5. _____

3 Main Ideas

LEARNING OUTCOMES

LO1 Use the SQ3R technique for better reading comprehension.

LO2 Find the topic of a reading passage.

LO3 Use knowledge of the topic to lead you to the author's main idea.

THEME – **Creating Better Relationships**

SPOTLIGHT ON LEARNING STYLES Write

Writing in a journal is a way many people process their thoughts and feelings. Another way is writing poetry or short stories. By writing in a journal and writing poetry I can think through my feelings and organize them so that I can understand myself and others better. It also helps me to read about people in relationships. By reading literature such as novels and short stories, true inspirational stories, and self-help books, I often learn more about life relationships. As I read about other people, I think of ways the characters are like people in my life. When I read self-help books, I may learn ways to deal with specific relationship issues.

Have you ever been reading and then realized you had turned several pages but did not remember what you just read? Maybe . . .

- Your mind wandered and you started thinking about something else (like your grocery list or your weekend plans), but your eyes kept moving along through the words.
- You concentrated on the text, but when you were finished reading, you realized that you did not know for sure what you read.

To comprehend the text, it is important to:

- focus on the overall subject, or topic, of the passage.
- know what point the author is trying to convey if you are going to comprehend what you are reading. This overall idea is called the *main idea*.

In this chapter you will learn to recognize and use the author's topic and main idea when you read. You will also learn the SQ3R technique for reading. SQ3R is a system for reading that will help you focus on and retain relevant information. It is especially useful for reading college textbooks and journal articles.

While you are improving your skill at finding the main idea, you'll also be improving your understanding of the relationships in your life. The examples and practice in this chapter pertain to different types of life relationships including friends, co-workers, bosses, dates, partners, families, children, and even pets. So whether you are single or married, work outside the home or in, have children or pets, there should be information that will be useful to you in this chapter.

SQ3R (Survey, Question, Read, Recite, and Review for Better Comprehension)

If you've ever found yourself reading and then you couldn't remember what you just read, SQ3R will help. Or, if you read an assignment but then you didn't know what was important and what was

> **LO1**
> Use the SQ3R technique for better reading comprehension.

not, SQ3R could be the answer. Another good reason to use SQ3R is to help you obtain and retain information you'll need for research papers and exams.

SQ3R is simply an organized strategy for reading. The letters in the acronym represent the steps in the strategy: S is for Survey; Q is for Question; and 3R is for Read, Recite, and Review. It may seem strange at first, but once you've practiced it a few times, SQ3R will become a useful technique for you to use when you read. You'll be able to stay focused on the material and retain the important information.

First, let's go over the five steps of SQ3R and then practice using them.

Survey	Skim over the material. Read the title, subtitle, subheadings, first and last paragraphs, pictures, charts, and graphics. Note italics and bold print.
Question	Ask yourself questions before you read. What do you want to know? Turn headings and subheadings into questions and/or read questions if provided.
Read	Read the material in manageable chunks. This may be one or two paragraphs at a time or the material under one subheading.
Recite	Recite the answer to each question in your own words. This is a good time to write notes as you read each section. Repeat the question-read-recite cycle.
Review	Look over your notes at the end of the chapter, article, or material. Review what you learned and write a summary in your own words.

S—Survey Look over the article or textbook assignment. Look at titles, subtitles, bold print, italics, pictures, charts, and graphs. Also, read the first and last paragraph if it is an article, or the introduction and summary if it is a chapter in a textbook. Remember—you are just surveying, or skimming, the material to get an overview. For an article, it may only take a minute. For a textbook chapter, you may need 3–5 minutes. When you survey, ask yourself, "What are the overall topics that are included in the material I am about to read?"

Q—Question After you have done the survey, you can ask, "What do I want to learn from this material?" The survey revealed the major topics. Now you can ask questions you hope the material will answer. This step will help you stay focused because the material will have some real purpose for you. When you ask the questions and want to know the answers, it is easier to pay attention and keep your mind from wandering.

With a textbook, you might use the chapter overview or summary questions. But, don't stop there. Another good idea is to turn the bold print headings and subheadings in the chapter into questions by adding *who, what, where, when,* or *why* to the headings. For example, if the subheading is "Non-Verbal Expression of Emotion," you might ask "What are non-verbal expressions of emotions?" Asking yourself questions as you read will help you seek and find relevant information. This will improve your reading comprehension.

R—Read This step may seem obvious. But here is an important tip: Read manageable chunks of material, maybe a paragraph or two under just one subheading at a time. For example, once you have turned the subheading into a question, you can read and focus on just that one section. Then you can Recite the answer to your question before you go on to the next section.

R—Recite Remember, you should read in manageable chunks, such as a paragraph or two under one subheading. So, if you write the answer to a question just after you read that chunk of text, you will be able to record the important information in your own words. As you work your way through a longer article or chapter, you should repeat the Question—Read—Recite steps with each paragraph or two or with each subheading. This keeps you focused on one key idea at a time and allows you to stop and take a break without forgetting what you've already read.

A suggestion that works well for many people is to read with a pencil in your hand. If you own the book or have a copy of the article, write your questions and answers on the page as you go through the material. If you don't own the book or don't want to write in it, then write in a notebook or on a separate sheet of paper. Either way, the practice of creating the questions and reciting the answers in your own words, and writing them for later review will help you etch the information into your memory.

R—Review Once you have finished reading the article or the chapter, look over all of your notes (your questions and answers). Read and reread all of the important information (not the entire article, just your notes). This is a good time to write a summary in your own words. Every time you process the reading material through your own mind, you enable yourself to better understand and remember it.

The amount of review you do will depend on the purpose of your reading. For example, if you read a newspaper article and you want to tell your friend about what you learned about the new non-smoking ordinance in your town, your purpose for reading will be different than if you need to retain and recall the information from your textbook for an exam in three weeks.

EXAMPLE

Survey	Skim over the material. Read the title, subtitle, subheadings, first and last paragraphs, pictures, charts, and graphics. Note italics and bold print.
Question	Ask yourself questions before you read. What do you want to know? Turn headings and subheadings into questions and/or read questions if provided.
Read	Read the material in manageable chunks. This may be one or two paragraphs at a time or under the material under one subheading.
Recite	Recite the answer to each question in your own words. This is a good time to write notes as you read each section. Repeat the question—read—recite cycle.
Review	Look over your notes at the end of the chapter, article, or material. Review what you learned and write a summary in your own words.

Directions: Practice the SQ3R strategy as you read the article below.

S—Survey

What are you going to be focusing on when you read this article?

_____

_____

Q—Questions (Turn the headings into questions and write them in the spaces provided.)

R—Read (Read one section at a time.)

The following text is taken from a book called *The Definitive Book of Book of Body Language.* This section talks about the distance that people stand from each other. This is called a "zone." People allow others into each "zone" based on how well they know each other.

Zone Distances

There is an "*air bubble*" around suburban middle-class people living in places such as Australia, New Zealand, Great Britain, North America, Northern Europe, Scandinavia, Canada, or anywhere else a culture is "*Westernized*" such as Singapore, Guam, and Iceland. The country in which you personally live may have larger or smaller territories than those we discuss here, but they will be *proportionally* the same as the ones we discuss here. Children have learned this spacing by age twelve and it can be broken down into four distinct zone distances:

1. **The Intimate Zone** between six and eighteen inches. Of all the zone distractions, this is by far the most important, as it is this zone that a person guards as if it were his own property. Only those who are emotionally close to us are permitted to enter. These include lovers, parents, spouse, children, close friends, relatives, and pets. There is a subzone that extends up to six inches from the body that can be entered only during intimate physical contact. This is the close Intimate Zone.

2. **The Personal Zone** between eighteen inches and forty-eight inches. This is the distance that we stand from others at cocktail parties, office parties, social functions, and friendly gatherings.

3. **The Social Zone** between four and twelve feet. We stand at this distance from strangers, the plumber or carpenter doing repairs around our home, the postman, the local shopkeeper, the new employee at work, and people whom we don't know very well.

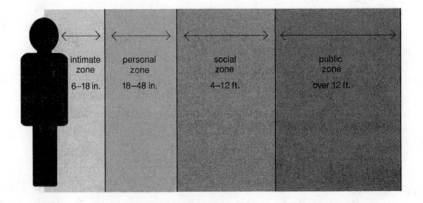

| intimate zone | personal zone | social zone | public zone |
| 6–18 in. | 18–48 in. | 4–12 ft. | over 12 ft. |

Air bubble—the personal space we all carry around us
Westernized—Eastern cultures that adopt behaviors similar to those in the Western hemisphere
Proportionally—properly related in size

4. **The Public Zone** is over twelve feet. Whenever we address a large group of people, this is the comfortable distance at which we choose to stand.

All these distances tend to reduce between two women and increase between two men.

Source: Pease, Allan and Barbara Pease. (2006). *The Definitive Book of Body Language.*
New York: Bantam Dell, pp. 194–195.

Q—Questions (Turn the headings into questions, and write them in the spaces provided.)

R—Read (Read one section at a time.)

R—Recite (Answer your questions as you read, and write them in your own words in the spaces provided.)

Subheading: **1. Intimate Zone**
Question:_____?
Recite:_____
_____

Subheading: **2. The Personal Zone**
Question:_____?
Recite:_____
_____

Subheading: **3. The Social Zone**
Question:_____?
Recite:_____
_____

Subheading: **4. The Public Zone**
Question:_____?
Recite:_____
_____

R—Review (Review your notes and write a summary in your own words.)

Answers:

S—Survey

What are you going to be focusing on when you read this article?

Zone distances between people or distances people stand from each other.

Subheading: **1. Intimate Zone**

Question: What is the Intimate Zone?

Recite: It is 6 to 8 inches and only for people who know each other very well such as children or spouse, relatives, close friends, and pets.

Subheading: **2. The Personal Zone**

Question: What is the Personal Zone?

Recite: It is 18 to 48 inches and used for people at parties, offices, and friendly gatherings.

Subheading: **3. The Social Zone**

Question: What is the Social Zone?

Recite: It is 4 to 12 feet and used for strangers and people we don't know very well such as workers at our house doing repairs and new people at work.

Subheading: **4. The Public Zone**

Question: What is the Public Zone?

Recite: It is over 12 feet and used when we talk to a large group of people.

R—Review (Review your notes and write a summary in your own words.)

People in every culture expect others to stand a certain distance away depending on how well the people know each other. There are four zone distances. Each zone puts an invisible space around us. The less we know someone, the bigger the zone becomes.

PRACTICE THE NEW SKILL

Escaping the Anger Prison

Do the smallest things set you off? If you're experiencing uncontrollable rage, then in order to stop long term, you've got to get to the root of your anger.

- **Identify the emotion your anger covers.**
  Anger is nothing more than a cover for hurt, frustration or fear—or all three. Try talking about what you're really feeling without using the word "anger." Instead, try saying, "I am hurt/frustrated/afraid of . . ."

- **Identify the true source.**
  What is the real source of your anger? Who is the real culprit? Chances are, it's not the people or situations you are lashing out at.

- **Identify the unfulfilled need.**
  If you are experiencing uncontrollable rage, you have unfulfilled needs that should be addressed. Maybe you need to forgive yourself for the way you've behaved while angry. Perhaps you need to forgive others for their actions. What- ever the case, you need to *know* what your needs are before you can fill them.

- **Identify the constructive alternative action.**
  Instead of raging against people, figure out what you can do that is construc- tive. If you need to resolve an issue with a person you are really angry with, the constructive alternative behavior would be to resolve it. If you need to forgive yourself or someone else, the constructive action would be to forgive.

- **Take specific action.**
  Once you have identified your constructive alternative action, it's important that you take that specific action, as uncomfortable as it may be, and move on. Claim your right to resolve the source of your anger and reclaim your life.

Source: Retrieved from http://drphil.com/articles/article/224

ENGLISH 2.0

Set you off means: make you angry

Root of your anger means: the origin or cause of your anger

S—Survey

What are you going to be focusing on when you read this article?

_____

Q—Questions (Turn the headings into questions and write them in the spaces provided.)

R—Read (Read one section at a time.)

R—Recite (Answer your questions as you read, and write them in your own words in the spaces provided.)

Question: _____?

Recite: _____

_____

Question: _____?

Recite: _____

_____

Question: _____?

Recite:_____

_____

Question: _____?

Recite: _____

_____

Question: _____?

Recite:_____

_____

R—Review (Review your notes and write a summary in your own words.)

_____

_____

_____

_____

Finding the Topic (What is this about?)

The first step of SQ3R is to Survey the text. In surveying, you are trying to determine the **topic** of the material. How do you find the topic? Look for a word or phrase that the author uses several times throughout the paragraph or passage. For example, if you see the word *friends* three or four times

> **LO2**
> Find the topic of a reading passage.

in a paragraph, there is a good chance the topic is "friends." Another example is if you see the words *aunt, uncle, cousin, grandma,* and *grandpa,* the topic might be "relatives" since "relatives" is a general term that includes all of the individuals mentioned. The topic is the overall subject the paragraph or reading passage covers. It is also what you will be focusing on as you read.

According to www.dictionary.com, *comprehension* is "the capacity of the mind to perceive and understand; power to grasp ideas; ability to know." The first strategy to improve your comprehension in reading is to make sure you know the topic or subject of the paragraph or reading passage. Writers must choose a general topic before they decide what details they are specifically going to include. Knowing this topic will help you stay focused.

First, let's practice finding the topic.

EXAMPLE

Directions: Circle the word that identifies the topic, or most general idea in the group of words.

aunt   uncle   extended family   grandparent

If you circled "extended family," you would be correct. Your "extended family" includes all of the other people listed: aunt, uncle, and grandparent.

PRACTICE THE NEW SKILL

Directions: Circle the general topic in each group of words.

1. hermit crabs   dogs   pets   cats
2. Facebook   social networking   MySpace   Twitter
3. talking   e-mailing   texting   communicating

Another way to practice finding the general topic of a group of ideas is to read several sentences and try to determine what they have in common.

EXAMPLE

Directions: Choose a topic for the group of sentences.

1. Topic: friends   laughing   support

   a. True friends are people we can count on when life is hard.

   b. It is great to share good news with your friends.

   c. Friends can be there to share a good laugh.

If you chose *friends* as the topic, you are correct. All three sentences share the topic of *friends*.

PRACTICE THE NEW SKILL

Directions: Choose the topic for each group of sentences.

1. Topic: life skills   home   pets

   a. Pets make us laugh.

   b. No home is complete without at least one pet.

   c. Caring for pets teach children life skills.

2. Topic: laughter   going out   coffee

   a. We love to go out for coffee.

   b. We always laugh when we go out together.

   c. Going out to the movies is so much fun.

3. Topic: family   food   responsibilities

   a. There are many responsibilities when our family gets together.

   b. We prepare a lot of food for the family to share.

   c. Our family gets together often to celebrate something.

Now that you can identify a general topic for a group of sentences, let's try this skill with a paragraph.

EXAMPLE

Directions: Circle the topic of the paragraph below.

Women have more complex connections between both hemispheres of their brain, allowing them to take in more information more quickly. In contrast, men tend to use only one side of their brain at a time. In a social situation, this would allow a woman to absorb many messages from a man's body language and the surrounding environment simultaneously, whereas a man takes those messages in one at a time.

Source: Reiman, Tonya. (2007). *The Power of Body Language: How to Succeed in Every Business and Social Encounter.* New York: Pocket Books, pp. 18–19.

a. body language   c. men's brains

b. women's brains   d. differences between men and women's brains

In the paragraph above, (a) body language is too specific to be the topic or focus of the paragraph. Answers (b) and (c) are both discussed in the paragraph, so the best choice for the topic is (d) differences between men and women's brains.

PRACTICE THE NEW SKILL

Directions: Circle the topic of each of the following paragraphs.

1.   Some pet owners still fear that it is not socially acceptable to mourn for a pet as they would for a human. This causes enormous internal conflict and disturbing feelings for them because they seem to need approval and support in order to properly grieve for an animal. As a result, these individuals suffer much more than they normally would. Additionally, they run the risk of suppressing these feelings to the point where it could impair the healing process.

   Source: Sife, Wallace, Ph.D. (1998). *The Loss of a Pet: A Guide to Coping with the Grieving Process When a Pet Dies.* New York: Howell Book House, pp. 19–22.

   a. grieving the loss of a pet   **c.** suffering
   b. internal conflict   **d.** feelings

2.   Guilt trips wear many disguises, and it's not always easy to recognize when we're using guilt. As a single mother, I often felt guilty that I had to work late, that I couldn't always cook healthy dinners, and that I didn't have all the time, energy, or money that I wanted to give to Amanda. Instead of telling her directly how I felt, I'd unconsciously dump guilt on her. I'd sigh and buy her the expensive shoes instead of saying, "I can't afford those now." I'd snap and pick her up from a party instead of telling her that I was too tired and needed to go to bed early.

   Source: Ford, Judy and Amanda Ford (1999). *Between Mother and Daughter: A Teenager and Her Mom Share the Secrets of a Strong Relationship.* Berkeley, CA: Conari Press, p. 91.

   a. single mothers   **c.** tiredness
   b. disguises   **d.** guilt

3.   It is interesting to note that many societies, including Native Americans, had no word to classify animals. They were simply considered a people, just as humans were people. To the Lakota they were brothers, sisters, fathers, and mothers. They were extended kin. The word "animal" was hardly used

before the 1600s and then mostly by scholars. Animals were simply called "beasts" or "creatures" or some such designation.

Source: Andrews, Ted. (2008). *Animal Speak: The Spiritual & Magical Powers of Creatures Great & Small.* Woodbury, MN: Llewellyn Publications, p. 211.

a. kin   **b.** animals   **c.** Lakota   **d.** beasts

REVIEW WHAT YOU LEARNED

Finding the Topic

1. Circle the topic for the group of words.

movies   date activities   dinner   miniature golf

2. Circle the topic for the group of words.

gossip   start rumors   what not to do at work   insult people

3. Choose the topic for the group of sentences.

emotions   anger   stress

    a. Keep in mind the fact that anger is an emotion, and it gets hot almost automatically. You have to work at "coolness" to block it out—talk softer and relax your muscles.

    b. Remember that an outward show of anger can make you look foolish, help lose a friend, or cause the need for a later apology—none of which are worthwhile.

    c. Anger requires energy. Convince yourself to channel your anger to something more positive.

    d. Tell yourself that anger won't get you anywhere positive.

    e. Use the old suggestion of counting to 10 or 100; or improve by mentally reciting an appropriate phrase, prayer or poem.

    f. Usually anger is the outcome of several minor irritations with the current one being "the straw that broke the camel's back." Make a list of each irritant, and try to rid your mind of each one separately for better mind control.

Source: Budzik, Richard and Janet Budzik. (1988). *One-Minute Thoughts That Bring Wisdom, Harmony and Fulfillment.* New York: Warner Books, p. 21.

4. Choose the topic for the group of sentences.

unhealthy risks   positive risks   risk-taking

a. There is a difference between healthy risk-taking and dangerous risk-taking.

b. Unhealthy risks such as drinking and driving or unprotected sex have dire consequences.

c. Positive risks boost confidence and reduce anxieties; they allow your daughter to grow emotionally, physically, and mentally.

Source: Ford, Judy and Amanda Ford. (1999). *Between Mother and Daughter: A Teenager and Her Mom Share the Secrets of a Strong Relationship.* Berkeley, CA: Conari Press, p. 146.

5. Circle the topic in the paragraph below.

attitudes   smiles   facial signals and lies

The face is used more than any other part of the body to cover up lies. We use smiles, nods, and winks in an attempt to cover up, but unfortunately for us, our body signals will tell the truth when our body signals and facial signals don't agree. Our attitudes and emotions are continually revealed on our faces and we are completely unaware of it most of the time.

Source: Pease, Allan and Barbara Pease. (2006). *The Definitive Book of Body Language.* New York: Bantam Dell, p. 146.

REVIEW *WHAT YOU LEARNED*

Finding the Topic

1. Circle the topic for the group of words.

reading books   playing games   time with children   making crafts

2. Circle the topic for the group of words.

throwing a ball   fun with pets   playing with yarn   walking on trails

3. Circle the topic for the group of sentences.

mother-in-law   puppy training   learning

a. My mother-in-law is giving me a hard time about starting my puppy at seven weeks in puppy class.

    b. I told her, "The class is really for me."

    c. Once I know what I am doing, both my puppy and I will be a lot happier.

    d. She believes the puppy is too young to retain anything, but I figure the pup is going to be learning whether I know what I'm doing or not.

> *Source:* Hansen, Harold. (2000). *The Dog Trainer's Guide to Parenting: Rewarding Good Behavior, Practicing Patience and Other Positive Techniques That Work.* Naperville, IL: Sourcebooks, Inc., p. 34.

4. Circle the topic for the group of sentences.

apologies   relationships   insults

    a. Halfhearted or insincere apologies are often worse than not apologizing at all because the recipients find them insulting.

    b. If you've done something wrong in your dealing with another person, it's as if there's an infection in your relationship.

    c. A good apology is like an antibiotic; a bad apology is like rubbing salt in the wound.

> *Source:* Pausch, Randy with Jeffrey Zaslow. (2008). *The Last Lecture.* New York: Hyperion, p. 161.

5. Read the paragraph and circle the topic from the choices below.

It's hard enough being in emotional pain, but it's important not to compound the pain by keeping it all to yourself. When you are in pain, don't keep it a secret. Instead, use this time to reach out to others. Doing so will make you feel empowered and will help you heal more completely. Being with other people while you are suffering is often very comforting and nourishing. People are an important source of support and strength.

> *Source:* Carlson, Richard, Ph.D. (2000). *Don't Sweat the Small Stuff for Teens: Simple Ways to Keep Your Cool in Stressful Times.* New York: Hyperion, p. 105.

    a. emotional pain   **b.** support   **c.** physical pain

Determining the Main Idea (What does the author want me to know?)

LO3
Use knowledge of the topic to lead you to the author's main idea.

Once you are focused on the author's general **topic**, then you can determine what specific message the author is trying to convey about that topic—the main idea. How do you find the main idea? As a reader, you should be looking for the **main idea** in the text by asking, "What's the point of this paragraph?"

For example, have you ever been listening to someone talk, and it seemed like the person was rambling on and on? Perhaps the person appeared to be telling totally unrelated stories or facts. You may have wondered, "What's the point?" When you asked that question, you were looking for the **main idea** the person was trying to communicate.

The main idea must be the author's main point about the topic. The main idea is like an overview of the rest of the paragraph. It is also the idea the author is trying to convey about the topic or the author's attitude or opinion about that topic. Remember: The **main idea** is not just a word or two—that is the **topic.** The **main idea** is a complete thought or sentence about the **topic.** The remaining sentences may be the **supporting details**—specific details that support the main idea.

Let's use a visual aid to see the relationship of topic, main idea, and supporting details.

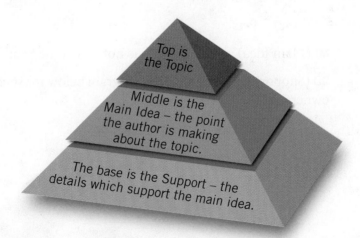

Top is the Topic

Middle is the Main Idea – the point the author is making about the topic.

The base is the Support – the details which support the main idea.

Think about the general topic "pets." If you were going to write about "pets," you'd need to decide what you want to say about pets. In other words, what point do you want to make? For instance, if you believe that "Living with pets has several positive effects on one's life," then you can discuss some of the advantages in the rest of the paragraph. See the diagram below.

T (Topic) = Pets

MI (Main Idea) = Living with pets has several positive effects on one's life.

SD (Supporting Details) = (See diagram for specific advantages for living with pets.)

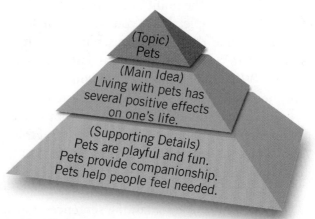

On the other hand, if you believe that "Owning pets is not worth the trouble," then you'd discuss the problems people have when they own a pet. See the diagram below.

T (Topic) = Pets

MI (Main Idea) = Owning pets is not worth the trouble.

SD (Supporting Details) = (See diagram below for specific problems with pet ownership.)

PRACTICE THE NEW SKILL

Directions: Look at each set of sentences. There is a **T** next to the general **Topic**, **MI** next to the **Main Idea,** and **SD** next to the specific or **Supporting Details** in each group below. Complete the pyramid using the information listed.

1. (T = Topic; MI = Main Idea; SD = Supporting Detail)

_____ 1. Unwritten rules for crowded situations

_____ 2. There are common unwritten rules most cultures follow when in a crowded situation such as elevator-riding.

____SD____ 3. There will be no talking to anyone, including a person you know.

____SD____ 4. Avoid eye contact at all times.

____SD____ 5. Maintain a "poker face"—no emotion is permitted to be shown.

Source: Pease, Allan and Barbara Pease. (2006). *The Definitive Book of Body Language.* New York: Bantam Dell, p. 197.

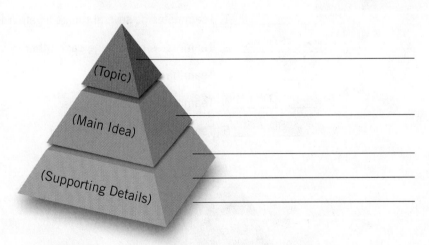

2. (T = Topic; MI = Main Idea; SD = Supporting Detail)

_____ 1. Dogs chew.

____MI____ 2. Some dogs misbehave when we're not home.

_____ 3. Dog misbehavior

_____SD_____4. Dogs get into our belongings.

_____SD_____5. Dogs knock things down.

Source: Hansen, Harold. (2000). *The Dog Trainer's Guide to Parenting: Rewarding Good Behavior, Practicing Patience and Other Positive Techniques That Work.* Naperville, IL: Sourcebooks, Inc., p. 56.

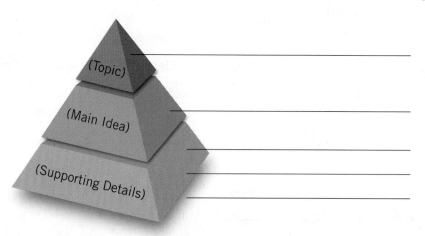

3. (T = Topic; MI = Main Idea; SD = Supporting Detail)

_____1. Teammates do several things together to win the game.

_____SD_____2. Teammates encourage each other.

_____3. Teammates

_____SD_____4. Teammates plan strategies.

_____SD_____5. Teammates work together.

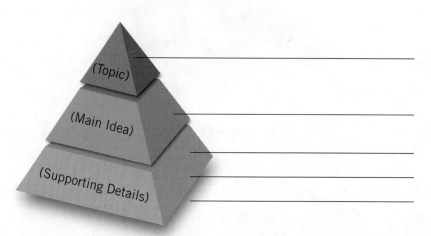

Another way to improve your skill at finding the topic is to create your own specific details related to the main idea.

EXAMPLE

Directions: Write your own specific details that support the main idea.

1. There are several types of social networking sites.

What are three social networking sites?

a. _____

b. _____

c. _____

Some specific social networking sites may include MySpace, Facebook, or Twitter.

PRACTICE *THE NEW SKILL*

Directions: Write your own specific details that support the main idea.

1. Love is more than just a feeling, it is an action.

What are three specific examples of showing love as an action?

a. _____

b. _____

c. _____

2. Working together with others for a good cause also builds relationships for the people participating in the project.

List three specific good causes where people work together.

a. _____

b. _____

c. _____

3. Caring for elderly parents or grandparents can be rewarding and challenging.

What are three specific examples of rewards or challenges in caring for elderly loved ones?

a. _____

b. _____

c. _____

Now let's revisit the SQ3R reading process to help you find the topic and main idea.

When you read using the SQ3R process, in the Survey step you find the **topic**. Then you survey each subheading and create Questions. The answers to those questions will lead you to the **main idea** of each paragraph. So, for example, when you survey the material, you have an idea about what the overall subject or topic will be. Then you can look for the point the author is trying to make about the topic.

Survey	Skim over the material. Read the title, subtitle, subheadings, first and last paragraphs, pictures, charts, and graphics. Note italics and bold print.
Question	Ask yourself questions before you read. What do you want to know? Turn headings and subheadings into questions and/or read questions if provided.
Read	Read the material in manageable chunks. This may be one or two paragraphs at a time or the material under one subheading.
Recite	Recite the answer to each question in your own words. This is a good time to write notes as you read each section. Repeat the question—read—recite cycle.
Review	Look over your notes at the end of the chapter, article, or material. Review what you learned and write a summary in your own words.

Example

Directions: Circle the topic and underline the main idea in the paragraph below.

Kind Words

Love is kind. If then we are to communicate love verbally, we must use kind words. That has to do with the way we speak. The same sentence can have two different meanings, depending on how you say it. The statement "I love you," when said with kindness and tenderness, can be a genuine expression of love. But what about the statement "I love you?" The question mark changes the whole meaning of those three words. Sometimes our words are saying one thing, but our tone of voice is saying another. We are sending double messages. Our spouse will usually interpret our message based on our tone of voice, not the words we use.

Source: Chapman, Gary. (2004). *The Five Love Languages: How to Express Heartfelt Commitment to Your Mate.* Chicago: Northfield Publishing, p. 45.

In the example above, when we Survey the paragraph we see the title, *Kind Words.* This gives us a strong hint about the topic. Skimming through the passage, we also see the words *love, I love you, words, kind words,* and *tone* used several times. The topic is *kind words.* Reading through the paragraph, we ask ourselves, "What is the author's opinion or attitude about kind words?" There are several sentences about how the tone of voice can change the meaning of words. The main idea is the last sentence, "Our spouse will usually interpret our message based on our tone of voice, not the words we use."

PRACTICE THE NEW SKILL

Directions: Survey the paragraph. Then circle the topic and underline the main idea in the paragraphs below.

1. Like it or not, first impressions are very important. I've heard it said that people form their initial opinions of us in the first minute of contact. The reason it's important to get off to a good start is that, once an opinion is formed, it's difficult to alter. So, if people see you as unfriendly, disrespectful, or lacking good manners (even if you didn't intend to come across that way), they will be unlikely to go out of their way to be nice or helpful to you, should that become necessary or desired. They might avoid you, talk behind your back, or share their negative feelings with others. In some instances, they might be downright mean or unfriendly to you. You've given them no reason to act otherwise. It's those negative first impressions that contribute to the phrase, "I don't know what it is about that person, but I don't like him."

Source: Carlson, Richard, Ph.D. (2000). *Don't Sweat the Small Stuff for Teens: Simple Ways to Keep Your Cool in Stressful Times.* New York: Hyperion, p. 107.

2. When you get off to a good start, your positive impression tends to feed on itself. You're nice, so the people you meet like you right away. They have a good feeling about you in positive terms. When they talk to you,

your discussions will be about positive things. When they talk to others, and your name comes up, you'll be discussed in a positive light. If you ever have questions, or need a favor, those people have no reason whatsoever to avoid helping you or answering your questions.

Source: Carlson, Richard, Ph.D. (2000). *Don't Sweat the Small Stuff for Teens: Simple Ways to Keep Your Cool in Stressful Times.* New York: Hyperion, p. 108.

3.   Actually, my father had a profound influence on my life. Both my philosophy of life and of coaching came largely from him. Even as a small boy I always had great respect for him because I always knew he would be fair with me and had my best interests at heart. And as soon as I learned that if he couldn't say something good about another person, he wouldn't say anything at all—a philosophy I've tried to follow.

Source: Wooden, John with Jack Tobin. (2004). *They Call Me Coach.* New York: McGraw-Hill, p. 25.

REVIEW *WHAT YOU LEARNED*

Finding the Topic and Main Idea

Directions: Circle the topic and underline the main idea in the paragraph below.

Blaming others for what's not going right in our lives is often more common than looking in the mirror and taking responsibility for what we have done to contribute or not contribute to our circumstances. If you ever watch the *Dr. Phil* show on TV you know that he is always telling his guests that they create their own experience. If things are not going right for you and you find yourself pointing the finger at others, turn that finger back on yourself, because that's where you need to begin to make changes in your life. You and only you have the power to take charge of your circumstances and create the life you want. It may be true that your boss is a racist or a sexist, your husband or wife might be a liar and a cheater, your mother may have been a drug addict or an alcoholic, but, in light of those circumstances, you have to decide to assume your right to live the life that God intended for you.

Source: Jakes, T. D. (2008). *Before You Do: Making Great Decisions That You Won't Regret.* New York: Thorndike Press, pp. 58–59.

According to this passage, what should you do if things are not going right for you in your life? _____

_____

REVIEW WHAT YOU LEARNED

Finding the Main Idea

A Kiss Isn't Just a Kiss, It's a Chemical Spigot

CHICAGO—"Chemistry look what you've done to me," Donna Summer crooned in Science of Love, and so, it seems, she was right.

Just in time for Valentine's Day, a panel of scientists examined the mystery of what happens when hearts throb and lips lock. Kissing, it turns out, unleashes chemicals that ease stress hormones in both sexes and encourage bonding in men, though not so much in women.

Chemicals in the saliva may be a way to assess a mate, Wendy Hill, dean of the faculty and a professor of neuroscience at Lafayette College, told a meeting of the American Association for the Advancement of Science on Friday.

In an experiment, Hill explained, pairs of heterosexual college students who kissed for 15 minutes while listening to music experienced significant changes in their levels of the chemicals oxytocin, which affects pair bonding, and cortisol, which is associated with stress. Their blood and saliva levels of the chemicals were compared before and after the kiss.

Both men and women had a decline in cortisol after smooching, an indication their stress levels declined.

For men, oxytocin levels increased, indicating more interest in bonding, while oxytocin levels went down in women. "This was a surprise," Hill said.

Source: Schmid, Randolph E. (2009, February 14). "A Kiss Isn't Just A Kiss, It's a Chemical Spigot." *Journal & Courier.*

Survey the newspaper article. Look at the title and the picture. Also read the first and last paragraph of the article.

1. What is the article about? (Topic) _____

_____

Question—Write a question about the article based on your survey.

2. _____

_____

Recite—Answer your question.

3. _____

_____

Review—Write a one-sentence summary of the article (Main Idea).

4–5. _____

_____

_____

NAME: _____   DATE: _____

Finding the Topic and Main Idea

Directions: Circle the topic and underline the main idea in each paragraph.

On a simple, practical level, kindness creates a sense of warmth and openness that allows us to communicate much more easily with other people. We discover that all human beings are just like us, so we are able to relate to them more easily. That generates a spirit of friendship in which there is less need to hide what we feel or what we are doing. As a result, feelings of fear, self-doubt, and insecurity are automatically dispelled, while at the same time other people find it easier to trust us, too. What is more, there is increasing evidence that cultivating positive mental states like kindness and compassion definitely leads to better psychological health and happiness.

It is tremendously important that we try to make something positive of our lives. We were not born for the purpose of causing trouble and harming others. For our life to be of value we need to foster and nurture such basic good human qualities as warmth, kindness, and compassion. If we can do that, our lives will become meaningful, happier, and more peaceful; we will make a positive contribution to the world around us. —His Holiness the Dalai Lama, May 2004

Source: Ferrucci, Piero. (2006). *Forward by H. H. The Dalai Lama. The Power of Kindness: The Unexpected Benefits of Leading a Compassionate Life.* New York: Penguin, Preface.

Directions: Answer the following questions about the article.

What does kindness create, according to the author?

_____

_____

_____

_____

_____

What do we realize that helps us communicate more easily with people?

_____

_____

_____

_____

_____

What is the result when we have a spirit of friendship?

_____

_____

_____

_____

_____

How can we make a positive contribution to the world around us?

_____

_____

_____

_____

_____

MASTER THE LESSON

Finding the Topic and Main Idea

Learning to mirror our parents begins early. (*Note:* "mirroring" is moving or gesturing the same way as another person as a way of bonding or being accepted.)

Creating the Right Vibes

1   Studies into **synchronous** body-language behavior show that people who feel similar emotions, or are on the same wave-length and are likely to be experiencing a rapport, will also begin to match each other's body language and expressions. Being "in sync" to bond with another person begins early in the womb when our body functions and heartbeat match the rhythm of our mother, so mirroring is a state to which we are naturally inclined.

2   When a couple are in the early stages of courtship it's common to see them behave with synchronous movements, almost as if they are dancing. For example, when a woman takes a mouthful of food the man wipes the corner of his mouth; or he begins a sentence and she finishes it for him. When she gets PMS, he develops a strong desire for chocolate; and when she feels bloated, he farts.

3   When a person says "the vibes are right" or that they "feel right" around another person, they are unknowingly referring to mirroring and synchronous behavior. For example, at a restaurant, one person can be reluctant to eat or drink alone for fear of being out of sync with the others. When it comes to ordering the meal, each may check with the others before ordering. "What are you having?" they ask as they try to mirror their meals. This is one of the reasons why playing background music during a date is so effective—the music gets a couple to beat and tap in time together.

Source: Pease, Allen and Barbara Pease. (2004). *The Definitive Book of Body Language: The Hidden Meaning Behind People's Gestures and Expressions.* New York: Bantam, p. 252.

What does *synchronous* mean?

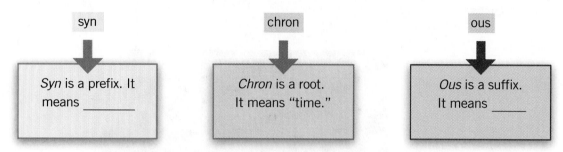

syn

Syn is a prefix. It means _____

chron

Chron is a root. It means "time."

ous

Ous is a suffix. It means _____

Studies into *synchronous* body-language behavior show that people who feel similar emotions, or are on the same wave-length and are likely to be experiencing a rapport, will also begin to match each other's body language and expressions. Being "in sync" to bond with another person begins early in the womb when our body functions and heartbeat match the rhythm of our mother, so mirroring is a state to which we are naturally inclined.

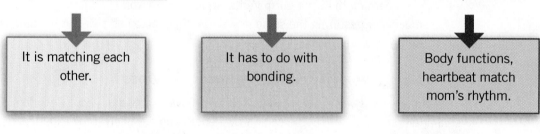

It is matching each other.

It has to do with bonding.

Body functions, heartbeat match mom's rhythm.

Together, these facts let you infer that *synchronous* means:

_____

Check on the word meaning in the dictionary: _____

_____

Look at paragraph 2. Create a pyramid with the information.

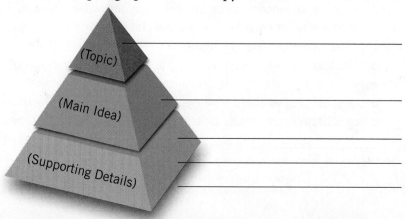

(Topic) _____

(Main Idea) _____

(Supporting Details) _____

_____

(T = Topic; MI = Main Idea; SD = Supporting Detail)

_____T_____ 1. _____   _____

_____MI_____ 2. _____ Studies into synchronous body-language behavior show that people who feel similar emotions, or are on the same wave-length and are likely to be experiencing a rapport, will also begin to match each other's body language and expressions.

_____SD_____ 3. _____

_____

_____SD_____ 4. _____

_____SD_____ 5. _____

_____

_____SD_____ 6. _____

LEARNING STYLE ACTIVITIES

*L*ook, *L*isten, *W*rite, *D*o

Directions: Find the lyrics for the song "You've Got a Friend" by James Taylor and Carole King from a source on the Internet, or from a CD or album cover.

👁 *L*ᴏᴏᴋ   Look at the picture. Describe what the picture shows about the relationship of the two people, James Taylor and Carole King. As you read the song lyrics, imagine a music video where the type of friendship in the song is shown.

🔊 *L*ɪsᴛᴇɴ   Listen to the song, "You've Got a Friend." You can find it on CD, iTunes download, or YouTube. Pay attention to which words are emphasized in the song by changes in the music or voices. You may also want to sing the song with your friends.

✏ *W*ʀɪᴛᴇ   As you read the lyrics, write notes about the meanings of the different figurative phrases such as "close your eyes and think of me and soon I will be there" or "when that old north wind should begin to blow."

👆 *D*ᴏ   As you read the song lyrics, think of your own friends. Describe situations you have experienced that different lines of the song bring to mind. Try to imagine what phrases such as "keep your head together" and "I'll come knocking upon your door" might mean as you think about your friends.

Reading Practice

The next section of the chapter will help refine your skills in finding the topic and main idea while you read a variety of materials. Remember to use SQ3R while you read. All five of the readings address topics related to life relationships.

The first reading, from the Internet, is "Rule of Thumbs: Love in the Age of Texting" from *TheWashingtonPost.com*.

The second reading is a section called "The Faces of Conflict" from the textbook *Cornerstone: Creating Success through Positive Change*.

The third reading is from literature. It is an excerpt from *The Notebook* by Nicholas Sparks.

The fourth reading is "Social Networking Sites: Safety Tips for Tweens and Teens" from the Federal Trade Commission.

The fifth reading is a visual image of friends hanging out together.

In each of the reading selections, several vocabulary words appear in bold. Use your knowledge of word parts and/or context clues to help determine the meanings. Answering the questions following each reading will help you continue to develop your vocabulary and reading comprehension. In the visual reading, you will need to find the main idea of the image.

Internet

READING 1

Rule of Thumbs: Love in the Age of Texting

1   I once had a boyfriend who was Mr. Text-o-Rama.

2   He never wanted to talk, but he always wanted to text. To him, the only way to communicate was via thumb.

3   I remember a Saturday afternoon I spent with a female friend when I didn't have my cell phone handy. By the evening, I had a *logjam* of text messages from him. The final mess of a message inquired whether our relationship was over because of my "lack of communication."

4   I called him. He didn't answer.

5   And so it went. During our relationship, he sent me *curt* texts reeking of attitude. He sent texts that had the *elocution* of an *August Wilson soliloquy*. If I tried to actually call him to work something out, he'd fire off a snippy "You're busy. I'll talk to you later." It got so I wished I could string him up by his thumbs.

6   Looking back, I see that relationship as the *embodiment* of how technology is slowly killing romance. It's draining the courting out of courtship. And frankly, I'm ready to hit "delete" on the whole thing.

7   A flirtatious text here and there is fine, but a text of more than 100 characters? That's overkill (not to mention hard to read). When the time comes, I don't want to see the words "will u marry me" in one-point font. Call me old-fashioned, but I wonder what's so "advanced" about these so-called advancements in communication. When they're abused, they can make a caveman's grunt seem refined. The same gadgets that allow you to be in touch all the time sometimes mask the fact that you never really touched at all.

8   "Texting is a way of life," says etiquette expert Joy Weaver, "but it cannot replace the human voice or touch." Tell me about it.

9   The relationship began sweetly enough. We met through mutual friends and quickly took a liking to each other. We visited museums and bookstores and

---

Logjam—massive accumulation
Curt—short
Elocution—a style or manner of speaking
August Wilson soliloquy—African American storyteller who used drama and intensity in a one-person act
Embodiment—expression or example of

camped out at *dive bars*. I liked that he was so expressive and open. And I had never dated a guy who liked to communicate quite so much in so many ways.

10   "I love you."

11   I looked down at my cell phone and read the text message. It was the first time he'd expressed those dreamy words. My heart fluttered. I immediately speed-dialed him back to hear him say it out loud. He didn't answer. "Call you later," he texted me back.

12   At the time, I was too *giddy* to notice—or care—how weird that was, or how even weirder the many scenarios that followed were: being forced to boost the allotment on my mobile text-messaging plan. So much passive aggression delivered via tiny rectangular pieces of plastic.

13   My thumbs becoming so tired.

14   Initially, texting with him was thrilling. Wherever I was—on assignment, at the airport, out with friends—his sweet messages triggered butterflies. It was like talking, or flirting, but better. We were always only a few keystrokes away from communicating at any time, night or day.

15   But soon that became the problem.

16   On the day of my birthday bash, he texted me that he was "uncomfortable" with our relationship and that we needed to talk before the party.

17   Say what? We hadn't had a fight. I called him. No answer. I called again and again and again. Finally, he answered with some lame excuse. I'm still not sure exactly what the problem was.

18   Repeat scenario. Add water and stir. He often seemed unable to articulate what made him mad or uneasy. But that didn't stop him from firing off messages accusing me of not communicating. Me. The girl who likes to hear or see the person she's talking to.

19   The final few weeks before we broke things off were a blur, one long string of digitally delivered *angst*. Once upon a time, drunken dialing could ruin a relationship. Ha. Try getting drunken, misspelled texts at 3 a.m.

20   What was I to make of this? According to Barb Iverson, a professor of new media at Columbia College Chicago, the latest technology revolution means that there are now two kinds of people in the world: "digital immigrants" and "digital natives." The digital immigrants came of age before the technology revolution and they struggle to adapt to the new language, rituals and protocol. The digital natives instinctively *emote* through their thumbs and don't consider a relationship "official" until their Facebook or MySpace profile says it is.

Dive bars—neighborhood bars
Giddy—excited
Angst—anxiety, torment, trouble, fear
Emote—to show emotion

21   Then there are the Gen-Xers like me who are somewhere in between.

22   In the United States, we have come fairly late to the texting game. The Chinese, who embraced this technology years before it arrived here, send 300 billion text messages a year, and the number is rising. Half the 13- to 15-year-olds in Australia own cellphones. In Japan, some experts have noted that thumbs are growing physically bigger and people are now using that digit—and not the index finger—to point and ring doorbells. Texting is so prevalent that Japanese teenagers are called the "tribe of the thumb."

23   Anthropologist Bella Ellwood-Clayton studied texting and dating in the Philippines, which she calls the texting capital of the world. In a 2005 study, she detailed how it works: A man might send an *innocuous* text message to a woman. If she replies quickly and with warmth, the texts back and forth increase in familiarity—and *innuendo*. "It is also a fairly nonthreatening way to initiate communication with someone versus a phone call or face-to-face methods, which demand greater bravery and often directness of intention," Ellwood-Clayton noted.

24   As we catch up here in the United States, we are *grappling* with the social implications that come along with texting.

25   As I learned, if emotions become involved, texting can quickly *devolve* into a power play. Because people usually keep their cell phones within reach, angry text forces the hand of the recipient: If you love me, you'll respond right now! It's not the same interruption as a phone call. You can work, watch television, sit in class or talk to a friend while texting.

26   My single friend Thomas says that "good morning" texts or short messages in the middle of the workday from a girlfriend are fine to let him know she's thinking of him. But receiving a text at 7 p.m. asking "How are you?" is a chicken way of saying "I want to talk to you without actually calling." He says the woman is probably at home willing the phone to ring. Her *recourse*? A text.

27   This *deranged* texting dance doesn't stop with singles. A married friend rolled her eyes as she *recounted* how her husband, sitting in another room in their house, sent her a sour text after an argument to cancel their night out on the town. It was widely reported that Britney Spears ended her marriage to Kevin Federline via text.

Innocuous—harmless, innocent, mild
Innuendo—suggestion, hint
Grappling—struggling
Devolve—to fall downward
Recourse—option, choice
Deranged—unbalanced, disturbed
Recounted—told, described

28   But in text, *nuances* in tone, mood and intent go by the wayside. Just like the pseudo lives of millions of addicted MySpacers, too much texting can create what media theorists call "parasocial" behavior. This term is applied to people who believe that constant virtual contact is more than just pretend intimacy.

29   In an online and magazine ad campaign, mobile phone company Helio put out guidelines on social etiquette and technology, filled with pop quizzes and diagrams. It includes a *primer* on emoticons and abbreviations (e.g. YMMFS—you make my fingers sweat).

30   The company suggests several texting rules for dating: Don't flirt too long virtually; if someone doesn't text you back in 24 hours, it's not happening; only cowards settle arguments via text, and text breakups don't count.

31   And the No. 1 text message rule: Keep it short.

32   The campaign is all *tongue-in-cheek*, but if you ask me, some people need to pay attention.

33   I now believe that texting should be reserved for the following notifications: "I'm running late." "I'm outside." "Meet me at [insert location.]" "It's noisy; I'll call you later." "What time are the reservations?"

34   And yes, "I love you" is fine—but only if you've already said those words in person.

Natalie Y. Moore is a public affairs reporter for Chicago Public Radio.
Source: Natalie Y. Moore. "Rule of Thumbs: Love in the Age of Texting." Retrieved from http://www.washingtonpost.com/.

Questions

Directions: Use the context clues to find the meanings of the highlighted words.

What was I to make of this? According to Barb Iverson, a professor of new media at Columbia College Chicago, the latest technology revolution means that there are now two kinds of people in the world: "***digital immigrants***" and "***digital natives***." The digital immigrants came of age before the technology revolution and they struggle to adapt to the new language, rituals and protocol. The digital natives instinctively emote through their thumbs and don't consider a relationship "official" until their Facebook or MySpace profile says it is.

1. What are *digital immigrants*? ———————————————

———————————————————————————

———————————————————————————

Nuances—shades, fine distinctions
Primer—introduction, basic coverage
Tongue-in-cheek—humorous

2. What are *digital natives*? _____

_____

3–4. *articulate*

Repeat scenario. Add water and stir. He often seemed unable to ***articulate*** what made him mad or uneasy. But that didn't stop him from firing off messages accusing me of not communicating. Me. The girl who likes to hear or see the person she's talking to.

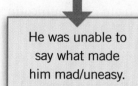

He was unable to say what made him mad/uneasy.

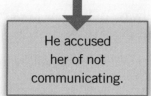

He accused her of not communicating.

He fired off messages.

Together, these facts let you infer that ***articulate*** means _____

_____

Check on the word meaning with the dictionary:

_____

5–6. *pseudo lives* and *parasocial*

But in text, nuances in tone, mood and intent go by the wayside. Just like the ***pseudo lives*** of millions of addicted MySpacers, too much texting can create what media theorists call "***parasocial***" behavior. This term is applied to people who believe that constant virtual contact is more than just pretend intimacy.

If *pseudo* is a root word that means "false or fake," what does ***pseudo lives*** mean?

_____

If *para* is a prefix that means "beyond," what does ***parasocial*** mean?

_____

7. What is the topic of the article?

    a. thumbs and texting   **c.** love and texting

    b. annoying boyfriends   **d.** international texting

8. What is the main idea of the following paragraph?

> Initially, texting with him was thrilling. Wherever I was—on assignment, at the airport, out with friends—his sweet messages triggered butterflies. It was like talking, or flirting, but better. We were always only a few keystrokes away from communicating at any time, night or day.

   a. Initially, texting with him was thrilling.

   b. Wherever I was—on assignment, at the airport, out with friends—his sweet messages triggered butterflies.

   c. It was like talking, or flirting, but better.

   d. We were always only a few keystrokes away from communicating at any time, night or day.

9. What is the main idea of the following paragraph?

> A flirtatious text here and there is fine, but a text of more than 100 characters? That's overkill (not to mention hard to read). When the time comes, I don't want to see the words "will u marry me" in one-point font. Call me old-fashioned, but I wonder what's so "advanced" about these so-called advancements in communication. When they're abused, they can make a caveman's grunt seem refined. The same gadgets that allow you to be in touch all the time sometimes mask the fact that you never really touched at all.

   a. A flirtatious text here and there is fine, but a text of more than 100 characters?

   b. When the time comes, I don't want to see the words "will u marry me" in one-point font.

   c. When they're abused, they can make a caveman's grunt seem refined.

   d. The same gadgets that allow you to be in touch all the time sometimes mask the fact that you never really touched at all.

10–13. What are the guidelines on social etiquette and technology from the on-line and magazine ad campaign from the mobile phone company, Helio?

   a. _____

   b. _____

   c. _____

   d. _____

14–15. What do you think about Helio's guidelines for using technology? Explain which of the suggestions make the most or the least sense to you.

_____

_____

_____

_____

_____

16–20. Explain whether you agree with the writer's conclusion. Give your own examples of how you use texting to communicate, and discuss any problems you've had with being understood in text messages or other electronic communication.

> I now believe that texting should be reserved for the following notifications: "I'm running late." "I'm outside." "Meet me at [insert location.]" "It's noisy; I'll call you later." "What time are the reservations?"
> And yes, "I love you" is fine—but only if you've already said those words in person.

_____

_____

_____

_____

_____

_____

_____

Textbook READING 2

THE FACES OF CONFLICT

Uggggg! How Do I Deal with Negative, Nasty, Difficult People?

We've all encountered them from time to time: DIFFICULT people who are negative, angry, unhappy, destructive, argumentative, sad, depressed, and/or judgmental. They are people who seem to walk around with a black cloud above their heads and seem to enjoy causing interpersonal conflict—like the negative people discussed in Chapter 1. They are likely to pop up everywhere—at work, in class, in traffic, in restaurants, and even in places of worship. They cannot be avoided. Figure 3.7 profiles the most common types of negative, difficult people. Perhaps you recognize some of them. Read the descriptions and try to develop at least two or three strategies to effectively deal with each type of difficult person. In developing your strategies, you may have to rely on others in your class for assistance, pull from your past experiences (what worked and what did not), and do some research on your own.

Learning to manage conflict and work with difficult people is a very important step in developing sound communication practices and healthy relationships. If you can learn to stay calm, put yourself in the other person's shoes, and try to find mutually beneficial solutions, you will gain admiration and respect from your friends, family, peers, and colleagues. As you consider conflicts in your life and relationships, take a moment to complete the Conflict Management Assessment (Figure 3.8) to determine your awareness of issues related to conflict and managing conflict.

STANDARDS FOR DEALING WITH DIFFICULT PEOPLE AND MANAGING CONFLICT

▶ Check your own behavior before doing anything else. Don't become the same type of difficult person as the people with whom you are dealing. Fighting fire with fire will only make the flame hotter. Learn to be the "cool" one.

▶ Don't take the other person's attitude or words personally. Most of the time, he or she doesn't know you or your life.

▶ AVOID physical contact with others at all expense.

▶ If you must give criticism, do so with a positive tone and attitude.

▶ Remember that everyone is sensitive about himself herself and his her situation. Avoid language that will set someone off.

▶ Do not verbally attack the other person; simply state your case and your ideas.

▶ Allow the other person to save face. Give the person a way to escape embarrassment. People may forgive you for stepping on their toes, but they will never forgive you for stepping on their feelings.

▶ If you have a problem with someone or someone's actions, be specific and let the person know before it gets out of hand. He or she can't read your mind.

▶ If someone shows signs of becoming physically aggressive toward you, get help early, stay calm, talk slowly and calmly to the other person, and, if necessary, walk away to safety.

▶ Allow the other person to vent fully before you begin any negotiation or resolution.

▶ Try to create "win-win" situations in which everyone can walk away having gained something.

▶ Determine whether the conflict is a "person" conflict or a "situation" conflict.

▶ Ask the other person or people what he/she/they need(s). Try to understand the situation.

▶ Realize that *you* may very well be "in the wrong."

▶ When dealing with conflict and other people, ask yourself, ***"If this were my last action on earth, would I be proud of how I acted?"***

Now answer the question in bold print at the beginning of the reading, **"Uggggg! How do I deal with negative, nasty, difficult people?"** Complete the chart on the next page. You may work on your own or with other people.

FIGURE

3.7 *Types of Difficult Behaviors and People*

Types of Difficult Behaviors by Difficult People	Description	What can you do to effectively deal with them?
Gossiping	They don't do a lot of work and would rather spread rumors and untruths about others to make themselves feel better.	
Manipulating	They constantly try to negotiate every aspect of life. I'll do this for you if you do this for me."	
Showing Off	They usually talk more than they work. They know everything about every subject and are not willing to listen to anything or anybody new.	
Goofing Off	They usually do very little and what they do is incorrect. They pretend to be involved, but spend more time looking busy more than actually being busy.	
Standing By	They do not get involved in anything or any cause but then complain because something did not go their way.	
Complaining	They may produce work and be involved, but complains about everything and everybody and seems to exist under a rain cloud. Nothing is ever good enough.	
Dooming and Glooming	They are so negative they make death look like a joy ride. They are constantly thinking about the "worst-case" scenario and don't mind voicing it.	

Source: Excerpt from *Cornerstone: Creating Success Through Positive Change,* 6th Edition by Robert M. Sherfield and Patricia G. Moody. Copyright © 2011 by Robert M. Sherfield and Patricia G. Moody. Printed and Electronically reproduced by permission of Pearson Education, Inc., Upper Saddle River, New Jersey.

Complete the Conflict Management Assessment on the next page. List your score, and discuss what it means about your ability to handle conflict.

_____

_____

_____

_____

_____

_____

FIGURE

3.8   *Conflict Management Assessment*

Read the following questions carefully and respond according to the key below. Take your time and be honest with yourself.

1 = NEVER typical of the way I address conflict
2 = SOMETIMES typical of the way I address conflict
3 = OFTEN typical of the way I address conflict
4 = ALMOST ALWAYS typical of the way I address conflict

1. When someone verbally attacks me, I can let it go and move on.	1	2	3	4
2. I would rather resolve an issue than have to "be right" about it.	1	2	3	4
3. I try to avoid arguments and verbal confrontations at all costs.	1	2	3	4
4. Once I've had a conflict with someone, I can forget it and get along with that person just fine.	1	2	3	4
5. I look at conflicts in my relationships as positive growth opportunities.	1	2	3	4
6. When I'm in a conflict, I will try many ways to resolve it.	1	2	3	4
7. When I'm in a conflict, I try not to verbally attack or abuse the other person.	1	2	3	4
8. When I'm in a conflict, I try never to blame the other person; rather, I look at every side.	1	2	3	4
9. When I'm in a conflict, I try not to avoid the other person.	1	2	3	4
10. When I'm in a conflict, I try to talk through the issue with the other person.	1	2	3	4
11. When I'm in a conflict, I often feel empathy for the other person.	1	2	3	4
12. When I'm in a conflict, I do not try to manipulate the other person.	1	2	3	4
13. When I'm in a conflict, I try never to withhold my love or affection for that person.	1	2	3	4
14. When I'm in a conflict, I try never to attack the person; I concentrate on their actions.	1	2	3	4
15. When I'm in a conflict, I try to never insult the other person.	1	2	3	4
16. I believe in give and take when trying to resolve a conflict.	1	2	3	4
17. I understand AND USE the concept that kindness can solve more conflicts than cruelty.	1	2	3	4
18. I am able to control my defensive attitude when I'm in a conflict.	1	2	3	4
19. I keep my temper in check and do not yell and scream during conflicts.	1	2	3	4
20. I am able to accept "defeat" at the end of a conflict.	1	2	3	4

Number of 1s _____   Number of 2s _____   Number of 3s _____   Number of 4s _____

If you have more 1s, you do not handle conflict very well and have few tools for conflict management. You have a tendency to anger quickly and lose your temper during the conflict. If you have more 2s, you have a tendency to want to work through conflict, but you lack the skills to carry this tendency through. You can hold your anger and temper for a while, but eventually, it gets the best of you. If you have more 3s, you have some helpful skills in handling conflict. You tend to work very hard for a peaceful and mutually beneficial outcome for all parties. If you have more 4s, you are very adept at handling conflict and do well with mediation, negotiation, and anger management. You are approachable; people turn to you for advice about conflicts and resolutions.

© Robert M. Sherfield, Ph.D.

Source: Excerpt from *Cornerstone: Creating Success Through Positive Change,* 6th Edition by Robert M. Sherfield and Patricia G. Moody. Copyright © 2011 by Robert M. Sherfield and Patricia G. Moody. Printed and Electronically reproduced by permission of Pearson Education, Inc., Upper Saddle River, New Jersey.

If you wanted to read more about conflict management and learn better ways to deal with people, how would you find relevant and useful materials? List 3 ways:

_____

_____

_____

_____

Literature   **READING 3**

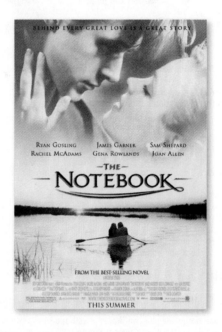

The Notebook is a story of an elderly man who reads to his wife every day from an old notebook. She has Alzheimer's disease, which has caused her to lose her memory. She thinks he is a stranger who is just visiting and reading to her. Their love story comes alive as he reads the details of their life from the old notebook, a diary she wrote when she was young. The following excerpt is just two pages from the beginning of the book. The man is describing himself and the love he has for his wife.

The Notebook

MIRACLES

1   Who am I? And how, I wonder, will this story end?

2   The sun has come up and I am sitting by a window that is foggy with the breath of a life gone by. I'm a sight this morning: two shirts, heavy pants, a scarf

wrapped twice around my neck and tucked into a thick sweater knitted by my daughter thirty birthdays ago. The thermostat in my room is set as high as it will go, and a smaller space heater sits directly behind me. It clicks and groans and spews hot air like a fairy-tale dragon, and still my body shivers with a cold that will never go away, a cold that has been eighty years in the making. Eighty years, I think sometimes, and despite my own acceptance of my age, it still amazes me that I haven't been warm since George Bush was president. I wonder if this is how it is for everyone my age.

3   My life? It isn't easy to explain. It has not been the rip-roaring spectacular I fancied it would be, but neither have I burrowed around with the gophers. I suppose it has most resembled a *blue-chip stock*: fairly stable, more ups than downs, and gradually trending upward over time. A good buy, a lucky buy, and I've learned that not everyone can say this about his life. But do not be misled. I am nothing special; of this I am sure. I am a common man with common thoughts, and I've led a common life. There are no monuments dedicated to me and my name will soon be forgotten, but I've loved another with all my heart and soul, and to me, this has always been enough.

Source: Sparks, Nicholas. (1996). *The Notebook.*
New York: Warner Books, Inc., pp. 1–2.

Questions

Directions: Use context clues, word parts, and/or the dictionary to find the meaning of the highlighted word.

1–2. *spews*

The thermostat in my room is set as high as it will go, and a smaller space heater sits directly behind me. It clicks and groans and ***spews*** hot air like a fairy-tale dragon, and still my body shivers with a cold that will never go away, a cold that has been eighty years in the making.

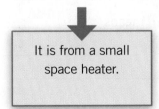

It is from a small space heater.

It involves hot air doing something.

The hot air is like a dragon.

Blue-chip stock—a stock investment in a company that has made money for the investor over years

Together, these facts let you infer that **spews** means _____.

Choose the best definition for **spews** from the dictionary. _____

_____

3–7. **spectacular** and **fancied**

My life? It isn't easy to explain. It has not been the rip-roaring **spectacular** I **fancied** it would be, but neither have I burrowed around with the gophers. I suppose it has most resembled a blue-chip stock: fairly stable, more ups than downs, and gradually trending upward over time.

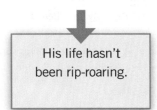

His life hasn't been rip-roaring.

Not burrowing around with gophers.

His life has been more stable.

3. Together, these facts let you infer that **spectacular** means _____

4. What word root is in **spectacular** that means "to see"? _____

5. Using the dictionary, what does **spectacular** mean? _____

_____

_____

6. Together, these facts let you infer that **fancied** means _____

7. Using the dictionary, what does **fancied** mean?_____

_____

8. What is the topic of the passage?

    a. growing old   **c.** true love

    b. regretting the past   **d.** care and concern

9. What is the main idea of the first paragraph?

   a. The thermostat in my room is set as high as it will go, and a smaller space heater sits directly behind me.

   b. I'm a sight this morning: two shirts, heavy pants, a scarf wrapped twice around my neck and tucked into a thick sweater knitted by my daughter thirty birthdays ago.

   c. I wonder if this is how it is for everyone my age.

10. What is the main idea of the second paragraph?

   a. There are no monuments dedicated to me and my name will soon be forgotten, but I've loved another with all my heart and soul, and to me, this has always been enough.

   b. A good buy, a lucky buy, and I've learned that not everyone can say this about his life.

   c. I am nothing special; of this I am sure. I am a common man with common thoughts, and I've led a common life.

Magazine/Periodical **READING 4**

Social Networking Sites: Safety Tips for Tweens and Teens

Apply the SQ3R technique to the reading.

Survey	Skim over the material. Read the title, subtitle, subheadings, first and last paragraphs, pictures, charts, and graphics. Note italics and bold print.
Question	Ask yourself questions before you read. What do you want to know? Turn headings and subheadings into questions and/or read questions if provided.
Read	Read the material in manageable chunks. This may be one or two paragraphs at a time or the material under one subheading.
Recite	Recite the answer to each question in your own words. This is a good time to write notes as you read each section. Repeat the question–read–recite cycle.
Review	Look over your notes at the end of the chapter, article, or material. Review what you learned, and write a summary in your own words.

1   You've probably learned a long list of important safety and privacy lessons already: Look both ways before crossing the street; buckle up; hide your diary where your nosy brother can't find it; don't talk to strangers.

2   The Federal Trade Commission, the nation's consumer protection agency, is urging kids to add one more lesson to the list: Don't post information about yourself online that you don't want the whole world to know. The Internet is the world's biggest information exchange: many more people could see your information than you intend, including your parents, your teachers, your employer, the police—and strangers, some of whom could be dangerous.

3   Social networking sites have added a new factor to the "friends of friends" equation. By providing information about yourself and using blogs, chat rooms, email, or instant messaging, you can communicate, either within a limited community, or with the world at large. But while the sites can increase your circle of friends, they also can increase your exposure to people who have less-than-friendly intentions. You've heard the stories about people who were stalked by someone they met online, had their identity stolen, or had their computer hacked.

YOUR SAFETY'S AT STAKE

The FTC suggests these tips for socializing safely online:

- Think about how different sites work before deciding to join a site. Some sites will allow only a defined community of users to access posted content; others allow anyone and everyone to view postings.

- Think about keeping some control over the information you post. Consider restricting access to your page to a select group of people, for example, your friends from school, your club, your team, your community groups, or your family.

- Keep your information to yourself. Don't post your full name, Social Security number, address, phone number, or bank and credit card account numbers—and don't post other people's information, either. Be cautious about posting information that could be used to identify you or locate you offline. This could include the name of your school, sports team, clubs, and where you work or hang out.

- Make sure your screen name doesn't say too much about you. Don't use your name, your age, or your hometown. Even if you think your screen name makes you anonymous, it doesn't take a genius to combine clues to figure out who you are and where you can be found.

- Post only information that you are comfortable with others seeing—and knowing—about you. Many people can see your page, including your parents, your teachers, the police, the college you might want to apply to next year, or the job you might want to apply for in five years.

- Remember that once you post information online, you can't take it back. Even if you delete the information from a site, older versions exist on other people's computers.

- Consider not posting your photo. It can be altered and broadcast in ways you may not be happy about. If you do post one, ask yourself whether it's one your mom would display in the living room.

- Flirting with strangers online could have serious consequences. Because some people lie about who they really are, you never really know who you're dealing with.

- Be wary if a new online friend wants to meet you in person. Before you decide to meet someone, do your research: Ask whether any of your friends know the person, and see what background you can dig up through online search engines. If you decide to meet them, be smart about it: Meet in a public place, during the day, with friends you trust. Tell an adult or a responsible sibling where you're going, and when you expect to be back.

- Trust your gut if you have suspicions. If you feel threatened by someone or uncomfortable because of something online, tell an adult you trust and report it to the police and the social networking site. You could end up preventing someone else from becoming a victim.

Source: http://www.ftc.gov/bcp/edu/pubs/consumer/tech/tec14.shtm
Retrieved from the Federal Trade Commission.

Questions

Survey—What is the article about? _____

_____

Question and Recite—Create your questions and then recite your answers. *Hint:* Each paragraph or bullet point may be used for a question.

    Question: What does the Federal Trade Commission urge kids to learn?

    Recite Answer: _____

    _____

    _____

    Question: What is the danger with "friends of friends"?

    Recite Answer: _____

    _____

    _____

Question: What should you know about how different sites work before you join?

Recite Answer: _____

_____

_____

Question: How should you keep some control over the information you post?

Recite Answer: _____

_____

_____

Question: What does it mean to keep information to yourself?

Recite Answer: _____

_____

_____

_____

Question: How do you make sure your screen name doesn't say too much?

Recite Answer: _____

_____

_____

Question: _____

_____

Recite Answer: _____

_____

_____

Question: _____

_____

Recite Answer: _____

_____

_____

Question: _____

_____

Recite Answer: _____

_____

_____

Question: _____

_____

Recite Answer: _____

_____

_____

Question: _____

_____

Recite Answer: _____

_____

_____

Question: _____

_____

Recite Answer: _____

_____

_____

Review—Write a brief summary of the article.

_____

_____

_____

_____

_____

Critical Thinking Application

Write a well-developed paragraph discussing which of these suggestions you could use to improve the safety of you or your children's safety online on social networking sites. Write your point (main idea) and then at least two specific supporting details to prove, illustrate, or explain the point (main idea) you are trying to make.

_____

_____

_____

_____

_____

_____

Visual Image **READING 5**

Directions: Answer the questions below based on the people and their use of body language in the picture.

1–3. Describe which people are most relaxed in the photo. What are the clues?

_____

_____

_____

_____

_____

_____

_____

4–6. Who is least relaxed in the photo? What are the clues?

_____

_____

_____

_____

_____

_____

_____

7–10. Write a conversation the people in the picture might be having. Include a topic and main idea in their dialogue.

_____

_____

_____

_____

_____

_____

4 Supporting Details

THEME – Using Your Time Wisely

SPOTLIGHT ON LEARNING STYLES Look Write

It is so easy to waste time, even when I have the best intentions. I've heard people say, "I lost track of the time" or "the time got away from me." When I'm doing things I enjoy, I rarely watch the clock. This makes it easy to forget about time and relax. However, when I need to get things done by a deadline, or when I have many things to do, I use a different approach—my See and Write learning style. Seeing my list of things to do that I have written on a planner keeps me on track. If my "to-do" list is really long, I group similar items together, such as putting the errands I need to run in order of location. When I fill out my planner, I see the times of my appointments and classes and then I fill it in with assignments in between. I used to cross things off as I finished them to get a sense of accomplishment. Lately, though, I've started erasing things as I get them done. This helps me see my list getting smaller throughout the day and week. Setting a reward and seeing it on the list works well. I plan something I enjoy as a special treat for accomplishing my goals each day. A small reward may be simply watching a favorite television show or taking a long walk in the park or the woods with my dog. The more difficult the goal, the bigger the reward I set. Using my See learning style really helps me stay motivated, use my time wisely, and get things done so I have more time to enjoy life!

Now that you are in college, you have new demands on your time. Whether you are returning to school with a family of your own, managing a job and school, living with a roommate or with your parents, it is your responsibility and choice to spend time on the aspects of your life that you value the most. Setting priorities and completing tasks more efficiently will help you make the most of your time and achieve your goals.

There is a lot of material to read in college. One important way to make the most of your time is to learn to read more effectively and efficiently. By finding the topic, the main idea, and the relevant details when you read, you will improve your reading effectiveness. In this chapter, you will develop your reading comprehension skills while learning more about managing your time—a very efficient plan!

In the previous chapter you learned how to identify the main idea of a paragraph. To better comprehend the text, it is also important to understand how the details in the paragraph support and develop the main idea. In this chapter you will learn to recognize and use the author's supporting details when you read. While you are improving your understanding of how the main idea relates to the supporting details within a text, you'll also be learning better ways to manage your time.

Reading the Other Sentences (What details are included in the paragraph?)

When an author writes a paragraph, there is usually a point she is trying to make. As you read a paragraph, notice that there are usually several sentences related to the main idea the author is presenting.

> **LO1**
> Determine what details are important for understanding the text.

If a sentence supports the author's point, it is called a **supporting detail**. For example, if the author's main idea involves alternative energy sources, sentences that offer supporting details might discuss biodiesel fuels, solar energy, or wind power. Similarly, an article on childhood obesity might support its main idea with sentences that discuss junk food or video games.

How can you recognize supporting details? Often these sentences will appear at the beginning of the paragraphs that follow the main idea in a longer passage or article. They will back up or give more information about the main idea. In a single paragraph, the supporting details are sentences that prove, illustrate, or explain the main idea.

EXAMPLE

Directions: For the group of statements below, write the topic in your own words on the line.

1. Topic _____

   a. Studying will take a significant amount of time for each of your classes.

   b. Maintaining old and new relationships requires time.

   c. In college, there are many demands on your time.

The statements refer to the general topic of *time*. You can clearly see that the author is writing about time because the word *time* is used in every sentence. Once you can focus on the general topic, then you can determine what point the author is trying to make.

PRACTICE THE NEW SKILL

Directions: Write the topic for the statements below.

1. Topic _____

   a. Managing your time is a must in college.

   b. There are many time management techniques you can easily use.

   c. Using planners is one way to manage your time.

2. Topic _____

   a. Stress can hurt your health.

   b. Running out of time may cause stress.

   c. Getting important work done may reduce your stress.

3. Topic _____

   a. One way to organize is to reduce clutter.

   b. Organizing your life gives you more personal time.

   c. Donating unneeded items is a good way to begin getting organized.

Using PIE (How do the sentences Prove, Illustrate, or Explain the author's point?)

The acronym **PIE** will help you remember what to look for in the supporting details. Ask yourself if the sentence Proves, Illustrates, or Explains (PIE) the author's main idea. Each supporting detail is like a piece of the "PIE."

LO2
Use PIE to remember the major supporting details (Prove, Illustrate, or Explain).

LO3
Use a diagram to better comprehend important ideas.

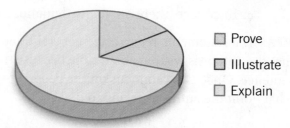

☐ Prove

☐ Illustrate

☐ Explain

You can approach the main idea/supporting details relationship from two directions: from general to specific or from specific to general. For instance, it might make more sense to identify the main idea first and then look for the supporting details. Or it might make more sense to see several related supporting details and then ask yourself what they are trying to prove, illustrate, or explain.

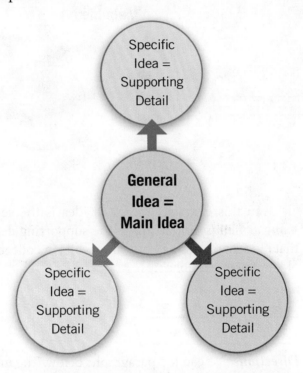

First, let's try it from general (main idea) to specific (supporting detail).

EXAMPLE

Directions: Read the sentences below. The main idea is underlined. Write supporting details that illustrate the main idea either on the lines or on the chart on the next page.

- In college there are many demands on your time.
- Studying will take significant time for each of your classes.
- Maintaining old and new relationships requires time.

a. _____

b. _____

Complete the chart (S.D. is Supporting Detail)

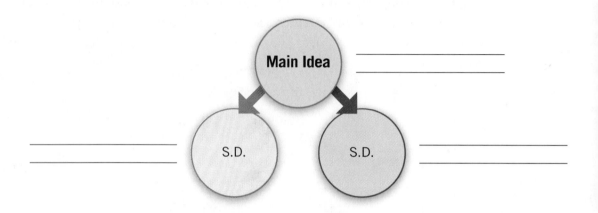

In this example, the main idea is the sentence, *In college there are many demands on your time.* The supporting details are examples of things that place demands on your time while in college: studying and maintaining old and new relationships.

PRACTICE *THE NEW SKILL*

Directions: Read the paragraphs below. The main idea is underlined. Write specific supporting details from the paragraph in the lines below or complete the charts.

1.   <u>There are several ideas to help you manage your time.</u> Using a daily planner helps you see where your time needs to be spent. Learning to say "no" will lead to using your time more wisely.

What supporting details illustrate the main idea? *HINT: What ideas from the passage may help manage your time?*

a. _____

b. _____

2.   <u>Working in blocks of time is more efficient than working piecemeal.</u> This applies not only to the batching of similar tasks such as telephone calls or to the handling of incoming mail, but also to project work, sales calls, or a marketing campaign. Peter Drucker suggests that the ideal span of time to work is 90 minutes. You will get more done in a concentrated period of 90 minutes than twice the time in an environment of regular interruptions.

Source: Gleeson, Kerry (2004). *The Personal Efficiency Program,* 3rd ed.: *How to Get Organized to Do More Work in Less Time.* Hoboken, NJ: John Wiley & Sons: Hoboken, p. 74.

What supporting details explain the main idea? *HINT: What is the ideal span of time to work and why is it better?*

a. _____

b. _____

_____

3.   <u>One of the new ailments of the technological age is an addiction to</u>
<u>being online.</u> Obviously the internet is a magnificent tool for research and
can save us vast amounts of time. It also offers the potential for each of us
to connect with every other person on the planet and thereby to achieve the
oneness we're all seeking. The possibilities for that are truly mind-boggling.
But according to research conducted at major universities around the
country, for many people being online has become a time-wasting habit.
For millions of others, it can be anything from a disturbing dependency to a
compulsive disorder.

> *Source:* St. James, Elaine. (2001). *Simplify Your Work Life: Ways to Change the Way You Work*
> *So You Have More Time to Live.* New York: Hyperion, p. 75.

What supporting details illustrate the main idea? *HINT: According to the
passage, what are three ways a person can show they are addicted to being
online?*

a. _____

b. _____

c. _____

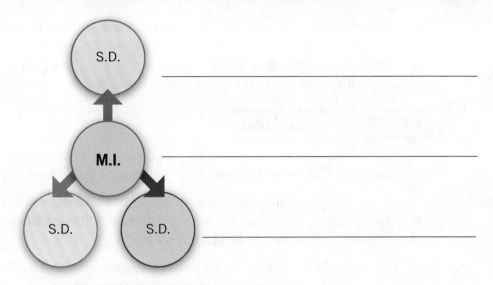

Now we'll try using the specific supporting details to help us find the general main idea.

EXAMPLE ──

Directions: Use the underlined supporting details to help identify the main idea. Write the main idea in the space below.

> I'm sure that at some time or other you've gotten to a place in a project, or in your life, where you just *had* to sit down and *make a list.* If so, you have a reference point for what I'm talking about. Most people, however, do that kind of list-making drill only when the confusion gets too unbearable and they just have to do something about it. They usually make a list only about the specific area that's bugging them. But if you made that kind of review a characteristic of your ongoing life- and work style, and you maintained it across all areas of your life (not just the most "urgent"), you'd be practicing the kind of *"black belt"* management style I'm describing.
>
> Source: Allen, David. (2001). *Getting Things Done: The Art of Stress-Free Productivity.* New York: Penguin Group, p. 22.

Main Idea

──

──

The main idea is the last sentence, "But if you made that kind of review a characteristic of your ongoing life- and work style, and you maintained it

---

Black belt—refers to the top level of martial arts, the most skilled.

across all areas of your life (not just the most "urgent"), you'd be practicing the kind of "black belt" management style I'm describing." The author is using the supporting details to describe the way most people write lists to make his point: There is a better way to use lists.

PRACTICE THE NEW SKILL

Directions: Use the underlined supporting details to help you identify the main idea. Write the main idea in the space that follows the paragraphs.

The paragraphs that follow are from *Unclutter Your Life: Transforming Your Physical, Mental, and Emotional Space* by Katherine Gibson (2004), Beyond Words Publishing: Hillsboro, Oregon.

1.   Clutter affects how we feel. It shows no mercy as it clouds life with anxiety and frustration. The chaos that clutter creates can make us feel overwhelmed and defeated. It creates tension in relationships when things become lost or misplaced. Clutter eats up time as we search for shoes, keys, and lunch bags and it creates work as we shop for, clean, and manage our stuff. It costs us money as we insure, repair, and transport our precious goods and replace things we cannot find. (p. 4)

Main Idea: _____

_____

_____

ENGLISH 2.0

Shows no mercy means: is unforgiving, harsh

Clouds means: adds despair to or makes gloomy like a cloud may cover the sun and make a gloomy day

Eats up means: uses too much, uses up, consumes

2.   File, don't pile. But before you put it away, be sure it's a document you need. Sources say that 80 percent of what we file is never accessed again. Set up a system of current files, inactive files, and permanent records. Current files should include employment contracts, credit card information, insurance policies, health records, warranties, that year's bank statements, and income tax information. Inactive files contain items from old files that may have relevance.

These files should be reviewed yearly. Nothing in them should be older than three years. <u>Permanent records</u> should be kept in a safe-deposit box to protect against fire or theft. These records include birth or death certificates, marriage or divorce papers, real estate deeds, automobile ownership papers, stocks and bonds, contracts, wills, and an inventory of household effects. (p. 47)

Main Idea: _____

_____

_____

3. Plan tomorrow today. I've kept the habit of <u>making an activity plan for the next day</u> from my years of teaching school. This might include <u>reminders to send a birthday card</u> or to <u>gas up the car</u>. Other days it lists <u>phone calls to return</u>, a <u>speech to research</u>, and <u>meetings to attend.</u> <u>Whatever is *on* the list is *off* my mind and I can enjoy my evening (and my sleep) without a flurry or to-dos floating around my head.</u> (p. 63)

Main Idea: _____

_____

_____

REVIEW *WHAT YOU LEARNED*

Make a date, write it down . . . every single time

1   Any system, whether handwritten or electronic, requires that you maintain it. Let's look at the time involved for this task. Taking time to keep going back to your calendar to jot down or modify appointments may seem like a waste at first if you're not used to doing it. But it takes no more than ten minutes a day to maintain and reference whatever system you choose.

2   Let me ask you this: How much of your time is spent in a frantic search for invitations? You know you have a social function to go to soon, but you don't know whether it's this weekend or next. Will you have time to shop for a gift? What about work assignments? Do you hit your head against the wall when you realize that you have less time than you remembered to turn in a proposal? These shocks to the system not only waste time but also drain you physically and emotionally.

3   If you agree to something, whether it's a meeting at work, attending your daughter's dance recital, or flying to Dallas on business, you must

immediately enter that commitment on your calendar. This is a wonderful habit to cultivate. Have you ever noticed how happily married couples never say "yes" to an invitation? They always say something like, "I think that date is clear but I have to check with my spouse." You must first check with your calendar. It holds the key to your time—that's the key to your future.

4   Commit your energies one hundred percent to the activities of the present moment. You can do this with ease when you consciously plan your life. When your schedule just seems to happen, it's more difficult to be in the present moment because there's a constant drama in your head. You wonder, "What's next on my agenda? Did I forget something? Should I be doing something else right now?" Getting organized using a calendar system takes time, but it requires far less time than hit-or-miss, "I've got it all in my head" system. Give it a try. What have you got to lose but a lot of stress, aggravation, and oh yes, wasted time?

Source: Leeds, Regina. (2009). *One Year to an Organized Work Life: From Your Desk to Your Deadlines, the Week-By-Week Guide to Eliminating Office Stress For Good.* Cambridge, MA: Da Capo Press, pp. 28–29.

Directions: Refer to the article and state the main idea and supporting details, using either the chart or the outline below.

Topic: _____

_____

Main Idea: _____

_____

SD: _____

_____

SD: _____

_____

_____

SD: _____

_____

REVIEW WHAT YOU LEARNED

Home habit of the month: Put things in their place

1   Are you a morning person or a night person? When do you feel you do your best work and are most alert? Carve out five minutes during your favorite time and walk through your home looking for anything out of place.

2   Carry a trash bag with you and set a timer. If you see old magazines, newspapers, or junk mail, toss them or recycle. If you spot items that belong in other parts of the house, gather them and, when your timer goes off, return them to their proper place. Is the blanket that lives on the couch tossed on the floor? Fold it neatly. Are CDs and DVDs languishing on the coffee table? Pop them back into their holders. You get the idea.

3   By the end of the month, you won't be able to enter or leave a room without noticing its true state. Never again will you turn a blind eye to piles, jumbles, and messes. If you can't do the entire house in five minutes, do one or two rooms with attention to detail. You'll gain speed with time.

Source: Leeds, Regina. (2009). *One Year to an Organized Work Life: From Your Desk to Your Deadlines, the Week-By-Week Guide to Eliminating Office Stress For Good.* Cambridge, MA: Da Capo Press, p. 125.

Directions: Refer to the passage and state the main idea and supporting details, using either the chart or the outline below.

Topic: _____

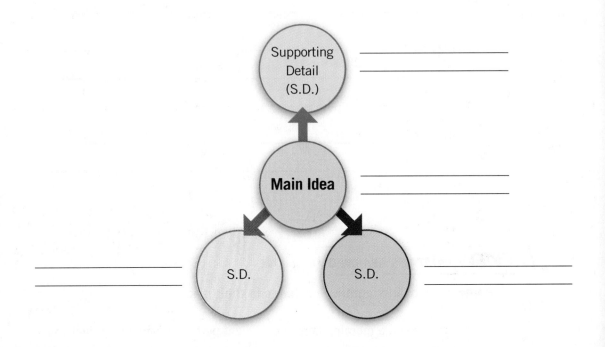

Main Idea: _____

_____

SD: _____

_____

SD: _____

_____

SD: _____

_____

/MASTER THE LESSON/

Supporting Details

(Photo by Mark McClenning, Sunset over Lake Michigan, July, 2009)

Take Time Out to Watch the Sunset

1   A cynic might say, "Oh right, that will be really helpful, especially to a teen," or "Could you be more superficial?" But do you know what? They're wrong. The truth is, many of the most powerful things you can do to improve your life are also very simple—and free.

2   When you learn to take time out to observe nature's beauty—sunset, sunrise, falling rain or snow, or a beautiful plant—on a regular basis, you are training yourself to slow down ever so slightly and appreciate life, beginning with the beauty around you. Like everything else, the more you do something, the better you become at it. If you keep it up, pretty soon you'll start noticing other aspects of life that are pretty special too. Indeed, when your life is filled with gratitude, everything looks less threatening and difficult. You spend less time irritated or wishing things were different and more time enjoying yourself and your day-to-day life.

3   The result is that, over time, rather than taking life quite as much for granted, you'll reexperience the magic of life. And when this happens, you'll be far less inclined, or even tempted, to search for artificial or harmful ways to create this magic. You won't need them because you'll already have it.

4   But that's not the only reason to take time out (every day) to watch the sunset. As you take time out to observe and appreciate the beauty in life,

not only will you feel happier and more nourished, but others around you will be influenced by your attitude as well. By way of example, it's as if you give permission to others to do the same thing.

5 I asked seventeen-year-old Jessica to take a few extra minutes a day to go out of her way to appreciate beauty—the sunset or some other type of nature. She reported back to me that within a few days, her family life had become noticeably calmer. Her parents, even her kid brother, started by asking her what she was doing and, very quickly, began following her lead and taking time out themselves.

6 What seems to be "the appreciation factor" kicks in, the stress in the entire household is reduced. For a moment, everyone is calm, perhaps silent. Perspective is enhanced. There is less rushing around and less frantic behavior. The appreciation acts as a kind of reset button, giving everyone a fresh start. When business as usual resumes a minute or two later, the atmosphere is more balanced.

7 I hope you'll start this strategy right away. You'll love the beauty you're going to see as well as the way it makes you feel.

Source: Carlson, Richard Ph.D. (2000). *Don't Sweat the Small Stuff for Teens: Simple Ways to Keep Your Cool in Stressful Times.* New York: Hyperion, pp. 120–121.

Directions: Answer the following questions about the passage.

1. According to the author, what are some examples of nature's beauty that you should observe on a regular basis?

_____

_____

_____

2. If you fill your life with gratitude, how will everything else look?

_____

_____

_____

3. What will you spend less time doing if you have gratitude?

_____

_____

_____

4. What will you spend more time doing with gratitude?

_____

_____

_____

5. Over time, you'll reexperience the magic of life and be less inclined or tempted to do what?

_____

_____

_____

6. What is the second reason to take time out every day to watch the sunset?

_____

_____

_____

7. What example did the author give about taking a few minutes to appreciate beauty?

_____

_____

_____

8. What were the benefits to the entire household?

_____

_____

_____

9–10. Describe things in nature that help (or could help) you become calmer and less stressed.

_____

_____

_____

MASTER THE LESSON

Supporting Details

Get Ready Early

1   I'm thrilled at the number of people who have told me how much this suggestion has helped them. I'm confident that, once you see the logic behind it, it will seem as obvious to you as the need to eat or sleep! The problem is, before you convince yourself of the importance of getting ready early, you'll see dozens of really good reasons why you "can't."

2   We live in busy times. Most of us feel that we're too busy and stretched for time. When you ask teens and adults alike what their perceived source of stress is, many will say, "Not enough time," or, "I'm always in a hurry."

3   Usually there are certain times of the day that are even crazier than the rest. In our family, for example, it's early morning. Although there are only four of us, it seems there are a hundred things to take care of and prepare for each and every day. If we're rushed, it's extremely stressful. If we're not, it's a nonissue.

4   It's fascinating to see how the same number of activities are experienced very differently, depending on how much time we allow. I'm convinced that one of the reasons people feel in such an enormous hurry is that they fail to give themselves adequate time to get ready. For example, if it takes an hour to do everything they need to do, most people will give themselves a *maximum* of one hour in which to do it. Never more, often far less. So, if everything goes smoothly and there are no unexpected problems, hassles, phone calls, lost items, or other time-consuming constraints, they will just make it if they hurry. The entire day is set up to be stressful, even if everything goes smoothly.

5   The nature of being in a hurry is stressful. You're rushing around, wondering if you'll make it and thinking about how busy you are. You might be thinking about what consequences there will be if you're late, or who might be mad at you. This type of thinking is stressful. It's also when you're hurried that you're most likely to misplace things, make mistakes, or forget something when you walk out the door. This too causes stress.

6   It's interesting, however, to listen to the excuses of people when they are late. "I didn't have enough time" is the number-one excuse. Number two is "I had too much to do." Seldom do you hear the truth, which is "I didn't give myself enough time." See the difference? In one instance you see yourself as a victim of time. You'll probably continue to do the same

thing often because you see the problem as being out of your control. In the other instance, however, you see yourself as empowered, as having the capacity to give yourself additional time.

7   Sometimes we do allow ourselves enough time, but instead of getting all the way, 100 percent ready, we get what I like to call "almost ready." Then, at the last minute, we scramble to do those remaining few things—make lunch, find our books, shave, gather our stuff, search for our shoes, make that urgent phone call, or whatever. We scramble and we feel pressured. This feeling of pressure can affect our entire day, encouraging us to feel uptight and to sweat the small stuff.

8   Most of this time stress can be eliminated from your life forever. All it takes is your willingness to see that the problem is self-created. As hard as it is to admit, it's usually not a lack of time that is the problem—instead, the problem is not giving yourself quite enough time. It's not getting *all* the way ready early enough.

9   If you usually give yourself an hour, for example, to get ready to go somewhere, experiment with 50 percent more time, or in this example, an extra thirty minutes. (You can adjust as needed.) Notice the difference in the quality of your experience—the lack of feeling pressured and stressed. Notice how the identical routine, with the same number of things to do, feels less stressful. And be sure, while you're at it, to get *all* the way ready (rather than almost ready) well before it's time to go. It's strange, but often as little as five or ten minutes can be the difference between a stressful day in which you're constantly "catching up" and a peaceful day in which you have plenty of time.

10   You can apply the same logic to longer-term projects as well. There is something quite peaceful about doing a book report, for example, well before the actual due date instead of cramming the night before. Or sending a birthday card a week early instead of hoping it will arrive on time. The number of actual applications for this strategy are vast. However you chose to use it, I hope it helps you as much as it has helped me.

Source: Carlson, Richard Ph.D. (2000). *Don't Sweat the Small Stuff for Teens: Simple Ways to Keep Your Cool in Stressful Times.* New York: Hyperion, pp. 86–88.

Directions: Answer the following questions about the passage.

1. What does the writer use as an example of a crazier time of day in his house?

_____

_____

_____

2. What is the number one excuse people give when they are late?

_____

_____

_____

3. What is the number two excuse people give when they are late?

_____

_____

_____

4. How are the two excuses different?

_____

_____

_____

5. What does the author mean by the phrase "almost ready"?

_____

_____

_____

6. Why does he say being "almost ready" is a problem?

_____

_____

_____

7. How does he suggest most stress can be eliminated from your life forever?

_____

_____

_____

8–10. List three ways you can apply this strategy to help manage your time better while you are in college.

_____

_____

_____

LEARNING STYLE ACTIVITIES

Look, Listen, Write, Do

Following are three different forms of the same reading about time. The first is a poem, the second is a song, and the last, a Bible passage. You may choose to read one or more. Complete one of the learning style activities that follow.

Poem

Take Time

Take time to think—
It is the source of all power.
Take time to read—
It is the fountain of wisdom.

Take time to play—
It is the source of perpetual youth.
Take time to be quiet—
It is the opportunity to seek God.

Take time to be aware—
It is the opportunity to help others.
Take time to love and be loved—
It is God's greatest gift.

Take time to laugh—
It is the music of the soul.
Take time to be friendly—
It is the road to happiness.

Take time to dream—
It is what the future is made of.
Take time to pray—
It is the greatest power on earth.

Take time to give—
It is too short a day to be selfish.
Take time to work—
It is the price of success.

There is a time for everything. . . .

Source: Retrieved from http://www.inspirational-poems.biz/Religion_Poems/
Ecclesiastes-3-1-8-Take-Time-to-Think-religious-poetry.html

Song

Find the song lyrics for "Turn! Turn! Turn!" by the Byrds. You might use the Internet, the library, or a CD at home.

Bible

A Time for Everything

For everything there is a season,
    A time for every activity under heaven.
A time to be born and a time to die.
    A time to plant and a time to harvest.
A time to kill and a time to heal.
    A time to tear down and a time to build up.
A time to cry and a time to laugh.
    A time to grieve and a time to dance.
A time to scatter stones and a time to gather stones.
    A time to embrace and a time to turn away.
A time to search and a time to quit searching.
    A time to keep and a time to throw away.
A time to teach and a time to mend.
    A time to be quiet and a time to speak.
A time to love and a time to hate.
    A time for war and a time for peace.

Source: Ecclesiastes 3:1-8 Holy Bible, New Living Translation (2004). Wheaton, IL: Tyndale House Publishers, p. 539.

Look   As you read the poem, song lyrics, or Bible verses, draw a concept map of the main idea and supporting details. Pay attention to the way two opposite concepts are paired together such as "a time to grieve and a time to dance" or "a time to dance, a time to mourn." You may also draw illustrations of the concepts on your map.

Listen   Listen to the song, "Turn! Turn! Turn!" You can find it on CD, iTunes download, or YouTube, or get a copy of the music and play it yourself on an instrument and sing along. If you prefer, read the poem or the Bible verse out loud or have someone read it to you. Listen for the main idea and the supporting details. Also listen for the way two opposite concepts are paired together such as "a time to grieve and a time to dance" or "a time to dance, a time to mourn."

✎ *W*RITE   As you read the poem, song lyrics, or Bible verses, write the main idea and supporting details as notes in your own words. You may prefer to write an outline of the material.

You may also add your own verses to the poem or song. Pay attention to the way two opposite concepts are paired together such as "a time to grieve and a time to dance" or "a time to dance, a time to mourn."

👆 *D*o   As you read the poem, song lyrics, or Bible verses, think of how you spend your own time. Describe lines in the poem, song, or verses that you can apply to an experience or situation in your life. Think especially about the way two opposite ideas are paired together, such as "a time to grieve and a time to dance" or "a time to dance, a time to mourn."

Reading Practice

The next section of the chapter will help refine your skills in determining the supporting details while you read a variety of materials. All five of the readings address topics related to establishing your priorities and managing your time.

The first reading is "Time Management—Getting It Done" from *Careers and College*. This article includes advice for first-time college students on how to manage their time. It was retrieved from Academic Search Premiere from the EBSCO online database.

The second reading, "Use Scheduling Techniques," comes from the textbook, *Keys to Success: Building Successful Intelligence for College, Career, and Life.*

The third reading is from contemporary literature, *Tuesdays with Morrie* by Mitch Albom.

The fourth reading is from an article titled "Beating the Odds" from the magazine, *Real Simple: Life Made Easier.*

The final reading is a visual image: "Working on the Beach."

READING 1

Time Management—Getting It Done

1   Freshmen in college consistently rank time management as one of their biggest challenges. Basically, if you don't stay on top of your schedule, it can lead to poor academic performance. So why are you wasting time? Grab your planner and jot this down! You'll be thanking us next year.

THE FIRST STEP: KNOW YOURSELF

2   Dr. Edward O'Keefe, author of *Self Management for College Students: The ABC Approach,* recommends that you look at the big picture of your life and figure out what's important to you, He suggests writing down your big goals for college. Don't limit yourself to academic ones. "You should use college to develop the rest of yourself, in addition to your academic side," explains O'Keefe.

3   Next, decide when, where, and how you work best. Ask yourself these questions:

- Do I work best with an intense or more laid back schedule? Some people thrive on having an ultra-packed lifestyle; others get overwhelmed.

- Am I a morning or evening person? Some students have a tough time in the morning, but others are like Leah McConaughey, from Bowdoin College in Brunswick, Maine. "I know that I get up early and can't stay up late at night," she says. "So forcing myself to study late is a waste of time."

- Can I tune out distractions easily? The answer will tell you whether you'll be able to study in a rowdy dorm or whether you'll have to head to the library.

STAYING ON TRACK

4   Once you've figured out how you operate best, start to make time management a habit. Follow these guidelines:

- Keep track. Students who write down all they have to do often find they have more free time than they thought. Using a laptop, a handheld organizer, day planner, or notebook, list your activities and deadlines in order of when they have to be done.

- Seek balance. Don't overload yourself. Scheduling all your classes on two or three days can turn ugly.

- Don't waste the daytime. Freshmen often wait until night to do their work. Instead of hanging out in the student lounge during free periods, use that hour between classes to hit the books.

ENGLISH 2.0

Hit the books means: study, spend time using your textbooks and reading

- Give yourself a break. Make sure your schedule includes short periods to recharge. If you can limit yourself to fifteen or twenty minutes, now is the time to relax in the student lounge. But if you'll get too distracted, reward yourself with a cup of tea or hot chocolate instead.
- Ask professors for help. Teachers are human and, for the most part, willing to consider solutions if you get into a jam.

ENGLISH 2.0

Get into a jam means: find yourself in a difficult situation

- Get credit for work you do outside of class. Jennifer Adams, from Mount Holyoke College in South Hadley, Massachusetts, took on the task of maintaining her school newspaper's website, and she was able to use that work for her final journalism project. Finding clever ways to "double up" like that can save time.
- Don't sweat the small stuff. Things like laundry can fall through the cracks and that's okay. "The only person who sees my dirty laundry is me," says Adams. "It needs to get done, but is the world going to stop if it doesn't? Probably not."

ENGLISH 2.0

Fall through the cracks means: not get done, like things that fall on the ground but then disappear in the cracks of the stones or bricks, they disappear and are forgotten

Is the world going to stop means: is it a really important issue?

TIME TIP

5   "Keep a calendar! It can be as simple as a notebook with the date and a list of stuff to do. No one will be there to nag you about homework. I live by my "to-do" lists. And when I cross things off, I can see how much I've accomplished."

—Crystal Tews, Wartburg College,
Waverly, Iowa

6   "School should be treated like a full-time job. People who work full time are at it from 8 am to 5 pm. Getting an education is your job, so in between classes do homework and study. You'll have a lot more time in the evenings to do things you enjoy."

—Colleen McAllister, The State
University of New York, Potsdam, NY

Source: Time Management–Getting It Done.
Careers & Colleges (Mar/Apr2006), Vol. 26 Issue 4, p. 12.
Retrieved from Ebsco host, Academic Search Premiere

Questions

1. For the first subheading, *The First Step: Know Yourself,* the article suggests you look at the bigger picture of your life and state your goals. Next, the article says to determine when, where, and how you work best. Fill in the concept map with the main idea and supporting details of the questions you should ask yourself.

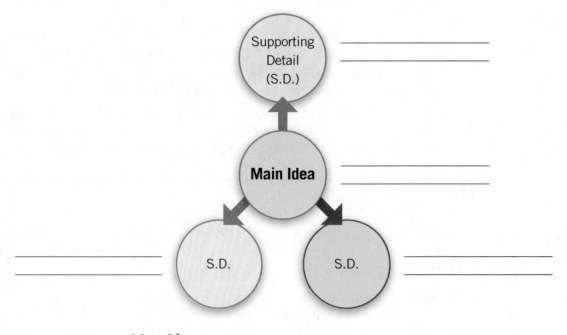

Main Idea: _____

_____

2. _____

_____

3. _____

_____

4. _____

_____

5. For the second subheading, _Staying on Track,_ use your own paper to create a concept map of the main idea and supporting details. (_HINT:_ There are 7 supporting details in the article under this subheading.)

Textbook

READING 2

**Directions:**   Use SQ3R to read this textbook selection below.

Survey	Skim over the material. Read the title, subtitle, subheadings, first and last paragraphs, pictures, charts, and graphics. Note italics and bold print.
Question	Ask yourself questions before you read. What do you want to know? Turn headings and subheadings into questions and/or read questions if provided.
Read	Read the material in manageable chunks. This may be one or two paragraphs at a time or the material under one subheading.
Recite	Recite the answer to each question in your own words. This is a good time to write notes as you read each section. Repeat the question—read—recite cycle.
Review	Look over your notes at the end of the chapter, article, or material. Review what you learned and write a summary in your own words.

S—Survey

What are you going to be focusing on when you read this article?

_____

_____

KEY 2.2 Note daily and weekly tasks.

Monday, March 14		
TIME	TASKS	PRIORITY
6:00 A.M.		
7:00		
8:00	Up at 8am — finish homew	
9:00		
10:00	Business Administration	
11:00	Renew driver's license @ D	
12:00 P.M.		
1:00	Lunch	
2:00	Writing Seminar (peer editi	
3:00	↓	
4:00	check on Ms. Schwartz's of	
5:00	5:30 work out	
6:00	↳6:30	
7:00	Dinner	
8:00	Read two chapters for	
9:00	Business Admin.	
10:00	↓	
11:00		
12:00		

Monday, March 28		
8	Call: Mike Blair	1
9	BIO 212	Financial Aid Office	2
10		EMS 262 *Paramedic	3
11	CHEM 203	role-play*	4
12		5
Evening 6pm yoga class		

Tuesday, March 29		
8	Finish reading assignment!	Work @ library	1
9		2
10	ENG 112	(study for quiz)	3
11	↓	4
12		5
Evening	↓ until 7pm	

Wednesday, March 30		
8	Meet w/advisor	1
9	BIO 212	2
10	EMS 262	3
11	CHEM 203 *Quiz	4
12	Pick up photos	5
Evening 6pm Dinner w/study group		

Use Scheduling Techniques

The following strategies will help you turn your scheduling activities into tools that move you closer to your goals:

Plan regularly. Set aside a regular time each day, and perhaps a longer time at the end of each week, to plan out your schedule. Being methodical about scheduling will help you reduce stress and save the hassle that might result if you forget something important. Your planner can help you only if you use it—so keep it with you and check it throughout the day.

Make and use to-do lists. Use a to-do list to record the things you want to accomplish on a given day or week. Write your to-do items on a separate piece of paper so you can set priorities. Then transfer the items you plan to accomplish each day to open time periods in your planner. To-do lists are critical time-management tools for exam week and major projects. They will help you rank your responsibilities so that you get things done in order of importance.

Post monthly and yearly calendars at home. Keeping track of your major commitments on a monthly wall calendar will give you the overview you need to focus on responsibilities and upcoming events. Key 2.3 shows a monthly calendar. If you live with family or friends, create a group calendar to stay aware of each other's plans and avoid scheduling conflicts.

Avoid time traps. Try to stay away from situations that eat up time unnecessarily. Say no graciously if you don't have time for a project; curb excess social time; declare your cell phone off-limits when you study, delegate chores. Rein in the time you spend surfing the Internet and instant-messaging with friends, because these activities can eat up hours before you know it.

Schedule down time. Leisure time is more than just a nice break—it's essential to your health and success. Even a half-hour of down time a day will refresh you and improve your productivity when you get back on task. Fill the time with whatever relaxes you—reading, watching television, chatting online, playing a game or sport, walking, writing, or just doing nothing.

KEY 2.3   Keep track of your time with a monthly calendar.

MARCH

SUNDAY	MONDAY	TUESDAY	WEDNESDAY	THURSDAY	FRIDAY	SATURDAY
	1 WORK	**2** Turn in English paper topic	**3** Dentist 2pm	**4** WORK	**5**	**6**
7 Frank's birthday	**8** Psych Test 9am WORK	**9**	**10** 6:30 pm Meeting @ Student Ctr.	**11** WORK	**12**	**13** Dinner @ Ryan's
14	**15** English paper due WORK	**16** Western Civ paper—Library research	**17**	**18** Library 6 pm WORK	**19** Western Civ makeup class	**20**
21	**22** WORK	**23** 2 pm meeting, psych group project	**24** Start running program: 2 miles	**25** WORK	**26** Run 2 miles	**27**
28 Run 3 miles	**29** WORK	**30** Western Civ paper due	**31** Run 2 miles			

get practical!

Make a To-Do List

Reduce stress by accomplishing practical goals. Make a to-do list for what you have to do on your busiest day this week. Include all the tasks and events you know about, including attending class and study time, and the activities you would like to do (working out at the gym, watching your favorite TV show) if you have extra time. Then prioritize your list using the coding system of your choice.

Date: _____

1. _____   7. _____
2. _____   8. _____
3. _____   9. _____
4. _____   10. _____
5. _____   11. _____
6. _____   12. _____

After examining this list, record your daily schedule in your planner (if you have a busy day, you may want to list Priority 3 items separately to complete if time permits). At the end of the day, evaluate this system. Did the list help you to manage your time and tasks effectively? If you liked it, use this exercise as a guide for using to-do lists regularly.

Source: Excerpts "Note Daily and Weekly Tasks," "Use Scheduling Techniques," "Keep Track of Your Time with a Monthly Calendar," and "Make a To-Do List" from *Keys to Success: Building Analytical, Creative, and Practical Skills,* 6th Edition by Carol Carter, Joyce Bishop, Sarah Kravits, Judy Block. Copyright © 2009 by Carol Carter, Joyce Bishop, Sarah Kravits, Judy Block. Printed and Electronically reproduced by permission of Pearson Education, Inc., Upper Saddle River, New Jersey.

Subheading **Plan regularly.**

Question: _____?

_____

Recite: _____

_____

_____

Subheading **Make and use to-do lists.**

Question: _____?

_____

Recite: _____

_____

Subheading **Post monthly and yearly calendars at home.**

Question: _____?

_____

Recite: _____

_____

_____

Subheading **Avoid time traps.**

Question: _____?

Recite: _____

_____

_____

Subheading **Schedule down time.**

Question: _____?

_____

Recite: _____

_____

_____

R—Review (Review your notes and write a summary in your own words.)

_____

_____

_____

_____

Vocabulary

Directions: Circle the letter of the best definition for the bold word as it is used in the sentence. Use the context clues in the surrounding paragraph and/or the word parts to help discover the meaning of the unknown word.

1. accomplish

    a. avoid   **b.** do

2. **rank**

   a. order   b. title

3. **curb**

   a. side of the road   b. cut back

4. **surfing**

   a. riding the waves   b. looking over something

5. **chatting**

   a. talking   b. buying

6. **leisure**

   a. free time   b. structured time

7. **essential**

   a. unnecessary   b. necessary

8. **down time**

   a. quiet time set aside for relaxation and low-key activity

   b. time when systems quit operating

9. **productivity**

   a. activity   b. output

Activity

Work with a group and discuss how you could use some of the time scheduling techniques from the textbook section you just read. Have you tried any of the author's ideas in your own life? How did they work for you? Give examples and share your ideas with the class.

Literature   READING 3

Tuesdays with Morrie

THE CURRICULUM

1   The last class of my old professor's life took place once a week in his house, by a window in the study where he could watch a small hibiscus plant shed its pink leaves. The class met on Tuesdays. It began after breakfast. The subject was The Meaning of Life. It was taught from experience.

2   No grades were given, but there were oral exams each week. You were expected to respond to questions, and you were expected to pose questions of your own. You were also required to perform physical tasks now and then, such as lifting the professor's head to a comfortable spot on the pillow or placing his glasses on the bridge of his nose. Kissing him good-bye earned you extra credit.

3   No books were required, yet many topics were covered, including love, work, community, family, aging, forgiveness, and, finally, death. The last lecture was brief, only a few words.

4   A funeral was held *in lieu of* graduation.

5   Although no final exam was given, you were expected to produce one long paper on what was learned. That paper is presented here.

6   The last class of my old professor's life had only one student.

7   I was the student.

(pp. 1–2)

In lieu of—instead of

THE FOURTH TUESDAY WE TALK ABOUT DEATH...

8   Here in Morrie's office, life went on one precious day at a time. Now we sat together, a few feet from the newest addition to the house: an oxygen machine. It was small and portable, about knee-high. On some nights, when he couldn't get enough air to swallow, Morrie attached the long plastic tubing to his nose, clamping on his nostrils like a *leech*. I hated the idea of Morrie connected to a machine of any kind, and I tried not to look at it as Morrie spoke.

9   "Everybody knows they're going to die," he said again, "but nobody believes it. If we did, we would do things differently."

10   So we kid ourselves about death, I said.

11   "Yes. But there's a better approach. To know you're going to die, and to be *prepared* for it at any time. That's better. That way you can actually be *more* involved in your life while you're living."

12   How can you ever be prepared to die?

13   "Do what the Buddhists do. Every day, have a little bird on your shoulder that asks, 'Is today the day? Am I ready? Am I doing all I need to do? Am I being the person I want to be?'"

14   He turned his head to his shoulder as if the bird were there now.

15   "Is today the day I die?" he said.

16   Morrie borrowed freely from all religions. He was born Jewish, but became agnostic when he was a teenager, partly because of all that had happened to him as a child. He enjoyed some of the philosophies of Buddhism and Christianity, and he still felt at home, culturally, in Judaism. He was a religious mutt, which made him even more open to the students he taught over the years. And the things he was saying in his final months on earth seemed to transcend all religious differences. Death has a way of doing that.

17   "The truth is, Mitch," he said, "once you learn how to die, you learn how to live."

18   I nodded.

19   "I'm going to say it again," he said. "Once you learn how to die, you learn how to live." He smiled, and I realized what he was doing. He was making sure I absorbed this point, without embarrassing me by asking. It was part of what made him a good teacher.

20   Did you think much about death before you got sick, I asked.

21   "No." Morrie smiled. "I was like everyone else. I once told a friend of mine, in a moment of exuberance, 'I'm gonna be the healthiest old man you ever met!'"

22   How old were you?

Leech—a bloodsucking worm which attached itself to its victim's skin

23   "In my sixties."

24   So you were optimistic.

25   "Why not? Like I said, no one really believes they're going to die."

26   But everyone knows someone who has died, I said. Why is it so hard to think about dying?

27   "Because," Morrie continued, "most of us all walk around as if we're sleep-walking. We really don't experience the world fully, because we're half-asleep, doing things we automatically think we have to do."

28   And facing death changes all that?

29   "Oh, yes. You strip away all that stuff and you focus on the essentials. When you realize you are going to die, you see everything much differently.

30   He sighed. "Learn you're to die, and you learn how to live."

31   I noticed that he quivered now when he moved his hands. His glasses hung around his neck, and when he lifted them to his eyes, they slid around his temples, as if he were trying to put them on someone else in the dark. I reached over to help guide them onto his ears.

32   "Thank you," Morrie whispered. He smiled when my hand brushed up against his head. The slightest human contact was immediate joy.

33   "Mitch. Can I tell you something?"

34   Of course, I said.

35   "You might not like it."

36   Why not?

37   "Well, the truth is, if you really listen to that bird on your shoulder, *if you accept that you can die at any time*—then you might not be as ambitious as you are."

38   I forced a small grin.

39   "The things you spend so much time on—all this work you do—might not seem important. You might have to make room for more spiritual things."

40   Spiritual things?

41   "You hate that word, don't you? 'Spiritual.' You think it's touchy-feely stuff."

42   Well, I said.

43   He tried to wink, a bad try, and I broke down and laughed.

44   "Mitch," he said, laughing along, "Even I don't know what 'spiritual development' really means. But I do know we're deficient in some way. We are too involved in materialistic things, and they don't satisfy us. The loving relationships we have, the universe around us, we take these for granted."

45   He nodded toward the window with the sunshine streaming in. "You see that? You can go out there, outside, anytime. You can run up and down the block and go crazy. I can't do that. I can't go out. I can't run. I can't go out there without fear of getting sick. But you know what? I *appreciate* that window more than you do."

46 Appreciate it?

47 "Yes. I look out that window every day. I notice the change in the trees, how strong the wind is blowing. It's as if I can see time actually passing through that windowpane. Because I know my time is almost done, I am drawn to nature like I'm seeing it for the first time."

48 He stopped, and for a moment we both just looked out the window. I tried to see time and seasons, my life passing in slow motion. Morrie dropped his head slightly and curled it toward his shoulder.

49 "Is it today, little bird?" he asked. "Is it today?"

(pp. 80–85)

Source: Albom, Mitch. (1997). *Tuesdays with Morrie: An Old Man, a Young Man, and Life's Greatest Lesson.* New York: Broadway Books, pp. 1–2 and 80–85.

Questions

1. Who is Morrie?

_____

_____

2. Who is Mitch?

_____

_____

3. Who has the oxygen machine?

_____

4. Use word parts and context clues to find the meaning of the word *portable.*

If port is a root word that means to carry, and able is a suffix that means able to, what does *portable* mean in this sentence?

Now we sat together, a few feet from the newest addition to the house: an oxygen machine. It was small and *portable*, about knee-high.

Portable means _____

_____

5. Why are Mitch and Morrie talking inside the house?

_____

_____

6. Is the little bird on Morrie's shoulder real?

_____

_____

_____

7. Use word parts and context clues to find the meaning of the word **mutt.**

Morrie borrowed freely from all religions. He was born Jewish, but became agnostic when he was a teenager, partly because of all that had happened to him as a child. He enjoyed some of the philosophies of Buddhism and Christianity, and he still felt at home, culturally, in Judaism. He was a religious **mutt**, which made him even more open to the students he taught over the years. And the things he was saying in his final months on earth seemed to transcend all religious differences.

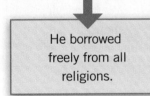
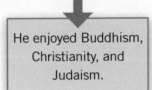

| He borrowed freely from all religions. | He enjoyed Buddhism, Christianity, and Judaism. | He transcended all religious differences. |

Together, these facts let you infer that **mutt** means _____

_____

Also, think about the word used when referring to a dog.

HINT: What does it mean when someone asks, "what kind of dog do you have?" and you answer, "We don't know—we got him from the animal shelter—he is a **mutt.**"

8. Read the text below and answer the question that follows.

"Because," Morrie continued, "most of us all walk around as if we're **sleepwalking**. We really don't experience the world fully, because we're half-asleep, doing things we automatically think we have to do."

And facing death changes all that?

"Oh, yes. You strip away all that stuff and you focus on the essentials. When you realize you are going to die, you see everything much differently."

What does Morrie mean by the term *sleepwalking*?

_____

_____

_____

9. Use word parts and context clues to find the meaning of the word *deficient.*

"Mitch," he said, laughing along, "Even I don't know what 'spiritual development' really means. But I do know we're deficient in some way. We are too involved in materialistic things, and they don't satisfy us. The loving relationships we have, the universe around us, we take these for granted."

We're too involved in materialistic things.	They don't satisfy us.	We take loving relationships and the universe for granted.

Together, these facts let you infer that *deficient* means _____

_____

10. What does the following comment mean? "Is it today, little bird?" he asked. "Is it today?"

_____

_____

"Beating the Odds"

1   Certain moments in life seem almost **insurmountable**—the moments when you think, *I'm not sure I can live through this.* Yet some people somehow, **miraculously,** find the strength to power through. As Sheri Lewis, who is battling breast cancer, puts it: "I realized I can lie down and die, or I can fight, kick, and scream—and live." Sheri shares how she **triumphed** over tragedy—and kept going.

Sheri Lewis, 42
Former public-relations executive, now a volunteer at her daughter's school; Grapevine, Texas

2   **Life-changing moment:** Learning that her breast cancer had *metastasized* to her liver.

3   **Prelude:** Sheri Lewis is, in her own words, "a classic firstborn **overachiever.**" This worked to her advantage during her 17-year career in public relations. A former senior vice president at Weber Shandwick, Sheri handled corporate communications for American Airlines in the wake of 9/11. "I learned how key preparation and teamwork are in a crisis," Sheri says. At the time, Sheri was **recovering** from her own personal crisis. She was recently divorced and had gone through a **contentious** child-custody battle (she and her ex-husband share custody of their daughter, Maddie), and then, in June 2002, Sheri found an ice cube-sized lump in her right breast.

4   **Turning Point:** Sheri, then 38, was sitting at her desk when her doctor called with the *biopsy* results: It was breast cancer. Sheri had a single *mastectomy* on August 21 and began **chemotherapy** immediately. "I had all the nasty side effects," she says. "Nausea, **fatigue,** hair loss." She cut back to a 25-hour workweek, and her parents, who live nearby, helped care for Maddie, then four. "She didn't really understand what was going on," Sheri recalls. "She'd say, 'Mommy, I love you even without hair.' That gave me strength."

5   After eight rounds of chemotherapy and 33 rounds of radiation, Sheri was declared cancer-free in January 2004. She returned to work "a kinder, gentler boss," she says, "**determined** to live life to its fullest." And that included flirting with Steve Lewis, a cute guy she met at a bar one night that April while she was waiting for some friends. The two exchanged e-mails, one thing led to another,

---

Metastasized—grown
Biopsy—examination of tissue to see if disease is present
Mastectomy—surgical operation to remove a breast

and around Christmas 2004 Steve **proposed.** "We decided to get married that March," Sheri says. "And then, one month before the wedding, I learned that my cancer had metastasized to my liver." *Shell-shocked*, Sheri suggested calling off the wedding. Steve refused. "He said, 'I love you, and I want to be with you for as long as you are here,'" she says. "So we had the minister **omit** the 'till death do us part' bit."

6   **Resolve:** Sheri started chemotherapy again in August 2005, and the new tumor had shrunk by January. But eight months later it started growing. Sheri is currently in a clinical trial, and the results are **promising.** It was in the *chemo-infusion* room that she came across a book called *I Will Not Die an Unlived Life*, by Dawna Markova. "I copied a poem from the book onto a piece of paper and taped it to my mirror," Sheri says. "It reminds me to not waste any time **wallowing.**" And yet moments of panic **puncture** her **optimism.** "When those hit, I set a timer and give myself 20 minutes to **wallow** in **self-pity,** crying in the *fetal* position on my bed," she says. "And when the timer goes off, I wash my face and go back to what I was doing."

7   Sheri decided to leave her job in the fall of 2005, and she now volunteers at Maddie's school. "All the kids say, 'Hi, Maddie's mom,'" she **enthuses.** She has made other life changes, too: "So what if clothes are lying on the bed?" she says. She believes cancer has made her a better person. "I found strength I didn't know existed," Sheri says. "I have breast cancer—it's **advanced.** But you can either sit down and wait to die or stand up and live every day."

Source: Welch, L. (April 2007). "Beating the Odds." *Real Simple: Life Made Easier,* p. 254.

Vocabulary

Directions: Circle the letter of the best definition for the bold word as it is used in the sentence. Use the context clues in the surrounding paragraph and/or the word parts to help discover the meaning of the unknown word.

1. **insurmountable** (see paragraph 1)

   a. easy   b. impossible

2. **miraculously** (see paragraph 1)

   a. amazingly   b. unremarkably

Shell-shocked—confused or upset because of extreme stress
Chemo-infusion—intravenous administration of chemotherapy
Fetal—curled up with legs against the chest and back hunched over

3. **triumphed** (see paragraph 1)

 a. gave up   b. succeeded

4. **pre**lude (see paragraph 3)

 a. introduction   b. ending

5. **overachiever** (see paragraph 3)

 a. high achiever   b. overwhelmed person

6. **recovering** (see paragraph 3)

 a. putting new upholstery on   b. getting better

7. **contentious** (see paragraph 3)

 a. touchy   b. satisfied

8. **chemotherapy** (see paragraph 4)

 a. physical therapy   b. chemicals to treat cancer

9. **fatigue** (see paragraph 4)

 a. energy   b. tiredness

10. **determined** (see paragraph 5)

 a. strong-minded   b. unsure about

11. **proposed** (see paragraph 5)

 a. made an offer   b. made a list

12. **omit** (see paragraph 5)

 a. decline   b. leave out

13. **promising** (see paragraph 6)

 a. hopeful   b. gifted

14. **wallowing** (see paragraph 6)

 a. avoiding, avoid   b. self-indulgent

15. **puncture** (see paragraph 6)

 a. let down   b. pump up

16. **optimism** (see paragraph 6)

 a. hopefulness   b. hopelessness

17. **self-pity** (see paragraph 6)

    a. feeling hatred for oneself   b. feeling sorry for oneself

18. **enthuses** (see paragraph 7)

    a. is bored with   b. is excited about

19. **advanced** (see paragraph 7)

    a. far along   b. easy to treat

Main Idea/Supporting Detail Questions

20. What is the main idea of paragraph 4?

_____

_____

_____

21. What gave her strength (see paragraph 4)?

_____

_____

22. What did the author do to "live life to the fullest" (see paragraph 5)?

_____

_____

_____

23. What is the main idea of paragraph 6?

_____

_____

_____

24. Why does the author say that cancer made her a better person (see paragraph 7)?

_____

_____

_____

Activity

Think about how you spend your time right now. If you learned that you had cancer, would you do anything differently? Write a paragraph, poem, or song, draw or paint your feelings, or discuss it with a friend.

Visual Image   ## READING 5

Directions: Use the supporting details in the picture to answer the questions.

1. Where is the man? _____

_____

_____

_____

2. What is he wearing? _____

_____

_____

_____

3. What is he doing? _____

_____

_____

_____

_____

4. Why is the man's right hand up?

_____

_____

_____

_____

_____

5. What do you think the picture is trying to show?

_____

_____

_____

_____

_____

6. Write a caption for the picture.

_____

_____

_____

_____

_____

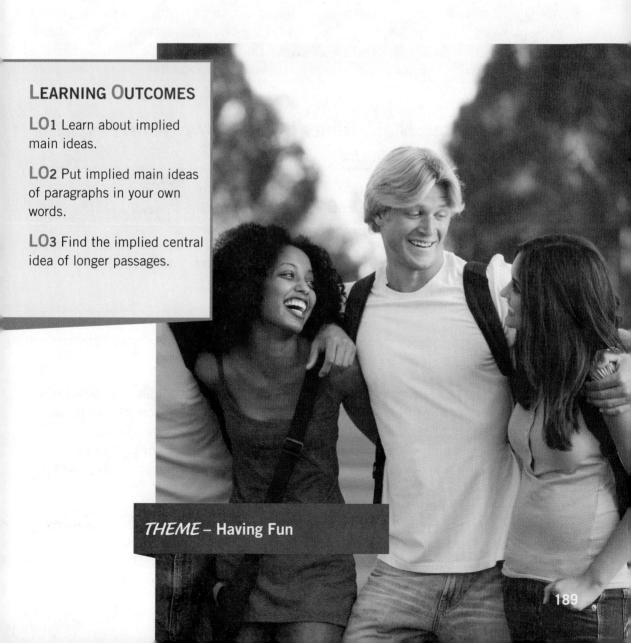

5

Implied Main Ideas

THEME – Having Fun

189

SPOTLIGHT ON LEARNING STYLES Do

As a learner who likes to "do," whenever I learn something new I automatically try to make connections to something else I have experienced in my life. My brain always searches for a place to attach the new ideas. When I taught myself to fly fish, I practiced in the back yard for several days to get the hang of it. It was tricky to get the right rhythm to keep the line from tangling into a mess. I thought about jumping rope and getting the rhythm just right so I could jump with my eyes closed. Once I connected the ideas in my brain, I was able to take my fly fishing skills to the lake and fill a fish basket with fresh bluegills in a couple hours.

Implied Main Ideas in Your Own Words (What is the unstated main idea?)

Many times an author does not directly state the main idea in a written sentence. Instead, the main idea may be implied through the details. In these

> **LO1**
> Learn about implied main ideas.

cases, the author is counting on the reader to figure out his point. Why might an author want the reader to figure out his point rather than simply stating it? List some of your ideas here.

_____

_____

_____

One reason the author might imply the main idea may be so readers can draw their own conclusions. For instance, in a creative or narrative piece, the author may draw you into the story with just enough details to keep you involved. When you have to solve a mystery or figure out a interesting situation, it makes the reading more exciting and probably makes you want to read more.

Another reason a writer may imply the main idea is to get you to "buy into" an idea for yourself. This is often used with persuasive writing or advertising. For example, if you decide for yourself that going to see a certain movie is a good idea based on the supporting details provided, such as your favorite actors, fast-paced action, or amazing effects, then you are more likely to act on that decision. If the message is stated directly in the first sentence, however, such as "You need to go see 'such and such' movie, and here are three reasons why," it is more likely you will "tune out" the message and ignore the supporting reasons.

Whenever you read:

- ask yourself what message, attitude, or opinion the author is trying to share.
- notice that sometimes the main idea message is stated directly.
- note that at other times you will put the main idea into your own words.
- look at the supporting details and decide for yourself what message the author is trying to get across.
- ask, "What point is the author trying to make about the topic?"

Let's review what we learned about finding the topic first to help us focus on the bigger ideas.

Finding the Implied Topic

EXAMPLE ───────────────────────────────────────

Directions: Read the terms and circle the best topic.

1. lions, tigers, bears

Topic: **a.** zoo animals   **b.** animals   **c.** pets

While all of the terms are animals, they are more specifically zoo animals; therefore, the best topic is (a).

PRACTICE THE NEW SKILL

Directions: Read the terms and circle the best topic.

1. coffee, cocoa, soda

Topic: **a.** snacks   **b.** products   **c.** beverages

  2. watch movies, play miniature golf, eat pizza

   Topic: **a.** businesses   **b.** things to do with friends   **c.** books to read

  3. basketball, tennis, soccer

   Topic: **a.** activities   **b.** sports   **c.** team sports

Finding the Implied Main Idea from a Group of Ideas

Authors may provide the reader with a list or a group of ideas or statistics. You need to ask yourself what the author is implying with this list of ideas. It may help to look at the details and ask what the individual items have in common.

EXAMPLE ——————————————————————————

Directions: Read the material; then select the implied main idea from the list below.

- Drive with a group of friends. Take frequent turns driving and talk with each other to reduce fatigue and drowsiness.
- Slow down and keep a larger following distance. Reaction time slows at night and it is more difficult to judge speed and distance after dark.
- Make frequent stops. Get out of your vehicle and walk or jog to increase blood flow and circulation and reduce drowsiness.
- Avoid smoking. Nicotine and carbon monoxide decrease night vision.
- If you are sleepy or drowsy, quit driving and get some rest.

Source: Retrieved from Spring Break 2011: Road Trip Safety Check List by Langdon & Emison—Trial Attorneys posted on Friday, March 11, 2011.

   Implied Main Idea:

   a. Driving a car on a road trip can be a lot of fun.

   b. Here are some things to do to be safe when taking a road trip at night.

   c. Night driving is dangerous.

All of the items on the list are related to driving at night. Therefore, the implied main idea is (b). If you must drive at night, here are some things to do.

PRACTICE THE NEW SKILL

Directions: Read the material; then select the implied main idea from the list below.

1. List of Things You Should Plan to Bring:

- Blanket or chair
- Cooler with refreshments (if permitted)
- Rain gear or warm jacket
- Book
- Tickets

Step 1

Purchase your tickets early. You may be able to buy them online. The most popular shows at the fair usually require a separate ticket in addition to fair admission.

Step 2

Check the fair's schedule on the Web site or in your local paper to see what musical groups are playing where and when. Most fairs include acts from various musical genres like rock, country, jazz and hip-hop.

Step 3

Check to see if you are allowed to bring a cooler into the show so that you can pack your own food and refreshments. Otherwise take extra cash to purchase food and drinks.

Step 4

Make a plan for how to get to the location. If parking is not available, you may be able to take public transportation.

Step 5

To make sure that you're comfortable during the show, bring a folding chair or blanket.

Step 6

Be prepared for changes in weather by packing a jacket or some rain gear since concerts at the fair are usually staged outdoors.

Step 7

Plan to arrive early to make sure you get a good spot. Bring along a book to pass the time before the show begins.

Implied Main Idea:

a. Several things could help you enjoy an outdoor concert at a state fair.

b. Several things could help you enjoy a trip to the beach.

c. Going on a summer outing has several advantages.

2.

- Get a view of the city from a tall building.
- See the Statue of Liberty.
- Walk around Central Park.
- Walk across the Brooklyn Bridge.
- Walk around downtown.

Implied Main Idea:

a. There are 5 things to see in the city.

b. Walking in a city is entertaining.

c. There are 5 top things to see in New York City.

3.

- Binoculars—these are always a great idea
- Microscope—is a lot of fun

- Small telescope
- Drawing tools like colored pencils, crayons, markers, and sketch pads
- Digital camera or disposable
- Tape recorder for recording sounds
- Magnifying glass
- Small vials or jars for collecting samples
- Backpack for carrying all your stuff
- Digging tools like a small shovel and hammer
- Walking sticks
- Metal detector

Implied Main Idea:

a. There are several things you should take with you on a nature walk.

b. Never leave the house without these important tools.

c. To have a great vacation, pack these items and take them with you.

Finding the Implied Main Idea in a Paragraph

Finding the implied main idea in a paragraph is similar to locating it in a list or group of ideas. Ask yourself what all or most of the supporting details have in common. Just as the supporting ideas helped you to find the stated main idea in a paragraph, they will also provide the clues to the author's point.

One word of caution, though: Don't let your own "issues" (meaning your own opinions, emotions, attitudes, etc.) get in the way of determining the *author's* point. We all have a tendency to mix our own experiences and attitudes with what we are reading. Often, the more experiences we have from life, the more difficult it is to see the author's point. That is why it is so important to recognize our prior knowledge and bias before we begin reading.

When I do the "Survey" step of SQ3R, I look over the material, and then I think about my own thoughts and attitudes as well as my prior knowledge about the topic. For instance, when I start to read something about smoking or smoking bans I have a lot of "issues" running through my head. My father was a smoker, had emphysema and a heart attack and died in his 70s; my brother was a smoker and had a fatal heart attack at age 39; my mother did not smoke, but lived with second-hand smoke and had a heart attack and triple bypass surgery at 76; my brother-in-law was a smoker and died of a heart attack in his 60s; my aunt was a smoker and died of emphysema in her early 70s; and I have asthma and have trouble breathing around any kind of smoke. If I read an article about tobacco and smoking, I have to put my own issues about smoking to the side temporarily in order to "hear" or comprehend the point the author is making.

When I read research information, opinions or editorials, organizational Web sites about smoking, or legislation to ban smoking, I might not understand the author's implied main idea if I let my own issues get in the way. For instance, when I read in our local newspaper that our city council was going to vote on a proposal to ban smoking in public places including most restaurants, I was so excited! All I could think was "It's about time! Larger cities have already done this, and even entire states. Why was our community so far behind?" I don't think I even read both sides of the argument. The article included interviews with smokers and non-smokers, restaurant and bar owners, and employees. There were many perspectives included, but my attention was only on my own desire to ban smoking. In order to determine the author's point, or implied main idea, we must carefully examine the supporting details in the reading without personal bias.

Here are some tools to help you remember all of the author's relevant information in the paragraph:

- Underline each relevant supporting detail as you read (if the book/magazine belongs to you).
- Write notes in the margin as you read.
- Include each specific detail mentioned in the paragraph that offers support.
- As you look over your notes and/or underlining, try to compose a sentence that addresses the meaning that the author wants to convey.
- Do not make your sentence too general or too specific.

Remember the previous examples from earlier in the chapter and note how you figured out the implied main ideas from the lists. When reading a paragraph, it is up to you to make the list by recognizing relevant supporting details.

EXAMPLE ───

Directions: Choose the answer that best matches the topic and the implied main idea in the paragraph below.

National Parks contain many of our nation's most treasured landscapes, from the majestic mountain ranges of Alaska to the vast sawgrass prairies of the Everglades. To safeguard these treasures, the National Park

Service combines the best available science with innovative education and stewardship programs, such as Biodiversity Discovery, the Climate Change Youth Initiative, and Geoscientists-in-Parks. We encourage you to "Explore Nature." Learn about the natural resources in parks, from the rocks under our feet to the sky overhead and everything in between. Discover the issues that affect our parks and how we join with neighbors and partners to address them. Meet the people who protect our parks and learn how you can help preserve these treasures for generations to come.

Source: http://www.nature.nps.gov/

Topic:

a. Nature

c. National parks

b. Biodiversity

d. Climate

Implied Main Idea

a. A National Park is not only fun to visit but also a place to learn about nature and why we need to preserve it.

b. National Parks contain many of our nation's most treasured landscapes, from the majestic mountain ranges of Alaska to the vast sawgrass prairies of the Everglades.

c. To safeguard these treasures, the National Park Service combines the best available science with innovative education and stewardship programs, such as Biodiversity Discovery, the Climate Change Youth Initiative, and Geoscientists-in-Parks.

d. Meet the people who protect our parks and learn how you can help preserve these treasures for generations to come.

In the paragraph above ask yourself what subject or topic is being discussed in most of the sentences. The topic is (c) National parks. The National parks are mentioned several times in the paragraph. Then ask yourself, "What point is the author trying to share about National parks?" The author's point or the implied main idea is answer (a) "A national park is not only fun to visit but also a place to learn about nature and why we need to preserve it. Answers (b), (c), and (d) are details mentioned in the paragraph, but they are not the author's main point.

PRACTICE THE NEW SKILL

Directions: Choose the answer that best matches the topic and the implied main idea of each paragraph.

1.   I'm not proud of my attitude as a child. Now, I understand that part of my problem was my diet. My parents usually let me eat what I wanted. They had little choice—I would throw a temper tantrum if I didn't get it. Not a little angry fit; these were atomic bombs of tantrums. I freaked out so much that my mom finally let me have my own shopping cart when we went to the grocery store. I filled it with junk food. I ate sugar-coated cereals and ice cream every day. I drank more Coke than water. All the sugar and caffeine cranked me up into a frenzy, and once it mixed with my overachieving determination, I could barely control myself.

Source: Hawk, Tony, with Seam Mortimer. (2002). *Tony Hawk: Professional Skateboarder.* New York: HarperCollins, pp. 11–12.

ENGLISH 2.0

Throw a temper tantrum means: be upset and be physically and verbally against the issue

Atomic bombs means: highly emotional and upsetting

Freaked out means: be upset and yell and scream

Topic:

a. temper tantrums

b. skateboarders

c. diet and a child's self control

d. junk food

Implied Main Idea:

a. Children throw temper tantrums when they don't get their way.

b. There are many ways to raise children.

c. Too much caffeine and sugar made it difficult for the child to control himself.

d. Children should not be allowed to eat junk food.

2.   It's not even worth getting mad when negative things happen. I still get sad, but every time that I've had to deal with loss, I have ended up growing so much as a person. And I can only be happy about that maturity. Challenges force us to grow. Unfortunately, since we're human, if everything worked out for the best and our lives were perfect, then we would have no *enticement* to improve. Personal growth takes somebody to boo you offstage. Life is about taking missteps, tripping, falling, dusting yourself off, getting back up, and working harder to get further than where you were in the first place. It's not worth wasting the time and the energy it takes to get upset and angry. That just holds you back. A lot of girls might have given up after losing on *Star Search*. But we were lucky my father saw the potential in us.

Source: Beyonce Knowles, Kelly Rowland, and Michelle Williams. (2002). *Soul Survivors: The Official Autobiography of Destiny's Child.* New York: Regan Books, HarperCollins, pp. 72–73.

Topic:

a. getting angry

b. *Star Search*

c. perfect lives

d. personal growth

Implied Main Idea:

a. Getting angry is a natural response to failure.

b. Doing well on *Star Search* was a good predictor of success in the music business.

c. Perfect lives lead to perfect musical careers.

d. The musicians used failure and frustration as an opportunity for personal growth.

Enticement—incentive

3.   In the 1870s, New England confectioner William Russell Frisbie opened a bakery that carried a line of homemade pies in circular tin pans embossed with the family surname. Bridgeport historians do not know if children in Frisbie's day tossed empty tins for amusement, but sailing the pans did become a popular diversion among students at Yale University in the mid-1940s. The school's New Haven campus was not far from the Bridgeport pie factory, which served stores throughout the region. The campus fad might have died out had it not been for a Californian, Walter Frederick Morrison, with an interest in flying saucers.

Source: Panati, Charles. (1987). *Extraordinary Origins of Everyday Things.* New York: Harper & Row, p. 372.

Topic:

a. William Russell Frisbie   c. Frisbie's pie tins

b. homemade pies   d. Yale University

Implied Main Idea:

a. William Russell Frisbie opened a bakery that carried homemade pies.

b. Frisbees we know today may have started with Yale University students sailing Frisbie pie tins to each other.

c. Children played with pie tins long before the Frisbee was invented.

d. Playing Frisbee with friends is a fun way to spend an afternoon.

Getting in the habit of putting the main idea of paragraphs in your own words is a skill that will help you concentrate and improve your reading comprehension. Remember to ask yourself these questions to help you determine the main idea:

- Who or what is the subject of the paragraph?
- What point is the author trying to convey about the topic?
- Do most of the sentences in the paragraph point to this main idea?

Putting the Implied Main Idea in Your Own Words

Most reading we will encounter does not come with multiple-choice questions. In real life we must determine the author's implied main idea

> **LO2**
> Put implied main ideas of paragraphs in your own words.

on our own. To understand the author's point, we need to concentrate on the specific words the author uses and think about the point she is trying to make with the details she gives.

EXAMPLE

Directions: Read the following quotation and write in your own words what you think the writer is implying.

> *I never lose sight of the fact that just being is fun.* —*Katharine Hepburn*

_____

_____

One possible answer is: She always remembers that just being alive and living your life is fun.

PRACTICE THE NEW SKILL

Directions: Read the following quotations and write in your own words what you think the writer is implying.

1. *Many a child who watches television for hours will go down in history—not to mention arithmetic, English and geography.*   —*Unknown*

_____

_____

_____

_____

_____

2. *By working faithfully eight hours a day, you may eventually get to be a boss and work twelve hours a day.*   —*Robert Frost*

_____

_____

_____

_____

3. *There is no pleasure in having nothing to do; the fun is having lots to do and not doing it.* —Andrew Jackson

_____

_____

_____

_____

Putting the Implied Main Idea in Your Own Words in Paragraphs

Determining the implied main idea from each individual paragraph may be required in order to comprehend the meaning of a longer reading passage. As you read, pause after each paragraph and put the author's main point in your own words.

EXAMPLE

Directions: Read through the paragraph. Identify the topic first and then write the implied main idea in your own words.

Music sets a mood and creates an ambiance. It can mellow you out, lift you up, or get you going. It can remind you of past memories, or create new ones. Music selections are shared in most of the chapters. So throughout your busy day, remember to "hear the music."

Source: Lee, Sandra. (2002). *Semi Homemade Cooking: Quick Marvelous Meals and Nothing is Made from Scratch.* New York: Hyperion, p. 16.

Topic: _____

_____

Implied Main Idea:

_____

_____

Answers will vary. One suggestion is the topic of the paragraph is music and moods. The implied main idea is that it is important to choose music to create the mood you desire.

PRACTICE THE NEW SKILL

Directions: In the following passages, identify the topic first. Then put the implied main idea in your own words.

1.   Fishing continues to be a favorite pastime in the United States. In 2001, 16% of the U.S. population 16 years old and older (34 million anglers) spent an average of 16 days fishing. Freshwater fishing was the most popular type of fishing with over 28 million anglers devoting nearly 467 million angler-days to the sport.

Source: http://www.recreation.gov/recFacilityActivitiesHomeAction.do?
goto=fishing.htm&activities=11&topTabIndex=RecreationArea

Topic: _____

_____

Main Idea: _____

_____

_____

2.   Unlike some of the wildlife that live within them, America's public land/recreation areas do not hibernate for the winter. Rather, many of these areas are open to a host of recreational opportunities unique to the season. Cross-country and downhill skiing as well as snowshoeing, snowboarding, and dog sledding are just a few of the activities that you can enjoy on public lands. Licensing, fees and seasonal restrictions vary from site to site.

Source: http://www.recreation.gov/recFacilityActivitiesHomeAction.do?
goto=winter_sports.htm&activities=22&topTabIndex=RecreationArea

Topic: _____

_____

Implied Main Idea: _____

_____

_____

3.   Financially strapped and emotionally depressed, Darrow spent hours at home devising gaming board amusements to occupy himself. The real-life scarcity of cash made easy money a key feature of his pastimes, and the business bankruptcies and property foreclosures carried daily in newspapers suggested play "deeds," "hotels," and "homes" that could be won—and lost—with the whimsy of a dice toss. One day in 1933, the elements of easy money and *ephemeral* ownership *congealed* as Darrow recalled vacation, taken during better times, in Atlantic City, New Jersey. The resort's streets, north to Baltic and south to Pacific avenues, became game board squares, as did prime real estate along the Boardwalk, on Park Place, and in Marvin Gardens.

Source: Panati, Charles (1987). *Extraordinary Origins of Everyday Things.* New York: Harper & Row, p. 378.

Topic: _____

Implied Main Idea:

_____

_____

Ephemeral—short-lived, temporary
Congealed—set

Finding the Implied Central Idea in Longer Passages

To find the implied central idea in a longer passage, use the same technique as you would to find
the implied main idea for a paragraph. You still

> **LO3**
> Find the implied central
> idea of longer passages.

need to pay attention to the supporting details and you still need to ask yourself "What is the author *really* saying?" The difference is that the point covers
several paragraphs instead of just one. After you read all of the paragraphs,
look for the message from the author. Ask yourself questions such as, "Why
is the author mentioning all of these details?" "What action does she want me
to take?" "What is his attitude about this topic?"

EXAMPLE

Directions: Read the passage and determine the implied central idea.

The consequences of a *sedentary* lifestyle are evidenced in the number
of deaths attributed to *cardiovascular* diseases and the ever-increasing
reports on the childhood obesity epidemic in the United States. To combat
this, fitness activities should be encouraged and included in the lifestyles of
young people. This is, at times, a difficult task because workouts can seem
like punishment or *drudgery*. However, exercising in the water can be an
exhilarating experience. Water that is clean, clear, and sparkling is *enticing*
and refreshing. Add fun and games to the workout plan and your participants will be excited, laughing, pleasantly surprised, and willing to come
back again. They will discover that they can do many things that they cannot do on land. They can do kickboxing or martial arts without falling. They
can try jumps and bounding activities that would normally create too much
impact for knees and ankles. They can also run around and play games that
become more challenging in the water without the added risks of injury.

Water workouts have a social and emotional component as well. Water
equalizes play because it is a foreign environment for everyone and almost
all can participate in some fashion. It doesn't matter who is on which team
because everyone has the same "disadvantage." Participation in interactive

---

Sedentary—inactive
Cardiovascular—of, pertaining to, or affecting the heart and blood vessels
Drudgery—hard work
Enticing—attractive, appealing, inviting

water games promotes self-esteem and provides opportunities to establish new friendships. Participants have the opportunity to forget the stresses of the day, play hard, and go home happy. And this is only the beginning.

Source: Lees, Terri. (2007). *Water Fun: 116 Fitness and Swimming Activities for All Ages*. Champaign, IL: Human Kinetics, p. 3.

Topic: —————————————————————

Implied Central Idea:

————————————————————————————

————————————————————————————

Answers will vary. One possibility is the topic is swimming. The implied central idea is that swimming is a great way to exercise and feel good.

PRACTICE THE NEW SKILL

Directions: Read the passage and determine the topic and the implied central idea.

1. Born in his great-grandparents' farmhouse about a mile from where his main chocolate factory stands today. Milton Hershey was a complex and colorful character who tried a number of businesses before he hit on chocolate. In the latter part of the nineteenth century, the recipe for making milk chocolate was a well-guarded European secret. Only the extremely well to do could afford to indulge in the velvety sweet.

    That is until candy maker Milton Hershey developed his own milk chocolate recipe. His goal was to produce the smooth, creamy chocolate in sufficient volume to be able to offer it to a wider customer base. Toward the end he built a factory in the rural village of Derry Church (often referred to as "the Factory in the Cornfield"), his own hometown in the heart of central Pennsylvania's dairy farmland.

Source: Odesser-Torpey, Marilyn. (2007). *The Hershey, Pennsylvania Cookbook: Fun Treats and Trivia from the Chocolate Capital of the World*. Guilford, CT: ThreeForks, p. vii.

Topic: ——————————————————————

Implied Central Idea:

————————————————————————————

————————————————————————————

2.   His friends thought that the Derry Township farm-country site Milton Hershey had chosen for his new chocolate factory was "too remote." His own wife suggested that he "have his head examined," according to company historic literature. But Hershey had done some extensive site—and soul—searching and determined that his old hometown could provide everything he needed to build a solid foundation for his growing company.

      Of course, there was the milk, a virtually endless supply produced fresh every day on surrounding farms. The area also provided plentiful quantities of clean water and access to the nearby ports of Philadelphia and New York, vital sources of essential ingredients, such as cocoa beans and sugar, that could not be produced in Derry. Just as important, the area offered a large potential workforce of Pennsylvania Dutch (the name variation on the word "Deutsch" referring to the Germans and Swiss Germans), like his own family, and Scots-Irish. Local limestone and brownstone quarries had also attracted a number of Italian stonecutters, who had brought their families along with them in their quest for employment and settled here when they found it.

      In 1903 Milton Hershey broke ground for his new factory about 1 mile from the family homestead on which he was born. Chocolate production began in 1905 in facilities that *Confectioners' Journal* described as "the most complete of their kind in the world," according to the Hershey-Derry Township Historical Society.

      From little Derry Township, Hershey's milk chocolate would become the first nationally marketed product of its kind. Because he had no predecessors in this area, Hershey either created or adapted most of the mass-production machinery for his factory.

But his goal was to build more than a business. Hershey wanted to build a town and, more than that, a model town that workers would be happy to call home. So Hershey authorized the construction of worker houses, and then he had a trolley system built so that workers living in neighboring communities could easily make the commute.

"Be sorry for people
    whoever they are,
Who live in a house
    Where there's no cookie jar!"

From an undated issue of Hershey's Kitchens' *Chocolate Town Bulletin*

Source: Odesser-Torpey, Marilyn. (2007). *The Hershey, Pennsylvania Cookbook: Fun Treats and Trivia from the Chocolate Capital of the World.* Guilford, CT: ThreeForks, pp. 23–24.

Topic: _____

Implied Central Idea: _____

_____

_____

Top 5 Streaming Music Sites

Listen to music while you surf the net

Streaming music sites offer you a huge library of music that you can listen to on-demand via your web browser. It's a great way to discover new music at zero cost while surfing the net. Simply type in the name of your favorite artist to start searching for music tracks; there are also recommendations displayed that are similar to what you are searching for. Many of them offer additional services that you can utilize, such as creating personalized playlists that you can share, watching videos, social networking, listening to radio, and even uploading your own music.

1. Spotify

Spotify is one of the top online services for streaming music. What makes this service unique is that you can use its Offline Mode to listen to thousands of music tracks without having to be connected to the Web. As well as subscription plans, this service also offers you the chance to try before you buy with its Spotify Free account. With facilities to stream music to mobile devices and home stereo systems, is this the ultimate digital music service?

2. Pandora Radio

If you're looking for a simple music discovery website that streams music, then Pandora is a good choice. Unlike Last.fm and imeem, Pandora is an intelligent Internet radio service that plays music based on your feedback. Once you have entered an artist's name or a song title, Pandora automatically suggests similar tracks which you can agree with, or reject; Pandora will remember your answers and fine-tune its subsequent recommendations. You can also buy albums and individual tracks from digital music services such as Amazon MP3, and the iTunes Store via links that are displayed on-screen.

3. Last.fm

Last.fm is one of the top sites to visit for streaming music. It has a whole host of features which include music and video streaming, custom playlist creation, uploading your photos, social networking, etc. You can also connect with people who have similar tastes. An interesting feature of Last.fm is 'scrobbling' which allows you (via a small widget download) to automatically add tracks to your Last.fm playlist while listening to music on your computer or iPod.

4. Maestro.fm

Maestro.fm is a social music network that not only makes it possible to search for new music, connect with friends, and share playlists, but also gives you the ability to store your own digital music library via remote storage.

5. Yahoo Music

Even though Yahoo has closed its Music Unlimited service and migrated its customers to *Rhapsody*, Yahoo Music continues to be one of the most popular music sites on the Internet. It provides a number of services which include, streaming music and video, information on artists, and current media news. Its LAUNCHcast and LAUNCHcast Plus Internet radio stations offer the user a selection of music that is based on their preferences. Unfortunately, Internet Explorer is the only compatible browser at the moment but Yahoo Music is still a top-notch service worth using.

Source: Mark Harris, About.com Guide http://mp3.about.com/od/ streamingaudio/tp/Best_Streaming_Music_Sites.htm About.com

3. Topic: _____

_____

4. Implied Central Idea: _____

_____

_____

REVIEW WHAT YOU LEARNED

Directions: Read the following passage and answer the questions that follow.

1–2.   A picnic can be a grand community celebration, complete with parades and fireworks. It can be a church gathering complete with hymn sings and dinner on the grounds, a tailgate party at the old alma mater, or a family gathering to show off new babies and remember old times. It can also be an intimate affair: dinner for four at twilight before a concert in the park, tea on the terrace for a small group of friends, or a romantic interlude for two—an apt setting for that perfect kiss or a quiet reaffirmation of abiding love. With the right attitude— that of celebration—even a solitary sandwich in the park can become a picnic to remember.

Source: Cronkhite, Russell. (2005). *A Return to Family Picnics.* Sisters, OR: Multnomah Gifts, Multnomah Publishers, p. 6.

Topic:

a. picnics

b. family gatherings

c. tailgate parties

d. celebrations

Implied Main Idea:

a. Picnics can be many different things

b. There are many ways to celebrate

c. Family gatherings are one type of picnic

d. A solitary sandwich in the park can be a picnic to remember

3–4.   Dogs are animals of the pack, eager to follow a leader, and even willing to accept a human being in that position, provided he or she feeds them. Cats are independent—leadership is not high on their list of demands—and it must have been quickly apparent that no cat was likely to look up at a human being with an adoring, trusting, or soulful expression in its eyes, or do anything on command.

Source: Korda, Michale and Margaret Korda. (2005). *Cat People: A Hilariously Entertaining Look at the World of Cat Lovers and Their Obsessive Devotion to Their Pets.* New York: HarperCollins, p. 3.

Topic:

a. cats

b. dogs

c. cats and dogs

d. pack behavior

Implied Main Idea:

a. Dogs and cats behave differently as pets.

b. Cats are independent.

c. Dogs are animals of the pack.

d. Dogs are better pets.

5.   Once, when asked what made the Beatles different from other sixties icons, Ringo said, "We don't hate our parents." British youth were only "junior versions of the men," "America had teenagers and everywhere else just had people," said John.

Source: Starke, Steven D. (1981). *Meet the Beatles: A Cultural History of the Band that Shook Youth, Gender, and the World.* New York: HarperCollins, p. 13.

Implied Main Idea:

_____

_____

_____

REVIEW WHAT YOU LEARNED

Directions: Read the following passage and answer the questions that follow.

1–2.   In addition to boosting alertness, coffee appears to enhance mood. Coffee consumption seems to decrease the risk of suicide, reduce irritability, and increase self-confidence and social skills. Coffee has been shown to help lift depression—even chronic depression. Coffee drinkers are also less likely to use anti-anxiety and anti-psychotic medications.

Source: Antol, Marie Nadine. (2002). *Confessions of a . . . Coffee Bean: The Complete Guide to Coffee Cuisine.* Garden City, NY: Square One, p. 68.

Topic:

a. coffee and moods   c. depression

b. caffeine   d. mood

Implied Main Idea:

a. Coffee drinkers are less likely to use anti-anxiety medications.

b. Caffeine consumption improves mood.

c. Coffee consumption improves mood.

d. Caffeine helps relieve depression.

3–4.   *Wheel of Fortune* had a shaky beginning, but has since gone on to become the longest running syndicated television game show in history. It is consistently the number one rated syndicated show, a spot that *Wheel* took over in 1984 and has held onto ever since. The co-hosts, simple format, and straightforward game play deliver an entertaining half-hour program every weekday evening across North America.

Source: http://gameshows.about.com/od/showprofiles/p/wheel_fortune.htm

Topic :

a. Game shows

b. Syndicated television

c. *Wheel of Fortune*

d. Entertainment

Implied Main Idea:

a. Game shows are very entertaining in North America.

b. *Wheel of Fortune* is one of the longest running and highest rated game shows.

c. Wheel of Fortune had a shaky beginning.

d. The co-hosts, simple format, and straightforward game play are enjoyed by everyone.

5.   A recent study of how men and women differ when it comes to the mall turned up this fact: Men, once you get them in the door, are much more interested in the social aspect of malls than the shopping part, whereas women say the social aspect is important but shopping comes first. Men enjoy the mall as a form of recreation—they like watching people and browsing around stores more than shopping. Maybe they'll spend fifteen minutes in a bookstore or a stereo store and leave without buying a thing. They treat it like an information-gathering trip. Men also like the non retail parts—the rock-climbing walls, the food courts, anything that doesn't actually require them to enter stores and look at, try on, or buy merchandise. Women, of course, are there for *exactly* those things. The only females who truly love the non-shopping aspects of the mall are teenage girls. They love shopping, of course, but they also love the food courts and video arcades and all that stuff, too. And that's probably because the mall is the only non-home, nonschool environment they have. But they outgrow that by the

time they're in college. From then on, they're at the mall to shop.

Source: Underhill, Paco. (2004). *Call of the Mall.* New York: Simon & Schuster, p. 69.

Implied Main Idea:

a. Men go to the mall to shop.

b. Teenagers spend significant amounts of time at the mall.

c. Women and men have different primary purposes for going to the mall.

d. Women prefer to socialize at the mall.

MASTER THE LESSON

A True Hero

1   The life of a major league baseball player involves more than playing baseball. Especially for those that are popular.

2   Jim Abbott was one of the most popular players from the moment he first donned a major-league uniform for the California Angels in 1989. Abbott, just twenty-one at the time, was one of the rare few who skips the minor leagues completely and begins his professional career in the big leagues.

3   But that's not what made Abbott so special to so many.

4   Abbott was born without a right hand. In fact, Abbott's right arm extended from his shoulder to just past the elbow joint.

5   Abbott, though, didn't make the big leagues because people felt sorry for him. Abbott could pitch.

6   The Angels took a chance on him by drafting him out of the University of Michigan and he proved in spring training that year that he was ready for the big leagues.

7   Using a skill he developed as a kid, Abbott could pitch with his left hand, then quickly transfer a right-hander's glove from the stub of his right arm onto his left hand, in case he had to field the ball.

8   If a ball was hit back to him, Abbott would catch it, stick the glove under his right armpit, then pull the ball out with his left hand so he could throw it again. And he did all of this in a second or two.

9   Abbott became a media magnet. Wherever he went, reporters wanted to hear his story. Abbott was overwhelmed, but never lost his pleasant disposition.

10   Abbott had a smile for everyone, writers and fans alike.

11   Many times the media relations department of a major-league team gets requests for fans to meet their favorite baseball players. Abbott was no different.

12   What was different about one particular fan was what made him similar to Abbott.

13   The Angels had set up a meeting between Abbott and a young boy from the Midwest. The boy, about nine or ten years old, had lost an arm in a farming accident.

14   Before one game during a long and arduous baseball season, the boy was brought onto the field to meet Abbott. The boy was obviously nervous, his body language telling the story. Head down, shoulders slumped forward, he had no idea what he was in for.

15   Abbott and the boy met on the field during batting practice before a game. But they weren't getting much privacy. The media are allowed to remain on the field up to forty-five minutes before game time, and there were plenty of curious onlookers.

16   So Abbott had an idea. He took the boy down the leftfield line and away from anyone who wanted to get close. The two stood in the outfield, talking, watching batting practice and laughing for about an hour.

17   When the two returned to the dugout after batting practice, the boy's eyes sparkled. His head was up and his chest was thrust forward. Abbott was asked what he said to the boy, but he wouldn't reveal what was said.

18   That was about ten years ago, and the boy is now an adult. I often wonder whatever became of him, but after his meeting with Abbott, I have no doubt he is leading a happy and productive life. Abbott, after all, was living proof for the boy that he could do anything he wanted. Even pitch in the big leagues.

Source: Haakenson, Joe, Canfield, Jack, Mark Victor Hansen, Chrissy, Donnelly, and Tommy, Lasorda. (2001). "A True Hero." In *Chicken Soup for the Baseball Fan's soul: Inspirational Stories of Baseball, Big-League Dreams and the Game of Life.* Deerfield Beach, FL: Health Communications, pp. 157–159.

1–2. What is the topic? _____

_____

3–5. Use the title, "A True Hero," and the topic to help you find the implied central idea. _____

_____

_____

6–10. What evidence or supporting details does the author provide to support his claim? _____

_____

_____

_____

_____

/MASTER THE LESSON/

Loretta Lynn

Directions: Read the article below and answer the questions that follow.

1   I waited as long as I could and finally announced that Jones was gonna be a no-show.

2   The fans crashed through Jones's dressing room door about the same time Doo and Jones peeled out of the parking lot. They broke the guitar and tore the room to pieces. Nobody bothered me because they knew I didn't have nothin' to do with Jones's carryin' on. But they smashed my guitar. Doo dumped Jones at our motel room just in case anyone knew what George's room number was. Then he came back to the venue for me.

3   I believe that Doolittle Lynn saved George Jones's life that night, and I'll believe it till the day I die. When a mess like the one with Jones happened, there wasn't nobody in this world I'd rather have there to fix things than Doo. Not the Wilburns, not even Ernest Tubb. Doo had a way of figgerin' out things and taking care of 'em. He could read a situation and take action in a second. But the times he wanted to go on the road with me got less and less. Apart from the fact that Doo was bored on the road, he got real sick of people making comments about his being married to a meal ticket. And no matter how many times I came back and said there wouldn't have been no Loretta meal ticket without Doo, it ate away at him.

> ### ENGLISH 2.0
>
> Crashed through means: went through quickly or in a hurry
>
> Peeled out means: drove fast to get out of
>
> Figgerin' out things means: Figuring out or thinking through a problem and understanding it
>
> Meal ticket means: someone who pays for everything so he doesn't have to
>
> Ate away at him means: upset him over a period of time

1–3. What is the implied central idea of the paragraphs above? _____

_____

_____

_____

4   By the 1960s and early seventies, I had a string of hit songs and a pile of awards. In 1967, I won Country Music Association's Female Vocalist of the Year for the first of three times, and in 1972, I became the first woman to win the CMA Entertainer of the Year. Things was going so good that promoters starting advertising me as America's most popular female country singer.

4–5. What is the implied main idea of the paragraph above? _____

_____

_____

5   I was making more money than Doo ever dreamed about. And Doo had figured out so many ways to spend it that it was a nightmare. Back then, I never spent a dime I didn't have to. I didn't even know how to use a credit card until the late 1970s when Conway Twitty taught me. Not that I needed to use one anyway. I signed for food and rooms on the road, and I didn't have time to run around and shop in any of them towns I played. Doo was the one who had his hand in the money pile, not me.

6–8. What is the implied main idea of the paragraph above? _____

_____

_____

6   I know he felt it was a man's job to bring in the biggest part of a family's income, but the sad fact is, an entertainer—if they work hard—can pull in more money than you can imagine. Certainly more than Doo could make as a farmer. In fact, I've always said that this is one thing that bothers me. Teachers, nurses, coal miners—where is their fair share? But until we can figure out a way to even things out, successful entertainers can count on a very good income. The problem turns out to be, in so many cases, how to hang on to it.

9–10. What is the implied main idea of the paragraph above? _____

_____

_____

Source: Lynn, Loretta with Patsi Bale Cox. (2002). *Still Woman Enough: A Memoir.* New York: Hyperion, pp. 105–106.

LEARNING STYLE ACTIVITIES

*L*ook, *L*isten, *W*rite, *D*o

Following is a list of 20 different ideas of things to do that are free. The Web site has 100 things to do during a money-free weekend. Complete one of the activities that follow.

100 Things to Do During a Money-Free Weekend

About a year ago, I offered up the idea of the money-free weekend:

1   For the last few months, my wife and I have been doing something every other weekend or so that we call a "money-free" weekend, in an effort to live more frugally. It's actually quite fun—here's how we do it.

2   **We are not allowed to spend any money on anything, no matter what.** In other words, we can't make a run to the store to buy food, we can't spend money on any sort of entertainment, and so on. Since we often do our grocery shopping on Saturdays, on a "money free" weekend, we delay it to Monday or Tuesday.

3   **We can use our utilities, but no extra expenses on these utilities.** No renting movies on cable, no text messages that aren't already covered by our cell phone plan, and so on.

4   I followed this up with fifteen things to do during such a weekend, fifteen more things to do, and fifteen deeply fulfilling things to do during such a weekend.

5   Since then, lots of people have sent me ideas for activities for money-free weekends, plus we've uncovered a bunch of our own. At the same time, many readers have asked for a master list of all of these ideas.

6   So, here we go—one hundred fun ways to spend a money-free weekend. The list below includes the first forty-five (with duplicates removed), plus about sixty new ones. Print this off and use it as a check-list or a thumbnail guide for your own money-free weekend. Please note that **everyone's interests are different**—you probably won't find everything on this list fun and neither will someone else, but the two lists won't overlap (I can think of countless things other people find fun that I find utterly dreadful). Anyway, here goes!

1. **Check out the community calendar.** Look at your town's website (as well as those of cities and towns nearby) or stop by city hall to find a list of events going on in the community, many of which are free. You'll often be surprised at how many interesting (and free) activities are going on *right now* in your area.

2. **Visit your community library.** Not only is a library a warehouse of books, most libraries also have extensive CD and DVD collections you can check out. Many libraries also have "story time" for young children, film nights, book clubs, and many other events that you may be unaware of—completely for free. Stop in and check out what they have to offer.

3. **Get involved in community sports.** Many towns have community sports fields where both youth and adult sports leagues and activities are regularly going on throughout the weekend. Stop by, watch a game or two, and if something intrigues you, look into joining either as a participant or as a volunteer.

4. **Get your financial papers in order.** This may not sound like a fun activity up front, but the peace of mind it gives you will make your life a lot more relaxing. Spend an hour or two organizing all of your statements and other financial documents. This is a perfect time to start your own filing system. If you're more adventurous, try initiating an electronic filing system, as it will save you significant space and make information retrieval easier (though it's more of a time investment up front).

5. **Check out some podcasts.** Podcasts are wonderful things—top-notch audio programs available for you to listen to for free. Give some a sample—you can do it easily by using iTunes. Visit the Podcast section of the store and check a few out. My favorites include The Splendid Table (on food topics), Marketplace (on economics and business), Speaking of Faith (on religion), Fresh Air

(interviews of general interest), This American Life (quirky general interest stuff), and This Week in Tech (technology news), among many others.

6. **Play board games.** We have a pile of board games, mostly received as gifts, that we often pull out and play, plus our closest friend has a few choice ones. Classic games like Monopoly and Pictionary can be great fun, but our favorites are Settlers of Catan, Cartagena, Puerto Rico, and especially Ticket to Ride. Just dig through the recesses of your closet, find an old board game you haven't played in ages, and bust it open!

7. **Bake a loaf of homemade bread.** You probably have everything you need to make a loaf of bread in your kitchen right now (except for maybe the yeast). Anyone can do it, and the bread turns out deliciously.

8. **Learn how to juggle.** All you really need is three balls and a video showing you how to do it. Not only is it a fun activity to learn, it's something that's fun to bust out as a party trick on occasion (trust me, you can always get people to smile if you juggle three fruits in the kitchen while preparing something).

9. **Teach yourself how to change the oil in your car.** If you're due for an oil change, just bring the oil you need home with you and teach yourself how to do it. All you really need is an old pan to catch the wasted oil and a funnel to pour the old oil back into the canisters for later disposal. Just use your car manual as a guide for the procedure and you might just find that not only is it a lot easier than you thought, but it's a useful skill to have *and* it's cheaper than taking your car into Jiffy-Lube (or wherever you take your car for oil changes).

10. **Meet your neighbors.** Make an effort to introduce yourself to your neighbors if you don't know them well. Invite any interesting ones over for a cup of coffee and a chat, just to get to know each other better. Your neighbors can not only become friends, but can also be a valuable resource—a friendly pair of eyes on your property when you're away or a helpful set of hands when you're trying to complete a challenging task.

...

90. **Visit a magazine room.** Most libraries have a "magazine room" where you can read all of the latest issues of many popular newspapers and magazines for free. Just grab a few, settle in a comfy chair, and read. Don't like the library environment? You can usually do the same thing at most bookstores.

91. **Attend a dress rehearsal.** Many performance groups have dress rehearsals that are open to the public if you call in advance, particularly if you have young children. Give the theater a ring and ask if there are open dress rehearsals for a particular show and then enjoy the show for free! It's a great way to give your kids a taste of theater without any cost.

92. **Attend a free community class.** Many institutions and stores offer free classes on the weekends on all sorts of topics. Stop by a local food store and catch a free cooking class, or a hardware store to learn about a home repair topic. Got kids? Try something like the Home Depot Kids Workshop, where they offer free how-to clinics for kids ages five to twelve—these can be a lot of fun (I've seen them ongoing when stopping by a Home Depot on a Saturday morning).

93. **Donate some unwanted things to charity.** If you've gone through your stuff but don't want to have a yard sale, consider giving the stuff to charity. Not only will you have a clean house, you'll have the good feeling of knowing your items are going to be used by someone who actually needs them, plus you'll have a pile of receipts to use for tax deductions next April.

94. **Discover new music that you like.** Download last.fm. It's a program that allows you to enter the name of your favorite musical artist and generates a radio station for you that plays songs similar to that artist. The songs are selected based on the enormous last.fm database, which collects information on what people listen to in iTunes and sorts it in different ways, finding songs by other artists that are popular among fans of a particular group. Give it a whirl—you'll be surprised at the good music you'll find for free.

95. **Build a cardboard castle.** This is a great one if you have kids. Stop by an appliance store and ask if they have any extra appliance boxes you can get, then flatten them and load up your vehicle. Get home, then use them as pieces in building a giant cardboard castle in your living room or in your back yard. Cut out doors and windows, and attach them together to make rooms. This can be a great afternoon of fun for free!

96. **Dig an old video game console out of the closet and play some of your favorites.** A lot of families have old video game consoles in the closet—an ancient PlayStation or Super Nintendo, long forgotten about, with a controller and a few games. Dig out that old console and hook it up to a television, then relive some of the memories of the games you used to play for hours. I did this not too long ago and found myself replaying a good chunk of *Final Fantasy IX*.

97. **Do some amateur stargazing.** Go outside on a clear evening, preferably away from city lights, and look up at the sky. Use some handy star maps to know what you're looking at. Spread out some blankets on the ground, lay flat on your back, stare upwards, and realize how magnificent the universe is around you.

98. **Go on a hike or a long walk.** Go to the local hiking or walking trails and just take off. Let yourself get absorbed into nature and simply enjoy the journey. Go at your own speed—this is for your own personal enjoyment, after all.

99. **Take a stab at writing poetry (or other forms of creative writing).** The basics of poetry are easier than you might think—just try writing down what's on your mind. Whatever you're thinking about, just write it down. That can provide the basics of any poem. Then, just read through the stuff you've written down, choose the words that seem beautiful to you, and assemble them until the whole work means something. This can be a deeply enlightening and personal experience, actually, and one that really stirs the creative juices.

100. **Go on a bike ride.** If you've got a bicycle and a helmet in your garage or closet, you already have everything you need for some good exercise and some good fun. Head outside and bike away. Almost every town and every state park around here has an extensive array of bike trails, so you can almost always find somewhere new and interesting to ride, plus it'll help get you into shape really quick.

   Hopefully, this list will provide for a ton of fun money-free weekends. Want some more tips? Here are 100 additional tips for saving money.

Source: 100 Things to Do During a Money Free Weekend. (July 17, 2008).
Retrieved from http://www.thesimpledollar.com/2008/07/17/
100-things-to-do-during-a-money-free-weekend/

Look   As you read some of the ideas in this article, highlight the ones you might want to try. Look around your home, your campus, and your community for other free things to do. Add your ideas to the list. You may also create a brochure for your campus or community with pictures of free things to do. Make sure to identify who will use the brochure, such as college students, parents of young children, etc.

■))) *L*ISTEN   As you read some of the ideas in this article, repeat the items you are most interested in trying. Tell a friend, your children, or classmate any of the suggestions you might do. Listen to a local radio station and talk to other people for more suggestions of free things to do in your community and/or on your campus.

✎ *W*RITE   As you read some of the ideas in the article, take notes on the ones that seem the most interesting to you. Jot down notes in the margin of the article and in your own words of the suggestions you are thinking of trying. Also, read your local newspaper for more ideas of fun and free things to do on your campus and in your community. You may also write an article for you college or local newspaper critiquing one of the fun and free adventures.

👆 *D*o   As you read through the article, choose a few of the suggestions you want to try. Imagine how you could implement the ideas in your own life. Then go out and try some suggestions for yourself and perhaps, include your family and/or friends. Add your own experiences to the list of free ideas. You may also submit your ideas to the blog on the Web site and/or share your fun ideas with your classmates.

Reading Practice

The following reading practice will help you further develop your ability to find the implied main idea and implied central idea while you are reading different material related to hobbies, sports, art, movies, music, and other recreational activities.

The first reading, "On-the-Job Video Gaming" is from the Web site www.businessweek.com.

The second reading, "The Art of Listening," is from the textbook *Understanding Music*.

The third reading is a passage titled "Make a Decision: Tigger or Eeyore," from a work of contemporary literature, *The Last Lecture* by Randy Pausch.

The fourth reading is an article titled "A Classroom with a View" from *National Parks Magazine*.

The final reading is a visual image of banana slugs.

Internet

READING 1

On-the-Job Video Gaming

Interactive training tools are captivating employees and saving companies money

1   Laura Holshouser's favorite video games include *Halo*, *Tetris*, and an online training game developed by her employer. A training game? That's right. The 24-year-old graduate student, who manages a Cold Stone Creamery ice-cream store in Riverside, Calif., stumbled across the game on the corporate Web site in October.

2   It teaches portion control and customer service in a cartoon-like simulation of a Cold Stone store. Players scoop cones against the clock and try to avoid serving too much ice cream. The company says more than 8,000 employees, or about 30% of the total, voluntarily downloaded the game in the first week. "It's so much fun," says Holshouser. "I e-mailed it to everyone at work."

1. What is the implied central idea of the paragraphs above? _____

_____

_____

3   The military has used video games as a training tool since the 1980s. Now the practice is catching on with companies, too, ranging from Cold Stone to Cisco Systems Inc. (CSCO) to Canon Inc. (CAJ). Corporate trainers are betting that games' interactivity and fun will hook young, *media-savvy* employees like Holshouser and help them grasp and retain sales, technical, and management skills. "Video games teach resource management, *collaboration*, critical thinking, and tolerance for failure," says Ben Sawyer, who runs Digitalmill Inc., a game consultancy in Portland, Me.

2. What is the implied main idea of the paragraph above? _____

_____

_____

4   The market for corporate training games is small but it's growing fast. Sawyer estimates that such games make up 15% of the "serious," or non-entertainment market, which also includes educational and medical training products. Over the next five years, Sawyer sees the serious-games market more than doubling, to

---

Media-savvy—experienced in using media
Collaboration—teamwork, cooperation

$100 million, with trainers accounting for nearly a third of that. It's numbers like those that prompted Cyberlore Studios Inc., maker of *Playboy: The Mansion*, to refocus on training games—albeit based on its *Playboy* title. And training games will be top of mind at the Game Developers Conference in San Jose, Calif., this month.

5   Companies like video games because they are cost-effective. Why pay for someone to fly to a central training campus when you can just plunk them down in front of a computer? Even better, employees often play the games at home on their own time. Besides, by industry standards, training games are cheap to make. A typical military game costs up to $10 million, while sophisticated entertainment games can cost twice that. Since the corporate variety don't require dramatic, warlike explosions or complex 3D graphics, they cost a lot less. BreakAway Games Ltd., which designs simulation games for the military, is finishing its first corporate product, V-bank, to train bank auditors. Its budget? Just $500,000.

3. What is the implied central idea of the paragraphs above?

_____

_____

_____

DRAG AND DROP

6   Games are especially well-suited to training technicians. In one used by Canon, repairmen must drag and drop parts into the right spot on a copier. As in the board game *Operation*, a light flashes and a buzzer sounds if the repairman gets it wrong. Workers who played the game showed a 5% to 8% improvement in their training scores compared with older training techniques such as manuals, says Chuck Reinders, who trains technical support staff at Canon. This spring, the company will unveil 11 new training games.

4. What is the implied main idea of the paragraph above?

_____

_____

_____

7   Games are also being developed to help teach customer service workers to be more empathetic. Cyberlore, now rechristened Minerva Software Inc., is developing a training tool for a retailer by rejiggering its *Playboy Mansion* game. In the original, guests had to persuade models to pose topless. The new game requires players to use the art of persuasion to sell products, and simulates a store, down to the carpet and point-of-purchase display details.

8   Don Field, director of certifications at Cisco, says games won't entirely replace traditional training methods such as videos and classes. But he says they should be part of the toolbox. Last year, Cisco rolled out six new training games—some of them designed to teach technicians how to build a computer network. It's hard to imagine a drier subject. Not so in the virtual world. In one Cisco game, players must put the network together on Mars. In a sandstorm. "Our employees learn without realizing they are learning," says Field. Sounds suspiciously like fun.

Source: On-the-Job Video Gaming. (March 27, 2006). *Bloomberg Business Week.*
Retrieved from http://www.businessweek.com/magazine/content/06_13/b3977062.htm

5. What is the implied central idea of the paragraphs above?

_____

_____

_____

6. What is the implied central idea of the entire article? _____

_____

_____

7–9. List three supporting details that prove, illustrate, or explain the writer's implied central idea.

a. _____

_____

b. _____

_____

c. _____

_____

10. If inter is a prefix that means "between" or "among," what does ***inter-activity*** mean in the sentence below? *HINT:* Think of the type of activity when people are playing video games.

    Corporate trainers are betting that games' ***interactivity*** and fun will hook young, media-savvy employees like Holshouser and help them grasp and retain sales, technical, and management skills.

Interactivity means _____

_____

11. If the root word capt means to "take" or "hold," what does *captivating*

mean in the sentence below? _____

_____

> Interactive training tools are ***captivating*** employees and saving compa-
> nies money . . . The company says more than 8,000 employees, or about
> 30% of the total, voluntarily downloaded the game in the first week. "It's
> so much fun," says Holshouser. "I e-mailed it to everyone at work."

| They are interactive. | Many employees voluntarily downloaded it. | One said, "It's so much fun!" |

12. Together, these facts let you infer that *captivating* means _____

_____

13. What is the topic of the article? _____

_____

14–15. Think of a place you have worked. What was your training like? Did
you have an interactive training video game? Would you have liked
one? Do you think it would make training better to play video games
while you learn?

_____

_____

_____

_____

Textbook **READING 2**

The Art of Listening

1   When all is said and done, the most important part of the musical experience is listening. There are many ways of listening to music. One of the most common is a **passive** kind of listening, the kind we do when music is playing as we are doing something else: eating at a restaurant, talking at a party, reading a book. There is even a kind of **unconscious** listening—on some movie soundtracks, for example, or in supermarkets, when the music creates a particular mood without our focusing on how or why.

2   The kind of listening this book encourages is a **conscious**, active, committed kind of listening, in which we really concentrate on everything that is happening, just as we would when reading a great work of literature. This kind of listening takes a great deal of concentration. It also offers very special rewards.

    1. What is the implied central idea of paragraphs 1 and 2?

_____

_____

    2–4. Give three supporting details for the implied central idea in the paragraphs. (*HINT*: three kinds of listening)

        a. _____

        b. _____

        c. _____

3   The previous chapter, on the **fundamentals** of music, presented some of the building blocks of the art of music; it also introduced you to some of the vocabulary that musicians and educated listeners use to talk and think about music. We shall use some of this vocabulary in what follows because it provides a clear means of describing what we hear. However, much of what we experience in listening to great music cannot be described in words, and this is the magic of music. It expresses things that cannot be expressed any other way.

4   The first and most important thing to know about listening to music is that you have to listen to a work several times to appreciate what is in it. Imagine reading a Shakespeare sonnet. The first time you read it, some of the meaning comes across, but a great deal is missed. Each **successive** reading provides you with greater insight into the thoughts and feelings expressed, the rhythm and sound of the words, the **interplay** of form and meaning. The words remain the same, but

your understanding of them changes. The same is true of music. A great composition repays repeated hearings, and some of the greatest works **reveal** something new every time you listen.

5   This type of active listening is not easy at first. It takes practice. The secret of enjoying music, especially complicated and unfamiliar music, lies in your willingness to listen to a work more than once, and in the quality of your concentration as you listen.

5. Write the implied central idea of the paragraphs above.

_____

_____

_____

6–8. Give three supporting details for the central idea in the paragraphs. *HINT*: Why listen several times?

a. _____

_____

_____

b. _____

_____

_____

c. _____

_____

_____

6   In this chapter, you will be introduced to five very different pieces of music. Each one has something special about it, and the way we talk about each piece will differ according to the type of music under discussion. In each case, however, we shall try to capture something of the **essence** of the work: what makes it special, what sorts of feelings it expresses, and how it does so.

Vocabulary

Directions: Circle the letter of the best definition for the bold word as it is used in the sentence. Use the context clues in the surrounding paragraph and/or the word parts to help you discover the meaning of the unknown word.

9. **passive** (see paragraph 1)

    a. active   **c.** focused

    b. inactive   **d.** romantic

10. **unconscious** (see paragraph 1)

    a. unaware   **c.** active

    b. asleep   **d.** aggressive

11. **conscious** (see paragraph 2)

    a. unaware   **c.** aggressive

    b. aware   **d.** romantic

12. **fundamentals** (see paragraph 3)

    a. fun parts   **c.** table of contents

    b. history   **d.** basics

13. **successive** (see paragraph 4)

    a. successful   **c.** first

    b. following   **d.** meaningful

14. **interplay** (see paragraph 4)

    a. interaction   **c.** intermission

    b. intramural   **d.** reading

15. **reveal** (see paragraph 4)

    a. hide   **c.** uncover

    b. repeat   **d.** understand

16. **essence** (see paragraph 6)

    a. fragrance   **c.** sounds

    b. sights   **d.** spirit

READING 3

The Last Lecture

"We cannot change the cards we are dealt, just how we play the hand."
—Randy Pausch

A lot of professors give talks titled "The Last Lecture." Professors are asked to consider their demise and to ruminate on what matters most to them. And while they speak, audiences can't help but mull the same question: What wisdom would we impart to the world if we knew it was our last chance? If we had to vanish tomorrow, what would we want as our legacy?

When Randy Pausch, a computer science professor at Carnegie Mellon, was asked to give such a lecture, he didn't have to imagine it as his last, since he had recently been diagnosed with terminal cancer. But the lecture he gave—"Really Achieving Your Childhood Dreams"—wasn't about dying. It was about the importance of overcoming obstacles, of enabling the dreams of others, of seizing every moment (because "time is all you have . . . and you may find one day that you have less than you think"). It was a summation of everything Randy had come to believe. It was about *living*.

In this book, Randy Pausch has combined the humor, inspiration and intelligence that made his lecture such a phenomenon and given it an indelible form. It is a book that will be shared for generations to come.

Source: Retrieved from http://www.thelastlecture.com/aboutbk.htm

MAKE A DECISION: TIGGER OR EEYORE

1   When I told Carnegie Mellon's president, Jared Chon, that I would be giving a last lecture, he said, "Please tell them about having fun, because that's what I will remember you for."

2   And I said, "I can do that, but it's kind of like a fish talking about the importance of water."

3   I mean, I don't know how *not* to have fun. I'm dying and I'm having fun. And I'm going to keep having fun every day I have left. Because there's no other way to play it.

4   I came to a realization about this very early in my life. As I see it, there's a decision we all have to make, and it seems perfectly captured in the Winnie-the-Pooh characters created by A. A. Milne. Each of us must decide: Am I a fun-loving Tigger or am I a sad-sack Eeyore? Pick a camp. I think it's clear where I stand on the great Tigger/Eeyore debate.

5   For my last Halloween, I had great fun. Jai and I dressed up as the Incredibles, and so did our three kids. I put a photo of us on my Web site letting everyone know what an "Incredible" family we were. The kids looked pretty super. I looked invincible with my fake cartoon muscles. I explained that chemo had not dramatically affected my superpowers, and I got tons of smiling emails in response.

6   I recently went on a short scuba-diving vacation with three of my best friends: my high school friend Jack Sheriff, my college roommate Scot Sherman, and my friend from Electronic Arts, Steve Seabolt. We all were aware of the subtext. These were my friends from various times in my life, and they were banding together to give me a farewell weekend.

7   My three friends didn't know each other well, but strong bonds formed quickly. All of us are grown men, but for much of the vacation it was as if we were thirteen years old. And we were all Tiggers.

8   We successfully avoided any emotional "I love you, man" dialogue related to my cancer. Instead, we just had fun. We reminisced, we horsed around and we made fun of each other. (Actually, it was mostly them making fun of *me* for the "St. Randy of Pittsburgh" reputation I've gotten since my last lecture. They know me, and they were having none of it.)

9   I won't let go of the Tigger inside me. I just can't see the upside in becoming Eeyore. Someone asked me what I want on my tombstone. I replied: "Randy Pausch: He Lived Thirty Years After a Terminal Diagnosis."

10   I promise you. I could pack a lot of fun into those thirty years. But if that's not to be, then I'll just pack fun into whatever time I do have.

Source: Pausch, Randy. (2008). *The Last Lecture.* New York: Hyperion, pp. 179–182.

Questions

1. Use context clues to find the meaning of the word ***camp.***

> Each of us must decide: Am I a fun-loving Tigger or am I a sad-sack Eeyore?
> Pick a ***camp.*** I think it's clear where I stand on the great Tigger/Eeyore debate.

Each of us must decide.	We must pick.	It is where he stands on the debate.

Together, these facts let you infer that ***camp*** means _____
_____

Now check with www.dictionary.com and select the best meaning for ***camp*** as it is used in the sentence.

> **camp** [*kamp*]
>
> −*noun*
>
> 1. a place where an army or other group of persons or an individual is lodged in a tent or tents or other temporary means of shelter.
>
> 2. such tents or shelters collectively: *The regiment transported its camp in trucks.*
>
> 3. the persons so sheltered: *The camp slept through the <u>storm</u>.*
>
> 4. the act of camping out: *Camp is far more pleasant in the summer than in winter.*
>
> 5. any temporary structure, as a tent or cabin, used on an outing or vacation.
>
> 6. a group of troops, workers, etc., camping and moving together.
>
> 7. army life.
>
> 8. a group of people favoring the same ideals, doctrines, etc.: *Most American voters are divided into two camps, Republicans and Democrats.*
>
> 9. any position in which ideals, doctrines, etc., are strongly entrenched: *After considering the other side's argument, he changed camps.*
>
> 10. a recreation area in the country, equipped with extensive facilities for sports.
>
> 11. <u>day camp.</u>
>
> 12. <u>summer camp.</u>

2. Which definition of *camp* best fits in the sentence? _____

_____

3–7. Use word parts and context clues to find the meaning of the word *incredible.*

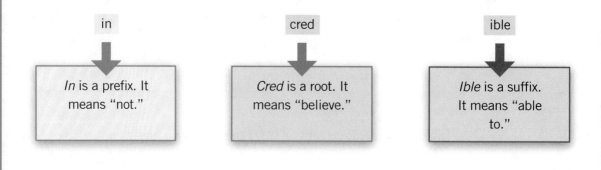

Word parts show us *incredible* means _____

_____

> For my last Halloween, I had great fun. Jai and I dressed up as the *Incredibles*, and so did our three kids. I put a photo of us on my Web site letting everyone know what an *"Incredible"* family we were. The kids looked pretty super. I looked invincible with my fake cartoon muscles. I explained that chemo had not dramatically affected my superpowers, and I got tons of smiling emails in response.

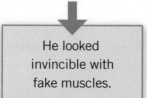

Together, these facts let you infer that *incredible* means_____

_____

8. What does Pausch mean when he says some people are Tiggers?

_____

_____

_____

9. What does he mean by saying some people are Eeyores?

_____

_____

_____

10. Why does Pausch believe you must choose a "camp"?

> I came to a realization about this very early in my life. As I see it, there's a decision we all have to make, and it seems perfectly captured in the Winnie-the-Pooh characters created by A. A. Milne. Each of us must decide: Am I a fun-loving Tigger or am I a sad-sack Eeyore? Pick a camp.

_____

_____

_____

_____

11–13. What supporting details does Pausch give to prove, illustrate, or explain that he is a Tigger?

_____

_____

_____

_____

14. What does Pausch imply when he says,

> Someone asked me what I want on my tombstone. I replied: "Randy Pausch: He Lived Thirty Years After a Terminal Diagnosis."

_____

_____

_____

15. What does Pausch imply when he says,

> I promise you. I could pack a lot of fun into those thirty years. But if that's not to be, then I'll just pack fun into whatever time I do have.

_____

_____

_____

16–20. What is the implied central idea of this reading? *HINT*: What is the major message the writer, Randy Pausch, wants to share?

_____

_____

_____

_____

_____

Magazine/Periodical   **READING 4**

A Classroom with a View

Together with nine other teenagers, Parker embarked on a weeklong "ed-venture" with Grand Canyon Youth (GCY), a nonprofit using one of the world's biggest classrooms. The Flagstaff-based program promotes stewardship for public lands and learning through participation in all aspects of a trip. Five guides, a student coordinator, and a U.S. Geological Survey (USGS) scientist act as mentors and instructors on this one.

After running a warm-up rapid at Badger Creek, the students are busy preparing lunch under leaden clouds that roil in typical monsoon season style. A rain shower later brings relief from three-digit temperatures. Drifting downstream in the rafts, the guides get acquainted with the students, whose interests and personalities quickly emerge. Their reasons for signing up are as diverse as their backgrounds. Matthew K., tall, blond, and politically astute, once stood on the South Rim during a geology school project and decided he had to hike to the river or float it someday. Joshua W., part Hopi and the son of a former Grand Canyon outfitter, has wanted to visit some of the canyon's powerful places since age 14.

"Aly" H., a South Korean fireplug, joined because a judge suggested she'd better stay out of trouble, but also because she likes going on private river trips.

Source: Engelhard, Michael, "A Classroom with a View," National Parks Association.

Questions

1. Use context clues to find the meaning of the word *ed-venture.*

   Together with nine other teenagers, Parker embarked on a weeklong "*ed-venture*" with Grand Canyon Youth (GCY), a nonprofit using one of the world's biggest classrooms.

   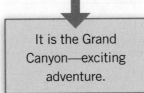

   | "Classrooms" reminds us of education. | It is the Grand Canyon—exciting adventure. | "With nine other teenagers" is a trip with peers. |

   Together, these facts let you infer that an *ed-venture* is _____

   _____

2. Use word context clues to find the meaning of the phrase *leaden clouds.*

   After running a warm-up rapid at Badger Creek, the students are busy preparing lunch under *leaden clouds* that roil in typical monsoon season style. A rain shower later brings relief from three-digit temperatures.

   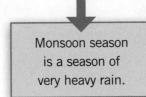

   | Roil is to move or proceed turbulently. | Monsoon season is a season of very heavy rain. | They are busy preparing lunch because it will storm soon. |

   Together, these facts let you infer that *leaden clouds* means _____

   _____

3. What is the topic of this article?

    a. Rain   **c.** Personalities

    b. Monsoon   **d.** Ed-venture

4–9. Complete the chart below with each person's description and reason for signing up.

NAME	DESCRIPTION	REASON
Matthew K.		
Joshua W.		
Aly H.		

10. What is the implied central idea of the article?

_____

_____

_____

_____

Visual Images **READING 5**

Banana Slug Mascot

1   The Banana Slug, a bright yellow, slimy, shell-less mollusk commonly found on the redwood forest floor, was the unofficial mascot for UC Santa Cruz coed teams since the university's early years. The students' embrace of such a lowly creature was their response to the fierce athletic competition fostered at most American universities.

2   In 1980, when some campus teams wanted more organized yet still low-key participation in extramural competition, UCSC joined Division III of the NCAA in five sports. Since the application required an official team name, UCSC's then chancellor polled student players; from this small group emerged a consensus for a new moniker—the sea lions.

3   The chancellor considered sea lions more dignified and suitable to serious play than Banana Slugs. But the new name did not find favor with the majority of students, who continued to root for the Slugs even after a sea lion was painted in the middle of the basketball floor.

4   After five years of dealing with the two-mascot problem, an overwhelming proslug straw vote by students in 1986 persuaded the chancellor to make the lowly but beloved Banana Slug UCSC's official mascot.

5   The Banana Slug has attracted a good deal of national attention over the years. In 2008, ESPN named it one of the 10 best college basketball mascots. Four years

earlier, *Reader's Digest* named it the best. *People* magazine once dedicated a full-page spread to the Santa Cruz Banana Slug movement. The National Directory of College Athletics named it the best college mascot and *Sports Illustrated* magazine once named the Banana Slug the nation's best college nickname.

6   The Banana Slug even figured in a court case involving campus mascots. Judge Terence Evans, writing the opinion for the Seventh Circuit Court of Appeals, stated: "We give the best college nickname nod to the University of California, Santa Cruz. Imagine the fear in the hearts of opponents who travel there to face the imaginatively named 'Banana Slugs'?" (Crue et al. v. Aiken, June 1, 2004)

7   Sammy the Slug mascot has been appearing around campus at sports events and other functions. And, when the men's tennis team played in the NCAA championships, their T-shirts read: "Banana Slugs-No Known Predators."

Source: Banana Slug Mascot. Retrieved from http://www.ucsc.edu/about/mascot.html

Questions

1. Why do you think the students chose the banana slug over the sea lion for their official mascot?

_____

_____

2. What do you think inspired the student body to *persevere* and fight the college for their choice?

_____

_____

3–5. Name three reasons why you would support the mascot being the banana slug over the sea lions. _____

    a. _____

    b. _____

    c. _____

_____
Persevere—keep trying

6–8. Look at the picture of the banana slugs in nature and compare it to the slug mascot. List the ways they are the same and the ways they are different.

_____

_____

_____

_____

9–10. If you had the choice of selecting the next mascot for your college, what would you choose and why?

_____

_____

_____

_____

6 Patterns of Organization

THEME – Money Matters

SPOTLIGHT ON LEARNING STYLES Do

When my daughter was in kindergarten, we went to an art fair in our town. It is an annual event for local and regional artists, who set up booths and sell their art. We were on a very tight budget at the time and did not have any extra money for art, but we liked to look. My daughter saw a stone sculpture of a cat she really wanted. With tax it cost around $100. I told her that we didn't have an extra $100, but we could save for it. I explained that if we put $2 every week in a jar, then after 50 weeks we would have $100 to buy it the next year. I asked my daughter what she could give up that was $2 each week. At the time, we had a weekly treat for her to eat and play at McDonald's while I studied. She asked how much her Happy Meal cost, and I told her $2. She said she could eat at home for free and save the money for the sculpture. She also said she would much rather own the cat than eat the kid's meals. So, every week we put $2 in a jar on my desk. We watched the money increase. The next year, we went back to the "Art around the Fountain" art sale and bought the stone cat sculpture from the artist. That was 12 years ago—the sculpture still sits on our fireplace mantel and my daughter is studying art and art education.

Writers Have a Plan (What are they trying to do?)

As we have already discussed in earlier chapters, most of the texts you read will have a clear purpose or main idea that the author is trying to convey.

> **LO1**
> Use the writer's plan to improve your comprehension.

Writers generally have a plan before they begin and they develop that plan throughout their writing. Think about the writing you have done, or are now doing, in your college writing classes.

- You may be asked to brainstorm or free write about a topic first to generate ideas.
- But the next step will probably be to clarify your purpose and your audience.
- You may also be asked to create an outline or a mind map before you begin writing.
- Writing is a process that requires some planning in the early stages.

As a reader, your comprehension will greatly improve when you identify the author's plan or "Pattern of Organization."

- Using the pattern of organization will help you look for relevant details that support the main idea.
- It will also help you stay focused on the major points throughout your reading.

How do you know which pattern of organization is being used by an author?

- Becoming familiar with the words authors use to set apart the patterns will help.
- Good examples are words you may recognize as transition or signal words used in your writing class.
- The more you work with the words in reading and in writing, the easier it will become to identify the pattern.
- Each pattern is used by the author to help convey a certain meaning.
- Being aware of the patterns of organization will help you understand the author's meaning.

Another important strategy is using graphic organizers when you read.

- These are visual aids such as charts, maps, flow charts, tables, etc.
- Learning to use graphic organizers will enable you to understand more clearly the author's meaning in a reading.
- You may also find that creating your own visual organizers as you read will help you process the information in a way that makes more sense to you.

In this chapter, we will use reading material related to money to help you practice using the patterns of organization.

Patterns of Organization

In this chapter you will learn to recognize and use the following patterns of organization:

> **LO2**
> Use patterns of organization in text.

- paragraphs developed with definition
- paragraphs developed with example
- paragraphs developed with time order/sequence
- paragraphs developed with simple listing

> *Finance is the art of passing currency from hand to hand until it finally disappears.*
> *– Robert W. Sarnoff*

Paragraphs Developed with Definition

LO3
Recognize paragraphs developed with definition.

Authors sometimes develop paragraphs by defining words or ideas in the text. This is common in both textbooks and technical articles. Often the definition follows the word in a straightforward manner. For example, according to the textbook *Principles of Accounting,* "*Interest* is the fee for using money." Sometimes the definition is in parentheses following the word or it is set apart with hyphens or dashes in the sentence. For example, the definition of *interest* might be presented a different way: "*Interest*—the fee for using money—is revenue earned by the payee for loaning the money; it is an expense incurred by the maker as the cost of borrowing money."

Signal Words

is defined as

also known as

is/are

the concept of . . .

Also watch for parentheses following a word (the definition is in parentheses) or a word followed by a dash—and then the definition.

EXAMPLE ─────────────────────────────────────

Directions: Use the text to find the definition of the words.

The Pell Grant is a need-based grant awarded to qualified undergraduate students who have not been awarded a previous degree. Amounts vary based on need and costs.

Source: Excerpt from *Cornerstone: Creating Success Through Positive Change,* 6th Edition by Robert M. Sherfield and Patricia G. Moody. Copyright © 2011 by Robert M. Sherfield and Patricia G. Moody. Printed and Electronically reproduced by permission of Pearson Education, Inc., Upper Saddle River, New Jersey.

Define *Pell Grant:* _____

──

The Pell Grant is a need-based grant awarded to qualified undergraduate students who have not been awarded a previous degree.

/ *PRACTICE* THE NEW SKILL /

Directions: Read each paragraph and answer the question that follows.

PRACTICE 1

Your credit score is referred to as the FICO score. FICO is the acronym for Fair Isaac Corporation, the company that created the widely used credit score model. This score is calculated using information from your credit history and files. The FICO score is the reason it matters if you accumulate large debts, if you go over your credit card limits, if you are late with payments—these offenses stick with you and are not easily changed. Based on this score, you can be denied credit, pay a lower or higher interest rate, be required to provide extensive asset information in order to even get credit, or sail right through when you seek a loan.

Source: Excerpt from *Cornerstone: Creating Success Through Positive Change,* 6th Edition by Robert M. Sherfield and Patricia G. Moody. Copyright © 2011 by Robert M. Sherfield and Patricia G. Moody. Printed and Electronically reproduced by permission of Pearson Education, Inc., Upper Saddle River, New Jersey.

Define *FICO:* _____

_____

PRACTICE 2

Slice costs with a simple request. When the doctor hands you a prescription, utter the following five-word mantra to cut its cost significantly: "Is there a cheaper alternative?"

"It's the easiest and most effective way to reduce your drug costs," says Dr. Levine, on staff at Montefiore Medical Center in the Bronx, New York. "But you'd be amazed how infrequently this is done."

It should be done more often, because outpatient drugs—that is, the ones your doctor prescribes in the course of an office visit—usually have a higher out-of-pocket cost than those administered in hospitals or other settings.

Source: Kirchheimer, Sid. (2006). *Scam-proof Your Life: 377 Smart Ways to Protect You & Your Family from Rip-offs, Bogus Deals & Other Consumer Headaches.* New York: AARP Sterling Publications, p. 211.

Define *outpatient drugs:* _____

_____

PRACTICE 3

Owning a home is a big deal. Besides being a major life goal, it is also a significant financial investment, since home values usually appreciate, or increase in value, over time (by contrast, even though buying a car is also a major purchase, almost any car depreciates, or decreases in value, the instant you drive it off the lot). Furthermore, a home is a double-duty investment that provides both financial security and a place to live.

Source: Excerpt from *Keys to Success: Building Analytical, Creative, and Practical Skills,* 6th Edition by Carol Carter, Joyce Bishop, Sarah Kravits, Judy Block. Copyright © 2009 by Carol Carter, Joyce Bishop, Sarah Kravits, Judy Block. Printed and Electronically reproduced by permission off Pearson Education, Inc., Upper Saddle River, New Jersey.

Define *appreciate:* _____

Define *depreciates:* _____

Paragraphs Developed with Example

Authors may develop their ideas by giving examples. Sometimes it is easier to get a point across through a specific example of a situation or an

> **LO4**
> Recognize paragraphs developed with example.

experience. How do you know when an author is using an example? Authors often use words such as *for instance, for example,* or *such as* to indicate they are providing an example or illustration. Or they may define a word first and then follow it with examples, combining both patterns of organization. For example: A *colleague* is considered your professional equal, such as a co-worker on the same level or a person in a similar job working at a different location. In this example, the word *colleague* is first defined and then an example is provided to help clarify the meaning of the word.

Signal Words

for example, one example, our first example, etc.

for instance

such as, including

one way to, another way, great ways to, etc.

> *Directions:*   Read the paragraphs below and answer the questions that follow. Determine the author's main idea based on the use of relevant, or useful examples.

Charity Cheats

> The scam: You receive a telephone call, letter, e-mail, or home visit soliciting a donation for a charity—be it hurricane relief, medical research, a police or fire department, or some other cause. Sometimes the request is made at the *behest* of a *bona fide* charity, such as the American Red Cross or the American Cancer Society, but scammers often claim to be collecting money for a sound-alike name, such as the American Cancer Research Society. Or they may invent new charities reflecting the latest crisis: In the wake of Hurricane Katrina, the FBI reported that at least 2,300 websites dealing with hurricane relief popped up. Most of them were fraudulent.

> *Source:* Kirchheimer, Sid. (2006). *Scam-proof Your Life: 377 Smart Ways to Protect You & Your Family from Rip-offs, Bogus Deals & Other Consumer Headaches.* New York: AARP Sterling Publications, p. 303.

What examples does the author use to help explain *charity cheats or scams?*

_____

_____

_____

What is the main idea?

_____

_____

_____

The author uses the example of a sound-alike name, the American Cancer Research Society, which sounds like a legitimate charity, American Cancer Society. The other example is how scammers invent new charities such as the 2,300 Web sites supposedly seeking aid for Hurricane Katrina victims. The main idea is that scammers try to collect money by sounding like legitimate charities.

Behest—strong request
Bona fide—honest or genuine

PRACTICE THE NEW SKILL

Directions: Read the paragraphs below. Determine the author's main idea based on the use of relevant examples.

PRACTICE 1

Get the Facts from Carfax

Don't even consider purchasing a used car without first getting a Carfax report. This document, which you can purchase yourself or get through a dealership, traces the history of the vehicle in question via its VIN. The exercise turns up information from sources such as extended-service companies and state Department of Motor Vehicles. It's not flawless, but the system provides the best record of a car's often checkered past, including previous owners, reported accidents, and flood damage.

Source: Kirchheimer, Sid. (2006). *Scam-proof Your Life: 377 Smart Ways to Protect You & Your Family from Rip-offs, Bogus Deals & Other Consumer Headaches.* New York: AARP Sterling Publications, p. 39.

What examples does the author use to help you understand the information from Carfax reports? _____

_____

_____

What is the main idea? _____

_____

_____

PRACTICE 2

The Cost of Carelessness

Men and women between the ages of eighteen and twenty-nine experienced the highest instances of identity-theft fraud in 2005, according to the FTC. This is in part because younger adults can be more careless than older workers and therefore are more likely to have their wallets and checkbooks lost or stolen, which is still the primary source of fraud involving personal information, as surveys done by Javelin Strategy & Research and the Better Business Bureau found. Younger adults may feel they're less likely to become victims of identity theft if they have relatively little in the way of finances, but as we've seen, thieves can use identities to create their own wealth. This age group also may be less aware of the dangers of giving out sensitive personal and financial information such as Social Security or bank-account numbers.

Source: Cullen, Terri. (2007). *The Wall Street Journal Complete Identity Theft Guidebook: How to Protect Yourself from the Most Pervasive Crime in America.* New York: Three Rivers Press, p. 11.

What examples does the author give for sensitive and personal information?

_____

_____

What is the author's main idea? _____

_____

_____

PRACTICE 3

Every time you pay with plastic, companies are gambling with your personal data. If hackers intercept your numbers, you may spend weeks straightening your mangled credit, though you can't be held liable for unauthorized charges. Even if your transaction isn't hacked, you still lose: Merchants pass to all their customers the costs they incur from fraud.

It took four months for Pamela LaMotte, 46, of Colchester, Vt., to fix the damage after two of her credit card accounts were tapped by hackers in a breach traced to a Hannaford Bros. grocery store. LaMotte, who was unemployed at the time, said she had to borrow money from her mother and boyfriend to pay $500 in overdraft and late fees—which were eventually refunded—while the banks investigated.

Source: Adapted from Robertson, Jordan. (2009, June 15). The Associated Press. Weak Security Opens the Door to Credit Card Hackers. *Journal & Courier.*

What example situation does the author give to show the problem with identity theft? _____

_____

_____

What is the main idea? _____

_____

Paragraphs Developed with Time Order/Sequence

LO5
Recognize paragraphs developed with time order/sequence.

Authors may also develop paragraphs according to a pattern of time order or sequence. In this case, it is critical to pay attention to the order in which the information is presented. If it is a time order pattern, then the author wants the reader to know that each item is presented in a specific time sequence. This pattern is often used in historical or narrative genres. For instance, if someone is telling a story, the order of the facts or events is very important to the reader's comprehension. Similarly, when information is presented in sequential order (a sequence pattern), then imagining the text as if you were watching a movie will aid comprehension. TRY IT ☺

Learning Styles TIPS

Look: Imagine you are watching a movie or draw a picture.

Listen: Read the passage aloud or have someone read it to you.

Read: Outline the important facts or events.

Do: Imagine you are in the story or events, or act it out.

Signal Words

first, second(ly), third(ly), etc.

last(ly), final(ly)

next, then, when, whenever, while, during, until

after, before, previous(ly), later, following, prior to

EXAMPLE ——————————————————————————————————

Directions: Use the signal words to help you understand the reading. Then, answer the questions.

> Forget $100 a month; Hollie Wulf of Algonquin, Illinois, saves $100 or more a *week* at the grocery store using coupons. She collects coupons from friends and family and uses them to buy sale and buy-one-get-one-free items. Recently, Hollie brought home $230 worth of groceries for just over $11. "After a year of coupon shopping, I was finally able to quit my job so I could stay home with my child," she says.

> *Source:* Roberts, Gretchen. (2007, July 10). 20 Ways to Save $100: Easy Ways to Stash Cash Right Now. *Woman's Day*, p. 116.

How did Hollie save money using coupons?

Recently _____

After a year _____

Recently, Hollie brought home $230 worth of groceries for just over $11. *After* a year of coupon shopping, she was *finally* able to quit her job so she could stay home with her child.

/ **PRACTICE** THE NEW SKILL /

Directions: Read the paragraphs. Use the signal words to aid your understanding of the readings. Then, answer the questions.

PRACTICE 1

Prior to going shopping for necessities that aren't everyday purchases (whether you're physically going shopping, sitting down with catalogs, or connecting to the huge marketplace known as the Internet), make a list of the items you're looking for and do some research first (*Consumer Reports* is a good starting point). After you're sure that you want an item; your research has helped you identify brands, models, and so on that are good values; and you've assessed your bank account to ensure that you can afford it, check various retailers and compare prices. When you set out to make a purchase, only buy what's on your list.

Source: Tyson, Eric. (2006). *Mind Over Money: Your Path to Wealth and Happiness*. New York: CDS Books, pp. 39–40.

What are the steps to stop overspending?

Prior to going shopping _____

_____

After you're sure that you want an item _____

_____

When you set out to make a purchase _____

_____

PRACTICE 2

Pay off your smallest high-interest debt.

Review your credit card debts. In addition to making the minimum payments on all your credit cards, focus on accelerating the payment of your smallest high-interest card first. You will be encouraged as you make progress, finally eliminating that debt.

Then, after you pay off the first credit card, apply its payment toward the next smallest one. After the second credit card is paid off, apply what you were paying on the first and second toward the third smallest credit card debt, and so forth. That's the snowball principle in action!

Source: Dayton, Howard. (2006). *Your Money Map: A Proven 7-step Guide to True Financial Freedom.* Chicago: Moody Publishers, pp. 134–135.

What are the steps in paying off your credit cards?

Review your credit card debts.

First, _____

_____

Then, _____

_____

After, _____

_____

PRACTICE 3

Insurance

There are many types of insurance: life, health, disability, homeowners, and liability for starters. Once you settle on the types of insurance you need, then determine how much you can afford. At this time, you may not be able to purchase all the insurance you need. If you are in this situation, prioritize which you should purchase first.

Source: Dayton, Howard. (2006). *Your Money Map: A Proven 7-step Guide to True Financial Freedom.* Chicago: Moody Publishers, p. 245.

List the signal words for time order used in the paragraph above:

_____

_____

Paragraphs Developed with Simple Listing

Sometimes authors convey a simple list of ideas in no particular sequence or order. If they are simply making several points in a row, they may state *first* for the first point, *second* for the next point, and *finally* for the last point. Here is an example of how an author might share a simple list of ways to invest money.

LO6
Recognize paragraphs developed with simple listing.

> There are several places to invest your money. First, a savings account provides the lowest risk but generally earns a lower interest rate. Second, a certificate of deposit offers the investor a fixed amount of time with a guaranteed interest rate, but the investor's funds are locked in for a period of time. Finally, a mutual fund offers investors more chance for higher returns but carries a higher risk since there is no guarantee on the return on investment.

The author also may use bullet points to indicate different ideas in a list. For example, here is a list of ways to invest your money:

- Savings Account
- Certificate of Deposit
- Mutual Fund

But remember, it may not be necessary that you remember or use the information in the same order as the author presented. (See the sequence or time order pattern of organization for examples of when this matters.)

Signal Words

one, for one thing, to begin with

first (of all), second(ly), third(ly)

further, furthermore, also, other, another, in addition, next, moreover

last(ly), (last of all), final(ly)

EXAMPLE ———————————————————————————————

Directions: Use the signal words to answer the questions that follow.

> The Internet can be a time-efficient tool for performing research and price comparisons, but be careful of two common online problems. The first is advertising that masquerades as informative articles. The second

problem is retailers that may be here today and gone tomorrow or who may be unresponsive after the purchase. Of course, this latter problem occurs with traditional bricks-and-mortar retailers, too.

Source: Tyson, Eric. (2006). *Mind over Money: Your Path to Wealth and Happiness.* New York: CDS Books, pp. 39–40.

What are two common online problems?

First

_____

Second

_____

The first is advertising that masquerades as informative articles. The second problem is retailers that may be here today and gone tomorrow or who may be unresponsive after the purchase.

PRACTICE *THE NEW SKILL*

Directions: Use the signal words to aid your understanding of the readings. Then, answer the questions that follow.

PRACTICE 1

How to Stop Going into Debt Each Month

If you are using your credit cards each month, and not paying off the balance in full, then you are going further into debt each month. This is a bad situation to be in, because you are making your financial situation worse. It is important to take control of your current situation immediately so that you can change your financial future, into a positive one.

Difficulty: Easy

Time Required: A few weeks

Here's How:

1.   The first step is to create a list of your income, and your expenses. You need to make sure that you are making enough to cover your necessities. This is your food, your shelter, your utilities and your clothing (but not designer labels). If you do not make enough to cover these basic expenses then you need to bring up your income and slash all other expenses in your budget. You may need to look at your housing costs to see if your house

payment is taking up more than twenty five percent of your income. If it is you may need to consider moving.

2.   Next you need to create a monthly budget. This step is important because it gives you control over where your money is going. It helps you to track your spending, so that you can find your trouble areas, and fix your spending habits. It also helps you to stop spending when you are out of money for the month. You many want to change to a cash only or envelope budget if you are having problems sticking to your limits.

3.   You also need to find extra money to apply to your current debt. This means that you may need to cut back on your cable and cell phone plan or cancel your gym membership so that you can take care of this debt. You may also want to sell some items or get a temporary second job to get out of debt.

4.   Once you are out of debt you need to start saving for the major purchases so that you do not go into debt for them. For example you can pay for your car with cash or for your home repairs and improvements with cash. Additionally you should save up an emergency fund of three to six months of income, so that you will not go into debt when an emergency arises.

Source: Miriam Caldwell, About.com Guide http://moneyfor20s
.about.com/od/managingyourdebt/ht/stopgoingindebt.htm

List the steps to help you stop going into debt each month:

_____

_____

_____

_____

_____

PRACTICE 2

Paying Off Auto Debt

Car debt is one of the biggest obstacles for most people on their journey to true financial freedom because people never get out of it. Just when they are ready to pay off a car, they trade it in and purchase a newer one with credit.

Unlike a home, which usually appreciates in value, the moment you drive a car off the lot it depreciates in value. It's worth less than you paid for it.

Take these four steps to get out of auto debt:

1. Decide to keep your car at least three years longer than your car loan.
2. Pay off your car loan.
3. After your last payment, keep making the payment, but pay it to yourself. Put it into an account that you will use to buy your next car.
4. When you are ready to replace your car, the cash you have saved plus your car's trade-in value should be sufficient to buy a car without credit. It may not be a new car, but a newer low-mileage used car without any debt is a better value anyway.

Source: Dayton, Howard. (2006). *Your Money Map: A Proven 7-step Guide to True Financial Freedom.* Chicago: Moody Publishers, pp. 147–148.

What are the four steps to get out of auto debt?

_____

_____

_____

_____

_____

_____

PRACTICE 3

Top Five Money Mistakes College Students Make

Debt Ranks Among the Biggest Problems for Most Students

College students face many hard financial decisions. As a young adult they need to figure out how to pay for college, earn some spending money, and still get a good education. This is a tall order for anyone, so it's no wonder that many college students end up making some costly money mistakes. Unfortunately, these mistakes can actually cause damage that lingers for decades, so making sure your finances are in order even as a college student can go a long way in helping you get a good start after school.

College Student Money Mistake #1: Credit Card Debt

Credit cards have become a way of life. They make paying for things extremely easy and with many cards offering rewards programs or cash back it's easy to see their appeal. The problem is that the appeal often overshadows the drawbacks. Many cards have high interest rates, unfavorable terms, and allow students to spend more money than they actually have. In fact, if you get into the habit of only paying the minimum payment each month you could be stuck trying to pay off the card for over ten years!

Keep in mind that credit cards can play a vital role in establishing your credit history, so that doesn't mean credit cards should be avoided. Instead, credit cards should be used to help build a solid credit history and the balance should be paid off in full each month. This will allow you to still collect the rewards or earn cash back while not having to deal with finance charges and long repayment periods.

College Student Money Mistake #2: Ruining Your Credit Score

While we're on the topic of credit cards it's important to highlight the dangers that can come with going into credit card debt. Many college students end up completely trashing their credit history by just making a few poor decisions. Remember, missed payments or other negative marks will remain on your credit history for seven years and trash your credit score. Yes, seven years! That one late payment you made back in college will be haunting you years after you graduate and are trying to get a loan for a new car or buy a house.

Don't get careless with your finances just because you're in college. It's easy to make a mistake, but realize that those mistakes can prove costly even later in life. If you are going to utilize credit cards or other loans, just make sure you make your payments on time and don't get in over your head.

College Student Money Mistake #3: Lack of Budgeting

Does a college student really need to create a budget? You bet! In fact, this is one of the most important times to start budgeting. As a student it's easy to get complacent when you don't have a mortgage to pay, kids to feed, or other significant money worries. The problem is that students often have a limited or even sporadic income and if you don't track this spending carefully it's easy to waste money on things that you could otherwise save.

Start by creating a simple budget. It doesn't take long, but if you take the time to analyze your income and where you're spending money you can get a better idea of where your money is going and where you can cut back. After all, if you end up spending more money than you have coming in you're likely to end up with the problems above of getting into credit card debt and possibly ruining your credit.

College Student Money Mistake #4: *Using Student Loan Money Inappropriately*

Many students have to rely on student loans, and that's fine. College tuition has gone up dramatically in recent years so it's hard to keep up if your parents can't help out that much. If the loans are actually used for school expenses that's one thing, but all too often students will use some of this money to buy things that aren't essential for school.

Using some of your student loan money to fund a spring break trip in Mexico might make for a good time, but all you're doing is hurting yourself by digging an even deeper hole that you'll need to climb out of after you graduate. A lot of students assume that student loans will be easy to pay off once they graduate and get a good job, but things don't always work out that way. So, if you use your student loan money appropriately you can be sure that you're only taking on as much debt as you need to in order to receive the education you want.

College Student Money Mistake #5: Reaching for an Expensive College

Does the name of the school on your diploma really matter? In some cases it certainly does. In other cases, not so much. A lot of students have dreams of going to a prestigious school or head out of state, but this may not be the best decision financially. With some degrees it may not matter as much where your degree comes from so spending an extra $100,000 on that four year degree might not be the best use of money.

Another option is to go to an inexpensive school for your first year or two and then transfer. This allows you to save money and more time to build up additional savings to help pay for the rest of your degree. So, before enrolling in your dream school that you can't afford, take some time to consider other options and see if you really need to attend that school to find the same job or if you can get some basic schooling done in your first year or two before transferring. It could end up being a savings of six-figures or more.

Source: Jeremy Vohwinkle, About.com Guide http://financialplan
.about.com/od/students/a/college-student-money-mistakes.htm

List the five mistakes college students make about money.

_____

_____

_____

_____

_____

REVIEW WHAT YOU LEARNED

Directions: Read the passage and answer the questions that follow.

Top 6 Free and Legal Music Download Sites

Discover new talent by downloading free and legal MP3s

There is a mass of free music on the Internet that is produced by artists just waiting to be discovered. Most of this music is usually covered by the creative commons license which allows you to listen, copy, share, or burn the tracks to CD. Here is an essential selection that will give you access to literally thousands of tracks for free.

1. Jamendo

Jamendo hosts over 7,000 albums for you to download for free. You have the opportunity to review, share and even make a donation to the artist if you like what you hear.

2. SoundClick

SoundClick, which has been live since 1997, has over 2 million full-length tracks available; many for free download. Streaming audio is also used for free videos and radio stations.

3. BeSonic

Once you have registered for free, you will be able to gain access to over 12,000 songs to download or listen to via streaming audio. As with most music websites, there is a search tool which you can use to quickly find the music that interests you. BeSonic also has music charts for you to consult so you can quickly see what's popular in your chosen genre.

4. PureVolume

A smart and user friendly site that contains music from more than 400,000 artists to listen to for free. A search tool is available for your convenience along with a facility to browse through their catalog of artists if you prefer. They have a charts system showing you what's popular and regularly feature artists.

5. ArtistServer

A social media website that hosts over 8000 free and legal songs. This social media service also provides free MP3 ringtones, photos, blogs, and a place to talk via its forums.

6. **Audio Archive**
   Audio Archive is an audio and MP3 library that hosts over 100,000 free digital files. A range of different subjects are available, including news and public affairs, radio shows, book and poetry readings and live music recordings.

   Source: Mark Harris, About.com Guide http://mp3.about
   .com/od/freebies/tp/freemusictp.htm About.com

1. What is the organizational pattern of the article?

   a. definition   **c.** simple listing

   b. example   **d.** time order/sequence

2. What is the implied central idea of the article?

   _____

   _____

3–5. What are the six major supporting details of the article?

   1. _____

   2. _____

   3. _____

   4. _____

   5. _____

   6. _____

REVIEW WHAT YOU LEARNED

Directions: Read the passage and answer the questions that follow.

Snowball the Consumer Debt

Consumer debt is all debt other than credit card debt, the home mortgage, and business loans.

How do you decide which consumer debt to pay off first? The same way you decided which credit card to pay off first. Continue making the minimum payments on consumer debts, but focus on accelerating the payment of your smallest higher-interest consumer debt first.

Then after you pay off the first consumer debt, apply its payment toward the next smallest one. After the second one is paid off, apply what you were paying on the first and second toward the third smallest consumer debt, and so forth. Snowball your consumer debt.

Source: Dayton, Howard. (2006). *Your Money Map: A Proven 7-step Guide to True Financial Freedom.* Chicago: Moody Publishers, p. 147.

1–2. Define consumer debt. _____

_____

3–5. Identify the steps in deciding which consumer debt to pay off first.

_____

_____

_____

_____

_____

_____

Patterns of Organization

Directions: Read the passage and answer the questions that follow.

Recycle Old Clothes for the New Style

Go Green on the Runway

1   Recycling your old clothes can be a really refreshing and energizing idea to help your closet space and the environment as well. After doing a little bit of research I found out some interesting information that has influenced my own decision to keep giving and recycling my own clothes. I used to just give old clothes away to clean out my closet, but I actually found out that somebody else can benefit from my old frocks! Let's take a look at some neat and great ideas to recycle clothes.

2   First of all 96% percent of textile materials are recyclable and can be used to create something new. So never think some old pair of jeans or shoes are just pure trash because that simply is not true. Donation centers such as the Goodwill, Salvation Army and consignment shops will be happy to help you out. Even if your clothes that you want to donate are not in condition to be resold, still donate them. Why, well the answer is simple. The donation centers have a system to sort through what they want to sell and what material is going to be used strictly for recycling purposes. The material from your clothes can be used anywhere from the automobile industry to back to clothing industry, to perhaps even create the new Pravda!

3   If you want to be a bit more creative then a great way to recycle your clothes is to simply start brainstorming as you are sorting out what you want and don't want. Plenty of clothes have beautiful prints and embellishments such as beads and buttons that are easy to use for a crafty project or a new piece of garment. I actually shredded some old skirts of mine to make my own "rag yarn." I used the rag yarn to make a colorful scarf for my sister. It really was an appreciated and more personal garment. If you have little girls then they would love to make some doll clothes or make their own dress up clothes. It is important to understand that the material can be used to create some of the most unique and environmental friendly designs.

4   Some lines of clothes such as Patagonia have started their own campaigns to recycle the clothes they make. Patagonia in 2005 created the Common Threads Garment Program to allow consumers to donate their long underwear and Polartec fleeces to help the production line remain an Eco-friendly and green efficient line of clothing. Another example of this was actually on the hit

TV series, *The Apprentice*. One of the teams created a donation bin just for the plastic shoes "Crocs." They set up bins in local department stores that would allow consumers to donate their old Crocs to make new Crocs!

5   There are so many great ideas to help you get in the recycle mode for your clothes. Thrift stores and consignment shops are a quick alternative to letting the clothes pile up or throwing them away to build up the trash. If you want to have a creative flair, brainstorming to make your own clothes or craft projects can be a way to use up your pretty dresses and fancy duds. Finally some clothing lines themselves are becoming more environmentally friendly and creating campaigns and ways to let the consumer put back into the product what they got out of it. All of these innovative approaches are great ways to get started and go green on the runway.

Source: Hashemzadeh, Kim. (2009, April 2). *Recycle Old Clothes for the New Style*. Retrieved from Associated Content from Yahoo http://www.associatedcontent.com/article/1615162/recycle_old_clothes_for_the_new_style.html?cat=46

1. What is the organizational pattern of the article?

   a. definition   c. simple listing

   b. example   d. time order/sequence

2. What is the implied central idea of the article?

   _____

   _____

3–5. What are some of the major supporting details of this article?

   _____

   _____

   _____

   _____

6–10. Discuss how you might use the information from this article in your life.

   _____

   _____

   _____

   _____

MASTER THE LESSON

Patterns of Organization

Directions: Read the passage below and answer the questions that follow.

Money

What does money represent to you? When it comes to working with our dreams the answer to this is crucial. Most people will acknowledge that they want it, and almost certainly that they need it, but beyond that our responses can differ markedly from person to person. Perhaps you see it as a means to an end, or an end in itself; maybe you think that it represents freedom and can liberate people, or you might see it as an enslaver. Our own and others' attitudes to money in real life will inevitably be reflected in our dreams; how much there is, where it came from and what we do with it will also be significant.

What are four ways you can see money (according to the passage)?

1. _____

2. _____

3. _____

4. _____

What Money Can Buy

It is what we can have and do with money—as well as what is unavailable to us if we don't have it—that gives it much of its value. We may feel that it gives us the freedom to have the things we want, including leisure time and opportunities to see and do things that aren't free. But having acquired wealth, we may feel burdened by our possessions and afraid of losing them, and we may also feel trapped by the need to carry on generating it.

Dreams of money may be simple wish fulfilment, or we may find they show us how to get it, the frustrations of not having it, or the fear of being suddenly deprived of it. But we can also use money dreams as a more general symbol for greed and materialism, opportunity, the loss of something we value, or even of being trapped.

Source: O'Connell, Mark, Raje Airey, and Richard Craze. (2008). *The Complete Illustrated Encyclopedia of Symbols, Signs, and Dream Interpretation: Identification and Analysis of the Visual Vocabulary and Secret Language that Shape our Thoughts and Dreams and Dictate our Reactions to the World.* London, England: Anness Publishing, p. 412.

What are two examples of how money gives us freedom to have things we want?

5. _____

6. _____

According to the passage, money can be a general symbol for what four things?

7. _____

8. _____

9. _____

10. _____

LEARNING STYLE ACTIVITIES

*L*ook, *L*isten, *W*rite, *D*o

Directions: Read the chart on the next page and choose one of the Learning Style Activities to complete.

*L*ook   Look over the chart. Make a plan to find the information you need. Look around your campus for posters and signs of where you may find the information you need. Also look at your college's Web site for clues to the location of the answers. If your college has a student information video, watch it.

*L*isten   Read the list out loud or work with a partner and recite the questions to each other. Then find the information you need. You may prefer to ask people for answers, such as a financial aid advisor or a clerk at the bookstore. Ask professors and other students to tell you about their knowledge of specific questions. If your college has a student information video, listen to it.

*W*rite   Read through the list of information you need. Make a plan to gather the information from various written sources. Locate your college's student handbook and find the information you need. Write all of your information in a notebook and transfer the dollar amounts to the lines on the chart.

*D*o   After answering the "yes/no" questions, research the information you need from the chart. Your research may include gathering information from various offices and locations on campus and using the college Web site. Talk to other students and professors who may have experience with the situations.

FIGURE **11.6** *Economic Readiness Assessment*

In the spaces below, please read each question carefully, respond with Yes or No, and then answer the question based on your financial research for **next semester.** Be specific. You may have to visit the financial aid office, bookstore, or other campus resource center to answer the questions.

QUESTION	ANSWER	RESPONSE
I know exactly how much my tuition will cost next semester.	YES NO	Answer: $_____
I know the cost of lab fees, technology fees, and other fees associated with my courses.	YES NO	Answer: $_____
I know how much my textbooks will cost next semester.	YES NO	Answer: $_____
I know how much my transportation will cost next semester (car payment, gas, insurance, bus passes, etc.).	YES NO	Answer: $_____
I know how much I need to spend on supplies for next semester.	YES NO	Answer: $_____
I know how much child care will cost next semester.	YES NO	Answer: $_____
I know where my GPA must remain to keep my financial aid.	YES NO	Answer: _____
I know how much money I can borrow through the Guaranteed Student Loan Program in one academic year.	YES NO	Answer: $_____
I know how much money I need to manage my personal budget in a single semester.	YES NO	Answer: $_____
I have estimated miscellaneous and unexpected costs that might occur during the semester.	YES NO	Answer: $_____
I know what a FAFSA is and how and WHEN to apply.	YES NO	Answer: _____
I know how a drug arrest could affect my financial aid.	YES NO	Answer: _____
I know the scholarships available to me, how, when, and where to apply for them.	YES NO	Answer: _____
I know how and where to apply for work study.	YES NO	Answer: _____
I know how a felony charge affects my ability to get a job after graduation.	YES NO	Answer: _____
		TOTAL $_____

Source: Excerpt from *Cornerstone: Creating Success Through Positive Change,* 6th Edition by Robert M. Sherfield and Patricia G. Moody. Copyright © 2011 by Robert M. Sherfield and Patricia G. Moody. Printed and Electronically reproduced by permission of Pearson Education, Inc., Upper Saddle River, New Jersey.

Reading Practice

The next section of the chapter will help refine your skills in determining the pattern of organization while you read a variety of materials. All five of the readings address topics related to money.

The first reading, "Money Trouble? It's Your Own Fault," is from *Money Central* at www.msn.com.

The second readings, "Small Costs Add Up" and "B is for Budgeting" are from the textbook, *Cornerstone: Creating Success through Positive Change.*

The third reading is from literature, *Catch Me If You Can: The True Story of a Real Fake* by Frank W. Abignale.

The fourth reading is a magazine article titled "Fuel Economy: Save Money on Gas; *Consumer Reports'* Tests Show How to Get the Best Gas Mileage."

The final reading is a visual image: *We Can Help You Save a Latte.* It is an advertisement from a credit union.

Internet

READING 1

Money Trouble? It's Your Own Fault

1   All right, you financial crybabies: No matter how unfair, unreasonable or un-American it may seem, you have no choice but to live on what you make.

2   If you're having money problems, you probably have good reasons. Maybe you're getting less overtime or your expenses have unexpectedly climbed. Perhaps your ex left you with big debts. Maybe your parents never taught you about money.

3   You might blame the economy for the fix you're in. Then there's the whole credit industry, which hands out credit cards like confetti before slapping you with interest rates that would make a loan shark blush. Or maybe you're just not good with numbers.

ENGLISH 2.0

Crybabies means: people who complain and whine that little things upset them

Ex means: someone you had a very close non-family relationship with such as a spouse or boyfriend or girlfriend but the person is no longer your love

Like confetti means: too easily and too many; confetti is usually paper or material cut into little pieces, it is thrown by the handfuls in celebration such as a during a party or victory

Make a loan shark blush means: embarrass a person (make blush) who cheats others by lending money at an extremely unfair rate (loan shark). "Loan" is related to lending money and "shark" is like a predator, a dangerous person.

---

4   You may comfort yourself with the idea that your money fix isn't entirely your fault.

5   Here's the thing, though: Reasons have expiration dates. Rely on them too long and they harden into excuses.

6   I'm fully aware, writing this, that now is a challenging time for many Americans. Median incomes have stagnated, globalization and technology are wiping out whole industries, wealth is increasingly concentrated in fewer hands, and too many people—44.8 million, by the Census Bureau's most recent account—have no health insurance.

7   Meanwhile, lenders are lavishing credit on people who can't handle it, and mortgages that should never have been made are proving unpayable, causing people to lose their homes.

8   There's certainly plenty of blame to go around. But if that's as far as you get, you'll never get ahead.

ARE YOU A FINANCIAL ADOLESCENT?

9   Part of maturity is taking responsibility for ourselves. We need to see and acknowledge our role in the problems that befall us. Even if we're entirely blameless, which is rare, we still need to figure out how to play the cards we've been dealt—to find solutions instead of just complaining. That's what maturity is all about.

10   When it comes to money, though, a lot of people want to remain financial adolescents. How much easier it is to point fingers at other people, the government, the economy or lenders for our money woes than to acknowledge we're at least somewhat—and sometimes a lot more than somewhat—responsible for the fixes we're in.

11   Let's take a gut check right now. Are you nodding and saying, "Amen, sister?" Then you need read no further. If steam is coming out your ears and you're already searching for the feedback form to give me a piece of your mind, then hang in a bit longer. Because the madder you are, the more likely I've just hit home.

12   I'll give you some examples of what people say, in e-mails and Your Money message board posts, that illustrate the point. Let's start with a common one:

13   **"My parents never taught me about money."** The statute of limitations on that excuse expired when you turned 18 and could be held responsible for a legal contract, like a loan or a credit card agreement.

14   Besides, how many families do you know in which one child is good with money and another is seemingly hopeless? The parents may have imparted financial wisdom, but one child heard while the other tuned out. Or maybe the parents were terrible with money, and one child decided to avoid their fate by educating himself or herself while the other followed in the folks' spendthrift footsteps.

15   The good news is that the past doesn't have to dictate the future. If you're smart enough to have read this far, you can teach yourself to handle money, too. Spend a few hours on this site (I'd suggest starting here or with a good primer like Eric Tyson's "Personal Finance for Dummies"), and you'll be on your way.

16   **"My credit card company jacked up the rate/changed my terms/piled on fees."** Were you carrying a balance? Then you left yourself open for all manner of abuse from your credit card company.

17   You might try the defense that you didn't know any better. But in all my years of writing about personal finance, I've yet to come across someone who didn't know, at the core, that carrying a credit card balance was a bad idea.

18   There are also those who believe they had no choice. In some cases, such as when you're uninsured and trying to get medical care, I have sympathy. It's still not a good idea to put those balances on your cards but sometimes it can seem the only way to get treatment.

19   Either way, it's up to you to deal with this debt. Whining about it isn't getting you anywhere.

20   **"I should be able to live better than this."** We hear all kinds of *permutations* on this theme on the Your Money board. The idea is that it's the high cost of living, rather than your own spending, that's causing your problems.

21   One reader who made $75,000 a year and who lived in an expensive area huffed that his family "shouldn't have to live like we're on welfare" in order to make ends meet.

22   Another, a single woman who made $50,000, complained that her fixed expenses—taxes, insurance, mortgage, etc.—ate up more than half of her salary, leaving her "only" $22,000 a year for her other living costs. She was oblivious to the fact that 20% of American households live on less than $20,000, or that a total income of $22,000 would put her in the top 10% of wealth globally. Both of these readers, and others like them, want to shift the blame for their financial problems to outside forces.

23   You can grouse all you want about "the high cost of living," but it's still your responsibility to figure out how to live on what you make. Trust me: There are almost certainly families bigger than yours living on less in your community, and doing it without going into debt.

OK, NOW WHAT?

24   Where you live, what you eat, what you wear, what you drive and what you do with your time are all choices that *you* make and which have a powerful impact on your financial situation.

Permutations—versions, variations

25   Maybe you're convinced, or maybe you still think you're faultless. Either way, let me suggest an exercise that could prove enlightening:

26   **First, write down your five biggest money problems.** Are you struggling with credit card debt? Getting squeezed by a big mortgage payment? Constantly running out of cash before the end of the month? Not saving enough for retirement? Whatever your most pressing concerns, write them down.

27   **Figure out your part in creating them.** What choices did you make that put you in this position? Even if you're not entirely to blame—after all, things like bad health or bad luck can strike anybody—what decisions or actions did you make that made matters worse? For example, did you:

- Spend more than you made?
- Fail to have a rainy-day fund?
- Try to get by with too little insurance?
- Fail to pay attention to the terms of the loan you were getting?
- Figure "something will work out" rather than having a plan?
- Procrastinate on dealing with an issue until it became a big problem?

These are just a few ideas. If you sit and examine the situation, you may find others.

28   **Brainstorm some solutions.** For now, remove the words "can't," "won't" and "but" from your vocabulary—as in "I can't do that," "That won't work" and "Yeah, but. . ." Try to think of every possible solution you can, no matter how weird some of them might seem. If you're stumped, post your money problems on the Your Money message board and tap into the expertise of hundreds of other readers who have faced and conquered similar dilemmas.

29   **Make a plan—and follow through.** Pick some solutions and get to work on them. If you've fallen behind on your mortgage payments, for example, talk to a housing counselor. If you need a budget, create one. If you're truly sinking under credit card debt, contact a legitimate credit counseling agency, a bankruptcy attorney or both.

30   By doing this, you don't have to give governments, corporations and other institutions a pass. If you think taxes are too high or the health-care system's a mess, or credit card companies are getting away with murder, go ahead and contact your lawmakers to agitate for change.

31   But first make sure your own house is in order. Don't leave your financial well-being to the whims of others. Taking charge, taking responsibility and finding solutions is what empowers us and what ultimately lead to financial freedom.

Source: Weston, Liz Pulliam. (2007, March 29). *Money Trouble? It's Your Own Fault.* Retrieved from msn.com http://articles.moneycentral.msn.com/SavingandDebt/ LearnToBudget/MoneyTroubleItsYourOwnFault.aspx

Vocabulary

Directions: Use word parts to determine the meaning of the word ***unpayable***.

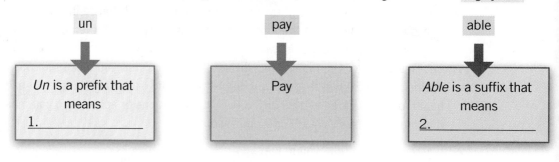

un	pay	able
Un is a prefix that means 1. _____	Pay	*Able* is a suffix that means 2. _____

3. *Unpayable* means _____

_____

Use context clues to find the meaning of ***unpayable***.

> Meanwhile, lenders are lavishing credit on people who can't handle it, and mortgages that should never have been made are proving ***unpayable***, causing people to lose their homes.

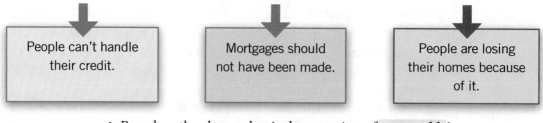

People can't handle their credit.	Mortgages should not have been made.	People are losing their homes because of it.

4. Based on the clues, what is the meaning of ***unpayable***? _____

Use context clues to find the meaning of ***grouse***.

> You can ***grouse*** all you want about "the high cost of living," but it's still your responsibility to figure out how to live on what you make. Trust me: There are almost certainly families bigger than yours living on less in your community, and doing it without going into debt.

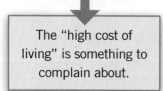
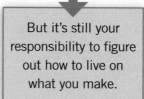
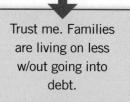

The "high cost of living" is something to complain about.	But it's still your responsibility to figure out how to live on what you make.	Trust me. Families are living on less w/out going into debt.

5. Based on the clues, what is the meaning of *grouse*? _____

_____

Main Idea

6. What is the central theme is the article?

_____

_____

_____

Supporting Details

Directions: Using the details in the article, circle **True** if the statement is correct or **False** if the statement is incorrect.

7. True or False: The author suggests you should write down your 5 biggest money concerns.

8. True or False: Remove the words "can't," "but" or "won't" from your vocabulary.

9. True or False: Whining about your debt helps you find a solution to the problem.

10. True or False: Pick some solutions and work on them.

Patterns of Organization

11–15. List examples from the article of what people say to avoid personal responsibility for financial troubles

_____

_____

_____

_____

_____

Textbook

READING 2

SMALL COSTS ADD UP!

How Much Money Will You Throw Down the Drain in 10 Years?

Many people pay more money for convenience. If you are on a tight budget, you might want to give up some of the conveniences so that you can hold onto more of your money. Although we want you to really live and enjoy life, we also want you to take a hard look at where your money goes. Those dimes, quarters, and dollars add up quickly. In fact, small-amount money drains for the typical person can add up to $175,000 over a 10-year period. What if you could hold onto some of that money and invest it? What would that money be worth to you when you are 65 and want to retire? Is having sausage biscuits and orange juice from a fast-food restaurant really worth $3.50 a day or $1,274 if you have that *every day for one year*? Did you ever stop to think that if you spend $3.50 every day on fast food or coffee or whatever for 10 *years*, you would be spending $12,740?

The 10-Year Plan

According to the Web site The Digerati Life (2008), some other prime causes of money drain are:

▶ **Gum**—a pack a day will cost you $5,488 in 10 years.

▶ **Bottled water**—One bottle a day will cost you almost $5,500 in 10 years. (Most bottled water comes from no special source and is no better than tap water.)

▶ **Eating lunch out daily**—Even if you spend only $9, this will cost you over $35,000 in 10 years. If you can eat lunch at home, you will save so much money.

▶ **Junk food, vending machine snacks**—This will cost you at least $4,000 in 10 years if you are a light snacker, and they are empty calories.

▶ **Unused memberships**—Those gym memberships that look so enticing and, for many people, go unused will total over $7,500 in 10 years.

▶ **Expensive salon visits**—Fake nails along with the salon visit can cost over $30,000 in 10 years. Is that really how you want to spend your money?

▶ **Cigarettes**—Not only will this terrible habit kill you and make people want to avoid you, it will cost you over $25,000 in 10 years if you smoke a pack a day.

These are just a few of the drains that take our money and keep us from being wealthy when we are older. Maybe you want to splurge at times and go for the convenience, but day in and day out, you can really save a lot of money if you budget your time and do some of these things for yourself.

Examine the following information about *The Latte Factor*™ (Figure 11.8), and apply it to your own spending habits.

FIGURE **11.8**   *The Latte Factor*™

In his book *The Finish Rich Notebook* (2003), Bach states, "How much you earn has no bearing on whether or not you will build wealth." As a rule, the more we make, the more we spend. Many people spend far more than they make and subject themselves to stress, exorbitant debt, fear, and an ultimate future of poverty.

Bach uses the Latte Factor™ to call people's attention to how much money we carelessly throw away when we should be saving and investing for the future. He uses the story of a young woman who said she could not invest because she had no money. Yet, almost every day she bought a large latte for $3.50 and a muffin for $1.50. If you add a candy bar here, a drink there, a shake at the gym, you could easily be spending $10 a day that could be invested.

If you take that $10 per day and invest it faithfully until retirement, you would have enough money to pay cash for a home and a new car, and have money left over. This is the power of compound interest! If you are a relatively young person, you will probably work that many years and more, so you could retire with an extra $1 million in addition to any other savings you might have accumulated.

The point is that most of us have the ability to become rich, but we either lack the knowledge or the discipline to do so. Remember the Latte Factor™ as you begin your college career and practice it, along with other sound financial strategies, if you want to become a millionaire.

Source: Excerpts "Small Costs Add Up!" and "The Latte Factor" from *Cornerstone: Creating Success Through Positive Change,* 6th Edition by Robert M. Sherfield and Patricia G. Moody. Copyright © 2011 by Robert M. Sherfield and Patricia G. Moody. Printed and Electronically reproduced by permission of Pearson Education, Inc., Upper Saddle River, New Jersey.

1. What are the prime causes of money drain? _____

_____

_____

_____

_____

_____

2. What could you do to change the drain on your money?

_____

_____

_____

_____

B IS FOR BUDGETING

Where Does My Money Go?

Most people have no idea where their money goes. Many just spend and spend and then borrow on credit cards to pay for additional expenses for which they had not budgeted. Knowing how much money you have and exactly how you spend it is a very important step toward financial security. Many college students pay more attention to buying than they do to budgeting, watching their credit scores, or controlling their credit card debt. If you fit that mold, this is one area where change is needed.

One of the main reasons to budget is to determine the exact amount of money you need to borrow to finance your college education. Poor planning while in college can easily result in a lower standard of life after you graduate and begin paying back enormous loans. Deciding how much to borrow will impact your life long after you have completed your degree. You should also remember that you will be required to repay your student loans even if you do not graduate. As previously mentioned, even bankruptcy won't eliminate student loans.

When budgeting, you must first determine how much income you earn monthly. Complete the following chart:

SOURCE OF INCOME	ESTIMATED AMOUNT
Work	$_____
Spouse/Partner/Parental Income	$_____
Scholarships/Loans	$_____
Savings/Investments	$_____
Alimony/Child Support	$_____
Other	$_____
TOTAL INCOME	$_____

Next, you must determine how much money you spend in a month. Complete the following chart:

SOURCE OF EXPENDITURE	ESTIMATED AMOUNT
Housing	$_____
Utilities (water, gas, power, etc.)	$_____
Phone (home and cell)	$_____
Internet Access	$_____
Car Payment	$_____
Car Insurance	$_____
Fuel	$_____
Clothing	$_____
Food	$_____
Household Items	$_____
Personal Hygiene Items	$_____
Health Care and/or Health Insurance	$_____
Entertainment/Fun	$_____

Savings $_____
Other $_____
TOTAL EXPENDITURES $_____
Total Income _____ **minus Total Expenses** _____ = **$**_____

If the amount of your total expenditures is smaller than your monthly income, you are on your way to controlling your finances. If your total expenditures figure is larger than your monthly income, you are heading for a financial crisis. Furthermore, you are establishing bad habits for money management that may carry over into your life after college.

Source: Excerpt from *Cornerstone: Creating Success Through Positive Change,* 6th Edition by Robert M. Sherfield and Patricia G. Moody. Copyright © 2011 by Robert M. Sherfield and Patricia G. Moody. Printed and Electronically reproduced by permission of Pearson Education, Inc., Upper Saddle River, New Jersey.

Main Idea

3. What is an important step to financial security?

_____

_____

_____

4. What is the main reason to budget?

_____

_____

_____

_____

Supporting Details

5. What are possible sources of income? _____

_____

_____

6. What are possible sources of expenses? _____

_____

_____

_____

Patterns of Organization

7. What is the pattern of organization for "Source of Income"?

_____

8. What is the pattern of organization for "Source of Expenditure"?

_____

Critical Thinking

9–10. If you were going to create a budget, what would you give up?

_____

_____

_____

_____

Literature   **READING 3**

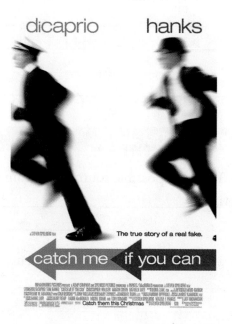

Catch Me If You Can

1   "I thought Kitty said your name was Frank Williams. This says your name is Frank W. Abignale, Jr."

2   I smiled. "It is. Frank William Abignale, Jr. You know Kitty. She had a little too much champagne last night. She kept introducing me to her friends as Frank Williams, too. But I thought she gave you my full name."

3   "She may have," agreed Miss Gunderson. "I had trouble hearing a lot of what she said. These damned Mexican telephones. Anyway, you're obviously a Pan Am pilot, and part of your name is Frank William, so you must be the one."

4   As instructed I had stopped and obtained two passport sized photographs. I gave those to Miss Gunderson, and walked out of the consulate building fifteen minutes later with a temporary passport in my pocket. I went back to the airport and changed in to a suit and bought a ticket for London at the British Overseas Airways counter, paying cash.

5   I was told the flight was delayed. It wouldn't depart until seven that evening.

6   I changed back into my pilot's uniform and spent six hours *papering* Mexico City with my decorative duds. I was $6,500 richer when I flew off to London, and the Mexican *federales* joined the posse on my tail.

7   In London I checked into the Royal Gardens Hotel in Kensington, using the name F. W. Adams and representing myself as a TWA pilot on furlough. I used my alternate alias on the premise that London police would soon be receiving queries on Frank W. Abignale, Jr., also known as Frank Williams, erst-while Pan Am pilot.

8   I stayed only a few days in London. I was beginning to feel pressure on me, the same uneasiness that had plagued me in the states. I realized in London that leaving the U.S. hadn't solved my problem, that Mexican police and Scotland Yard officers were in the same business as cops in New York and Los Angeles—that of catching crooks. And I was a crook.

ENGLISH 2.0

Decorative duds means: fancy clothing

Joined the posse on my tail means: started chasing him with the others

Feel pressure on me means: feel strong stress and constraint

Had plagued me means: had disturbed and followed me

---

9   I was actually incapable of sound judgment, I realize now, driven by compulsions over which I had no control. I was now living by rationalizations: I was the

---

Papering—using his counterfeit money all over the area
Federales—short for Federal police in Mexico

hunted, the police were the hunters, ergo, the police were the bad guys. I had to steal to survive, to finance my continual flight from the bad guys, consequently I was justified in my illegal means of support. So, after less than a week in England, I papered *Picadilly* with some of my picadillies and flew off to Paris, smug in the irrational assumption that I'd resorted to fraud again in self-defense.

10   A psychiatrist would have viewed my actions differently. He would have said I wanted to be caught. For now the British police began to put together a dossier on me.

11   Perhaps I was seeking to be caught. Perhaps I was subconsciously seeking help and my subliminal mind told me the authorities would offer that help, but I had no such conscious thoughts at the time.

Source: Abignale, F. (1980). *Catch Me If You Can: The True Story of a Real Fake.* New York: Random House, pp. 161–162.

Questions

1. What details let you know that Abignale is a fraud? _____

_____

_____

_____

_____

_____

_____

_____

_____

_____

2. How did Abignale hide his identity? _____

_____

_____

_____

_____

_____

_____

_____

Picadilly—a city in London, England

Fuel Economy: Save Money on Gas

CONSUMER REPORTS' TESTS SHOW HOW TO GET THE BEST GAS MILEAGE

1   The best way to burn less fuel is to buy a car that gets better gas mileage. But our tests with a Toyota Camry and other vehicles show there are ways to minimize what you spend at the pump with your current car.

Drive at a moderate speed

2   This is the biggest factor. You may have to be a little patient, but driving at 55 mph instead of 65 or 75 will save you money. When we increased the Camry's highway cruising speed from 55 mph to 65, the car's fuel economy dropped from 40 mpg to 35. Speeding up to 75 mph cost the car another 5 mpg. One reason is that aerodynamic drag increases exponentially the faster you drive; it simply takes more fuel to power the car through the air.

Drive smoothly

3   Avoid hard acceleration and braking whenever possible. In our tests, frequent bursts of acceleration and braking reduced the Camry's mileage by 2 to 3 mpg. Once up to speed on the highway, maintain a steady pace in top gear. Smooth acceleration, cornering, and braking also extend the life of the engine, transmission, brakes, and tires.

Reduce unnecessary drag

4   At highway speeds, more than 50 percent of engine power goes to overcoming aerodynamic drag. So don't carry things on top of your vehicle when you don't have to. Installing a large Thule Cascade 1700 car-top carrier on our Camry dropped its gas mileage from 35 mpg to 29 at 65 mph. Even driving with empty racks on the car reduces its fuel economy.

Don't use premium fuel if you don't have to

5   If your car specifies regular fuel, don't buy premium under the mistaken belief that your engine will run better. The only difference you'll see is about 20 cents more per gallon. Most cars are designed to run just fine on regular gasoline. Even many cars for which premium is recommended will run well on regular. We have found that the differences are imperceptible during normal driving. Check your owner's manual to find out if your engine really requires premium or if you can run on other grades.

Minimize driving with a cold engine

6   Engines run most efficiently when they're warm. In our city-driving tests, making multiple short trips and starting the engine from cold each time reduced fuel

economy by almost 4 mpg. Engines also produce more pollution and wear faster when they're cold. When possible, combine several short trips into one so that the engine stays warm.

Keep tires properly inflated

7 The Camry experienced a 1.3 mpg loss in highway fuel economy when the tires were underinflated by 10 psi. More important, underinflated tires compromise handling and braking, and wear faster. And they run much hotter, which can lead to tire failure. Check the pressure of your vehicle's tires at least once a month with a tire gauge. The owner's manual explains how to do it.

Buy tires with lower rolling resistance

8 A tire's rolling resistance can add or detract another 1 or 2 mpg. In our tire ratings, look for high-rated tires with low rolling resistance. They generally won't cost more, and replacing a worn tire could save you more than $100 a year in fuel.

Avoid idling for long periods

9 Think of it this way: When you're idling, your car is getting zero miles per gallon. When we let a Buick Lucerne, with a V8, idle for 10 minutes while warming up, it burned about an eighth of a gallon of gas. A smaller engine would probably burn less, but idling still adds up over time. As a rule, turn off your engine if you expect to sit for more than about 30 seconds. An engine warms up faster as it's driven anyway.

MYTH BUSTERS

Morning fill-ups

10 A common tip is to buy gasoline in the morning, when the air is cool, rather than in the heat of the day. The theory is that the cooler gasoline will be denser, so you will get more for your money. But the temperature of the gasoline coming out of the fuel nozzle changes very little, if at all, during any 24-hour stretch. Any extra gas you get will be negligible.

Air conditioning vs. opening windows

11 Some people advise you not to run the air conditioner because it puts more of a load on the engine, which can decrease fuel economy. But others say that opening the windows at highway speeds can affect gas mileage even more by disrupting the vehicle's aerodynamics. In our tests in a Honda Accord, using air conditioning while driving at 65 mph reduced the vehicle's gas mileage by over 3 mpg. The effect of opening the windows at 65 mph was not measurable.

A dirty air filter

12   Our tests show that driving with a dirty air filter no longer has any impact on fuel economy, as it did with older engines. That's because modern engines use computers to precisely control the air/fuel ratio, depending on the amount of air coming in through the filter. Reducing airflow causes the engine to automatically reduce the amount of fuel being used. Fuel economy didn't change, but the Camry accelerated much more slowly with a dirty filter.

Source: Fuel Economy: Save Money on Gas. ConsumerReports.org Retrieved from http://www.consumerreports.org/cro/cars/tires-auto-parts/car-maintenance/ fuel-economy-save-money-on-gas/overview/index.htm

Questions

What are the 8 ways to minimize what you spend for gasoline at the pump?

1. _____
2. _____
3. _____
4. _____
5. _____
6. _____
7. _____
8. _____

What are the true answers to the 3 myths of fuel economy?

9. _____
10. _____
11. _____

12–15. Discuss which idea are you most likely to adopt in your life.

_____
_____
_____
_____

Visual Image

READING 5

Directions: Look at the details in the advertisement above to answer the questions below.

1. Why is there a picture of a paper cup in the ad?

   _____

   _____

   _____

   _____

2. Why is there an "X" by the words "SAVE MORE" on the cup?

   _____

   _____

   _____

3. What does the ad suggest with the words "We can help you save a latte"? HINT: There are two meanings for the word "latte."

_____

_____

_____

4. Why does the advertisement state the credit union offers free coffee in the branches every day?

_____

_____

_____

5. How might the free coffee in the branches persuade a person?

_____

_____

_____

Read the section of the ad under the heading "A small sacrifice for a big goal."

6. What is the sacrifice?

_____

_____

7. What is the goal?

_____

_____

_____

Look at the box in the bottom right corner of the ad "$aving just makes cent$." What two meanings are they implying with the word "cent$"?

8. _____

9. _____

10. Discuss a habit you have that could be changed to help you reach your goals. Be specific about what you could substitute to save money, as the ad suggests.

_____

_____

_____

_____

7 Advanced Patterns of Organization

THEME – Life and Job Skills

SPOTLIGHT ON LEARNING STYLES ◀)) LISTEN

One of the most useful job and life skills I have learned is how to listen. Don't get me wrong, I really like to talk. I think talking might be considered one of my hobbies. When I was in junior high, my Algebra teacher called me "motor mouth." I like talking so much that I even made a career of talking—as a college professor. But I have found that I learn more when I listen. When I listen, I learn so much about life and about people. I love to listen to people tell their stories—their joy, their pain, and their adventures. A few years before my mother passed away, I recorded her telling her stories. My husband, daughter, and I brought our digital recorder to her house and listened for hours as she talked about her life and the people she loved. She told us about her parents, young immigrants who settled in Chicago in the early 1900s, learning a new language and culture, and making ends meet with a huge backyard garden. She shared vivid details of being young, taking the streetcar, and dancing with the servicemen at the USO at Navy Pier. We listened to stories of her love for my father, their Friday night "date nights," and their raising seven children together. Listening to my mother gave us beautiful stories about our roots. My mother also taught me that people need to "shine," so sincerely listening to others' accomplishments and complimenting them is a valuable and cherished gift.

Paragraphs Developed with Classification

Authors may organize paragraphs by classifying information into sorts, types, or categories. Usually there will be a sentence in the paragraph indicating that there are "several types," "three main catego-

LO1
Recognize paragraphs developed with classification.

ries," or some other way of classifying. As a reader, you should also watch for a description and perhaps examples of each classification. It may be easier to complete a chart of the relevant information so you can "see" the classifications.

Signal Words

sorts

types

categories

groups

areas

levels

styles

EXAMPLE ————————————————————————————————————

Directions: Read the paragraph below. Use the signal words to locate the major categories and examples to complete the chart.

Employers have to make their decision based on three areas relevant to any job:

* your qualifications and skills—what you know and what you can do;
* your experience and work background—where you have been and what you have done;
* your personality and character—who you are and how you behave.

Source: Corfield, Rebecca. (2009). *Successful Interview Skills: How to Prepare, Answer Tough Questions and Get Your Ideal Job.* Philadelphia: Kogan Page, p. 19.

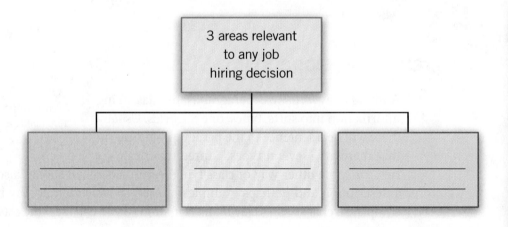

In the example above, the three areas relevant to any job are: your qualifications and skills; your experience and work background; and your personality and character.

PRACTICE THE NEW SKILL

Directions: Read the paragraph below. Use the signal words to locate the major categories and examples to complete the chart.

PRACTICE 1

When illness hits you, it can touch you on the physical, intellectual, emotional, or spiritual level. Physical symptoms might be headaches or stomach problems; intellectual symptoms might be absentmindedness or indecisiveness; emotional symptoms might be out of control answers or weeping. Even people who aren't religious recognize that we all have a spiritual part to ourselves, and spiritual stress can manifest in that feeling of emptiness or the feeling that we have nothing left to give. Burnout.

Source: Emmett, Rita. (2009). *Manage Your Time to Reduce Your Stress: A Handbook for the Overworked, Overscheduled, and Overwhelmed.* New York: Walker & Company, p. 12.

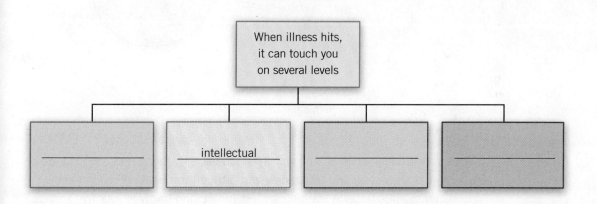

PRACTICE 2

Employers often require the following types of background checks: (1) criminal history, (2) employment history, (3) citizenship, (4) credit history, and (5) drug testing.

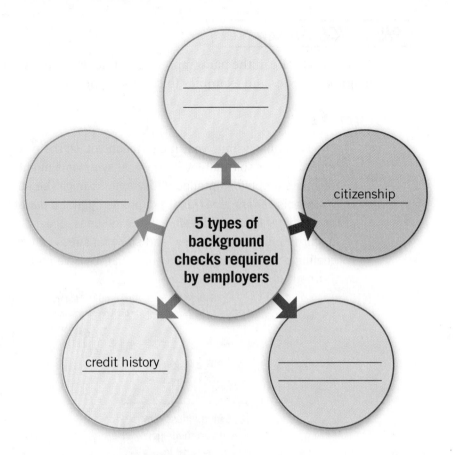

PRACTICE 3

A learning style is "the way in which each learner begins to concentrate on, process, and retain new and difficult information" (Dunn and Griggs, 2000). . . . A learning style is innate and involves your five senses. It is how you process information that comes to you . . . If you learn best by seeing information, you have a more dominant visual learning style. If you learn best by hearing information, you have a more dominant auditory learning style. If you learn best by touching or doing, you have a more dominant tactile learning style. You may also hear the tactile learning style referred to as kinesthetic or hands-on.

Source: Excerpt from *Cornerstone: Creating Success Through Positive Change,* 6th Edition by Robert M. Sherfield and Patricia G. Moody. Copyright © 2011 by Robert M. Sherfield and Patricia G. Moody. Printed and Electronically reproduced by permission of Pearson Education, Inc., Upper Saddle River, New Jersey.

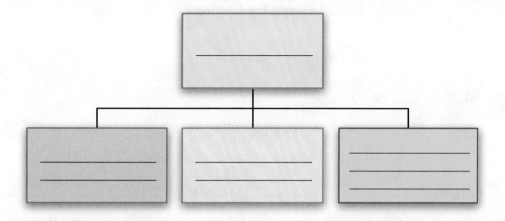

Paragraphs Developed with Compare/Contrast

When authors compare two things, they discuss the ways they are similar. For example, an author might discuss the similarities between having dogs or cats as pets—you give them both food and water, you must take them to the vet for check-ups and shots, they can both be cuddly, they can make you smile with their funny behaviors, and you can love them as part of the family.

> **LO2**
> Recognize paragraphs developed with compare/contrast.

When authors contrast two things, they discuss the ways they are different. For example, an author might discuss the differences between having dogs or cats as pets—a dog needs to be fed once or twice a day since it might eat all the food you give it at once, while a cat can be given enough food for a week and will only eat a little at a time. Another difference is that a dog can be trained more easily to learn words such as "sit" and "stay," while a cat more likely will ignore those commands and do what it pleases.

How do you know when an author is using a compare and/or contrast pattern of organization? Watch for words that signal when the author is comparing and/or contrasting ideas. This will help you focus on the main ideas and understand the author's point.

Signal Words for Comparison

similarly, is similar to

the same as, in the same manner, in the same way

like, likewise, is alike in . . .

just as

Signal Words for Contrast

in contrast

differently, different than

unlike

meanwhile

but, however, on the other hand

EXAMPLE ————————————————————————————————————

One of the fundamental differences you'll find between the world of college and the work world is in your ability to choose your attire: As a student, you have been able, in large part, to determine what you wanted to wear. Not so in the world of work. Most organizations have a policy or guidelines that dictate on-the-job dress, although policies vary from organization to organization, and what's acceptable and appropriate in one will be frowned upon at another. Your workplace attire is important beyond the issue of complying with company policy or practices. Your dress is part of your personal "brand"—the image you project. What you wear on the job can help or hurt you in your work life.

Source: *Job Choices 2010 for Science, Engineering, & Technology Students.*
National Association of Colleges and Employers, p. 50.

Directions: Complete the chart below listing the differences between college and work expectations about clothing.

COLLEGE CLOTHING	WORK CLOTHING

Answer:

COLLEGE CLOTHING	WORK CLOTHING
Choose what you want to wear.	*Follow expectations of the employer.*
	What you wear creates your image.

PRACTICE THE NEW SKILL

PRACTICE 1

> In the years since I started VocationVacations I've talked to many people who gave up "security" to start their dream jobs, and I've discovered that most people had an experience similar to mine. They spent *years* thinking about making the switch before finally taking action. Like me, they had found their fear insurmountable. They'd had a million reasons for not doing it: kids in school, mortgages and tuitions to pay, and impending promotion, not the right time . . . Every reason was completely legitimate, but somehow, at a certain point, those reasons ceased to matter. Sometimes the reasons actually went away (the kids graduated, the mortgage got paid off), but just as often the underlying situations didn't change. What changed was something inside the people. They had crossed a line. They had moved from a place where they were making *rational* arguments for not pursuing their dream to making an emotional choice to do so. And once that line was crossed, there was no turning back.

> *Source:* Kurth, Brian. (2008). *Test Drive Your Dream Job: A Step-by-step Guide to Finding and Creating the Work You Love.* New York: Hachette Book Group, pp. 33–34.

Directions: Underline the compare signal words. Then list three ways the author's experiences were similar to others who gave up "security" to start dream jobs.

PRACTICE 2

> People driving a car can react in a way that's often completely unlike their normal social, territorial behavior. A motor vehicle seems to have a magnifying effect on the size of a person's Personal Space. In some cases, this territory is magnified up to ten times the normal size, so the driver feels that he has claim to an area twenty-five to thirty feet in front of and behind his car. When another driver cuts in front of him, even if it wasn't dangerous, the driver may go through a physiological change, becoming angry

and even attacking the other driver in what is now known as "Road Rage." Compare this to the situation that occurs when the same person is stepping into an elevator and another person steps in front of him, invading his personal territory. His reaction in those circumstances is normally apologetic and he allows the other person to go first; dramatically different from what happens when the same person cuts in front of him on the open road.

Source: Pease, Allan and Barbara Pease. (2004). *The Definitive Book of Body Language.* New York: Bantam Books, pp. 206–207.

Directions: Complete the chart contrasting a person's social, territorial behavior in different settings.

PERSON IN THEIR CAR	PERSON NOT IN THEIR CAR

PRACTICE 3

The flexible individual listens receptively to new ideas or suggested approaches, doesn't get upset when plans change, shows respect to those in positions of authority when new policies or priorities are introduced, and looks for the positive side of proposed changes. A flexible person is empathetic toward others, showing a readiness to try to understand ideas or values that may be different from his or her own.

The body language of a flexible person is typically "open," with relaxed movements, steady eye contact, and a smile. In fact, flexible people always seem to have more fun and are more pleasant to be around.

An inflexible person presents quite a different picture. This individual tends to complain or to become easily upset about a sudden change in plans or a new way of doing things. His or her natural tendency is to cling to the old ways without presenting a solid rationale for maintaining the status quo. Because he or she is so quick to respond negatively to new information, the inflexible individual has little time to do active listening and tends to focus more on his or her own needs than on those of colleagues or of the organization as a whole. Sometimes the very idea of change can seem so threatening to this individual that his or her first response is simply to shut down. The rigid attitude of the inflexible person may be reflected in "closed" body language, such as crossed arms, pinched or pursed lips, darting eyes, frowning, and hunched posture. Inflexible people tend to be judgmental and uptight. In the absence of other redeeming personal traits, their negativity can be a turnoff to others.

Source: Jansen, Julie. (2006). *You Want Me to Work With Who?*
Eleven Keys to a Stress-free, Satisfying, and Successful Work Life…
No Matter Who You Work With. New York: Penguin Books, pp. 126–127.

Directions: Complete the chart contrasting flexible and inflexible people.

FLEXIBLE PERSON	INFLEXIBLE PERSON

"It's not whether you get knocked down, it's whether you get up."
—Vince Lombardi

Paragraphs Developed with Cause/Effect

LO3
Recognize paragraphs developed with cause/ effect.

When authors are trying to convey a point, they sometimes develop their ideas through the cause-and-effect pattern. How do you know when a cause-and-effect pattern is being used? If a cause pattern is being used, the author may give one or more reasons for something happening. For example, they may discuss the reasons why students have trouble paying for their college books, such as lower income from their part-time jobs or lower financial aid awards.

The author may also discuss the effects of a certain situation. For example, when the economy is doing poorly, business is down and people may get fewer hours at work. This results in lower income and less money to pay for college tuition and books.

Authors might discuss more than one cause and/or more than one effect. For example, the poor economy may cause people to get fewer hours at work and some people may even lose their jobs. This may result in more people going to community college instead of working, but it also results in more competition for the limited college financial aid. The point is that in order to make sense of what we are reading, we must be aware of how authors use the cause-and-effect pattern to demonstrate how one thing affects another.

Signal Words for Cause and Effect

because, because of
is due, due to, can be attributed to
if . . . then
leads to, has made us
since, so, in order to
accordingly, consequently
as a result, result in
therefore, thus

EXAMPLE ———————————————————————————————

Enthusiasm is also essential to success. When interviewing, you are likely to stand out in an employer's mind if you show excitement about the job. Prior to the interview, check out the company's Web site to learn about the business. Think of questions you might want answered, because asking questions is one way to show interest. Other strategies include arriving a few minutes early to the interview, dressing professionally, and staying engaged in the conversation. You should also bring a pad and pen so you can take notes during the interview; just make sure to ask if it is okay to take notes first. This shows the interviewer that you are actively engaged and paying close attention to what they are saying. It may also make it easier for you to think of additional questions to ask prior to accepting a job offer.

Source: http://publications.usa.gov/USAPubs.php?PubID=244Essential Skills to Getting a Job, What Young People with Disabilities Need to Know, Soft Skills: The Competitive Edge, What do employers look for in new employees?

Complete the cause and effect diagram.

Cause	LEADS TO	Effect
Think of questions and ask them	Leads to →	_____
Bring a pad and pen to the interview	Leads to →	_____
Take notes during the interview	Leads to →	_____
	Leads to →	_____

Answer:

Cause	LEADS TO	Effect
Think of questions and ask them	Leads to →	shows you are interested in the interview
Bring a pad and pen to the interview	Leads to →	so you can take notes
Taking notes during the interview	Leads to →	shows the interviewer you are engaged and paying attention
	Leads to →	makes it easier to think of additional questions

PRACTICE THE NEW SKILL

Directions: Complete the cause-and-effect diagram below the readings.

PRACTICE 1

Time management is not the only solution if you find yourself running like a hamster in a wheel, rushing to get too much done in too little time. In fact, if you are that busy, trying to do too many things is causing you stress. There is hidden, surprising pain in efficiency and productivity for its own sake—depression, broken relationships, financial difficulties, health problems, overwhelming schedules, and exhaustion all come under the general headings of stress and burnout.

Source: Emmett, Rita (2009). *Manage Your Time to Reduce Your Stress: A Handbook for the Overworked, Overscheduled, and Overwhelmed.* New York: Walker & Company, p. 24.

Complete the cause-and-effect diagram.

_____ **Leads to**   **stress**
                                        ⟶

PRACTICE 2

Stop Slouching!

Good posture boosts self-esteem

When you were growing up, your mother probably told you to sit up straight, because good posture helps you look confident and make a good impression. And now it turns out that sitting up straight can also improve how you feel about yourself, according to a study in the October 2009 issue of *European Journal of Social Psychology*. Researchers asked college students to rate themselves on how good they would be as job candidates and employees. Those told to sit up straight with their chests out gave themselves higher ratings than those instructed to slouch while filling out the rating form. Once again, Mom was right.

Source: Black, Harvey. (May/June 2010) *Scientific American Mind*, p. 10.

Complete the cause-and-effect diagram.

_____   **Leads to**   **feeling better about yourself**
                                        ⟶

"When you complain, all you do is broadcast, 'There's a victim in the neighborhood.'"   —*Maya Angelou*

PRACTICE 3

Don't Complain–Sell!

Grandma always said, to complain is foolish, to sell is holy. The point is, the world doesn't need a complainer. The reason we complain should be to get a result. What do you want? You need to know what result you want before you open your mouth. Suggest that solution. That's selling.

Source: The Art of Effective Complaining: Financial Expert Explains How to Get Results from your Gripes to Businesses. Retrieved from www.cbsnews.com.

Complete the cause-and-effect diagram.

_____   **Leads to**   _____
                                →

> *"Slow down and enjoy life. It's not only the scenery you miss by going too fast—you also miss the sense of where you are going and why."*
>
> —*Eddie Cantor*

Paragraphs Developed with a Combination of Patterns

Much of what we read uses a combination of several organizational patterns. Continue to watch for the words that signal a pattern and you'll improve your reading comprehension. The more you practice, the better you will be at recognizing patterns and knowing what to expect from the text.

LO4
Recognize paragraphs developed with a combination of patterns.

EXAMPLE ——————————————————————————

Controlling Nerves

Everybody suffers from nervous feelings in high anxiety situations. This nervous energy provides us with the extra impulse we need in order to put ourselves forward, speak up and perform impressively at an interview.

Some of our greatest actors are actually sick before every appearance on the stage, showing that the energy which is generated by nervous tension is crucial to giving a good performance.

When we feel nervous our bodies are reacting to the fact that the forthcoming event is important to us. We have spent time and trouble preparing and rehearsing for the interview and we are getting our response mechanism ready either to go into battle or flee. This is known as the 'fight or flight' mechanism. It is a throwback to the times when we had to either fight our way out of trouble or run away when faced with a threat in the wild, in order to survive. Today we need to harness our nerves to make sure we fight, or at least engage impressively with the interview, rather than panic and dry up. The trick is to make your nervous tension work *for* you, rather than against you. When your nerves work for you, you feel extra alive, highly conscious of everything that is happening around you, very focused on the task at hand and excited by the prospect of the performance ahead.

> *Source:* Corfield, Rebecca. (2009). *Successful Interview Skills: How to Prepare, Answer Tough Questions and Get Your Ideal Job,* 5th ed. Philadelphia: Kogan Page, pp. 60–61.

Directions: Underline the signal words and write the organizational patterns you find in the passage above.

Everybody suffers from nervous feelings in high anxiety situations. This nervous energy provides us with the extra impulse we need in order to put ourselves forward, speak up and perform impressively at an interview. Some of our greatest actors are actually sick before every appearance on the stage, showing that the energy which is generated by nervous tension is crucial to giving a good performance.

When we feel nervous our bodies are reacting to the fact that the forthcoming event is important to us. We have spent time and trouble preparing and rehearsing for the interview and we are getting our response mechanism ready either to go into battle or flee. This is known as the 'fight or flight' mechanism. It is a throwback to the times when we had to either fight our way out of trouble or run away when faced with a threat in the wild, in order to survive. Today we need to harness our nerves to make sure we fight, or at least engage impressively with the interview, rather than panic and dry up. The trick is to make your nervous tension work *for* you, rather than against you. When your nerves work for you, you feel extra alive, highly conscious of everything that is happening around you, very focused on the task at hand and excited by the prospect of the performance ahead.

Patterns of Organization:

In order to—cause and effect

Before, when, is a throwback to the times when, today—time order

Is known as—definition

Rather than—contrast

Last sentence (when your nerves work for you, you feel . . .)—simple

listing/cause and effect

PRACTICE THE NEW SKILL

Directions: Underline the signal words as you read each passage, and write the organizational patterns in the space below each passage.

PRACTICE 1

Relaxation Exercises

When you are feeling at your most nervous, you are at the mercy of many different physical symptoms which can seriously derail you from performing well in your interview. However, there are several exercises that you can do to help counter the effects of fear and dread. When we are experiencing the fight or flight mechanism, the body produces adrenalin to help us act to fight or flee from the threat facing us. Adrenalin gets our pulses racing by raising our heart rate ready for action. The body cuts off oxygen from the brain and the extremities, such as the hands and feet. After all, if you are engaged in a fight or running for your life, you do not need great thoughts or use tiny hand gestures. All available oxygen is being channeled to our muscles, ready for the fight or the flight that is to ensue. Our hands and feet feel numb and tingly as a result and our minds go blank. We cannot hear properly, sometimes we feel we cannot even see straight and it is difficult to concentrate on what we are trying to say.

All of these things are the result of the physical reactions of our body to a perceived threat, so you should not feel a failure if you feel nervous at times like this. Your churning stomach, clammy palms, sweating and confusion are rational reactions to a scary situation. However, a job interview is not a real threat; it is an opportunity, so we need to counter these reactions by taking control of what is happening to us physically. At a time like this we do not need powered-up arms and legs and a blank brain; we need the opposite—a calm body and powered-up mental faculties.

Source: Corfield, Rebecca. (2009). *Successful Interview Skills: How to Prepare, Answer Tough Questions and Get Your Ideal Job,* 5th ed. Philadelphia: Kogan Page, pp. 65–66.

Organizational Patterns:

_____

_____

_____

PRACTICE 2

Breathing Exercise

Breathing exercises are one way of managing feelings of nervousness. When we are under strain our breathing is likely to become shallow and we do not use all our lung capacity. The effect is to starve the brain of the vital oxygen it needs in order for you to think quickly and clearly. To counteract this you need to do some deeper breathing. Just before you enter the interview room, take several deep breaths. Inhale slowly, standing up if possible, breathe in through your nose and try to fill up with air. Hold this breath for a count of three, then exhale slowly through your mouth. Concentrate on expelling all of the air that you took in. Feel your shoulders relax and watch your stomach flatten as the air is sent out. Repeat for three or four deep breaths only. This will flood your system with oxygen which will counter the unhelpful effects of the flight or fight mechanism.

Source: Corfield, Rebecca. (2009). *Successful Interview Skills: How to Prepare, Answer Tough Questions and Get Your Ideal Job,* 5th ed. Philadelphia: Kogan Page, p. 66.

Organizational Patterns:

_____

_____

_____

PRACTICE 3

Taking some deep breaths is a very powerful way to handle nerves in any situation whether it is at a social event, before medical treatment, during college exams or any time that you feel scared. In the middle of a recent piano exam, I found my hands shaking uncontrollably and my mind unable to concentrate on the notes. I was unable to play at all. I fought my feelings of panic, told myself to breathe and soon the shaking stopped. Slowly my mind cleared and the notes in front of me came back into focus. I started playing again and passed the exam. The examiner told me afterwards that such attacks of nerves are very common and that I had controlled mine well, not to let it wreck the exam. Even if the situation looks as if it is going badly, you can still retrieve it and do better than you think. Attacks of nerves will happen to all of us but you can stop them from ruining your chances.

Source: Corfield, Rebecca. (2009). *Successful Interview Skills: How to Prepare, Answer Tough Questions and Get Your Ideal Job,* 5th ed. Philadelphia: Kogan Page, p. 68.

Organizational Patterns:

_____

_____

_____

REVIEW *WHAT YOU LEARNED*

Directions: Read the passage and answer the questions that follow.

Eliminate Distractions

Distractions are the enemy of focused attention. A successful race car driver said to me, "A little bit of distraction on the racetrack and you could have a really bad day." The same applies on the fast track to success. Entertainment, cell phones, video games, Web surfing, parties—they all defocus you and cause crashes and delays on the road to success. That's why successful people eliminate distractions. Renowned venture capitalist Steve Jurvetson says, "You can't do it all, so I cut out a lot of extraneous things. I haven't watched television for eighteen years. I don't miss it." Deborah McGuiness, senior research scientist at Stanford, said to me, "Getting my degree, every year I cut things out. I remember the year I sacrificed movies.

I just said, 'I can't afford the time. I'll put movies back in my life again once I finish the Ph.D.'" What distractions are *you* willing to eliminate today in order to achieve faster success tomorrow?

Source: Ettus, Samantha. (2008). *The Experts' Guide to Doing Things Faster: 100 Ways to Make Life More Efficient.* New York: Random House, p. 72.

ENGLISH 2.0

Enemy of means: something that destroys

Cause crashes and delays on the road to success means: keeps you from being successful such as when driving a car, crashes and delays would keep you from getting to where you want to go.

Cut things out means: removed certain activities from my life

---

Directions: Choose one of the patterns of organization from the list to answer the questions.

Definition	Example	Time Order/Sequence	Simple List
Classification	Compare/Contrast	Cause and Effect	

1–2. What two patterns of organization are used in the sentence below?

Entertainment, cell phones, video games, Web surfing, parties—they all defocus you and cause crashes and delays on the road to success.

_____

_____

3. What signal word is used for the second pattern (after the dash)?

_____

4. What pattern of organization is used in the sentence below?

What distractions are *you* willing to eliminate today in order to achieve faster success tomorrow?

_____

5. What signal words indicated the pattern of organization?

_____

REVIEW WHAT YOU LEARNED

Directions: Read the passage and answer the questions that follow.

Your Total Nonverbal Message

A combination of all the elements of nonverbal messages, taken together, can help or hinder you in the job interview. The way you manage your appearance and dress for the interview communicates to the employer whether you cared enough about the interview to clean up and dress appropriately. A slovenly appearance or inappropriate attire suggests that you either don't know any better, or don't care.

Your body language—eye contact, facial expression, and your vocal expressiveness—further conveys your interest or lack of interest throughout the interview. If all the aspects of your nonverbal behavior are congruent—that is, they communicate the same message and that message is the same as your verbal message—then you will communicate a strong message to the interviewer that should be believable. If some of the aspects of your message are at odds with the other aspects (for example, you say [verbally] you are interested in the job, but your nonverbal messages suggest otherwise and contradict the verbal), then the employer is likely to be confused. You say one thing, but act another. In this case the employer is likely to be uncomfortable with you for the job, and you are likely to lose out on the chance at being hired.

Source: Krannich, Ron and Caryl Krannich. (2004). *Job Interview Tips for People with Not-so-hot Backgrounds: How to Put Red Flags Behind You to Win the Job.* Manassas Park, VA: Impact Publications, pp. 62–63.

1. What patterns of organization are in the sentence below?

Your body language—eye contact, facial expression, and your vocal expressiveness—further conveys your interest or lack of interest throughout the interview.

2. What patterns of organization are in the sentence below?

If all the aspects of your nonverbal behavior are congruent—that is, they communicate the same message and that message is the same as your verbal message—then you will communicate a strong message to the interviewer that should be believable.

3. What signal words are used in the sentence above?

_____

4. What patterns of organization are used in the sentence below?

If some of the aspects of your message are at odds with the other aspects (for example, you say [verbally] you are interested in the job, but your nonverbal messages suggest otherwise and contradict the verbal), then the employer is likely to be confused.

_____

5. What signal words are used in the sentence above?

_____

/ **MASTER** THE LESSON /

Patterns of Organization

Directions: Read the passage and answer the questions that follow.

1. In offices across America, good people are engaging in some extremely obnoxious behavior: talking over each other in meetings, failing to respond to e-mails, showing up late to appointments or blowing them off entirely with a hurried text message. What gives?

2. Psychiatrist Edward M. Hallowell, M.D. says that the issue isn't that the human species is devolving into ill-mannered automations. Rather, the accelerated pace of office life has made us lose touch with common courtesies once taken for granted, like saying, "Good morning."

3. "We don't have a sudden epidemic of rudeness," says Hallowell, the author of *CrazyBusy: Overstretched, Overbooked and About to Snap!* "It's just that without meaning to we have allowed ourselves to be over-whelmed."

4. Hallowell says that much of the problem can be attributed to our relationship with technology, and the unrelenting stream of incoming information—from e-mails and IMs to cellphones and texts—that it offers. In order to cope, we screen things out. And all too frequently, it's the people around us who don't make the cut.

Source: Eckel, Sara. (June 12, 2010). *How Rude! Bad Office Behavior We're All Guilty Of: Information Overload Leads to Missed Meetings, Rude Habits.* Forbes.com. Retrieved from www.abcnews.go.com

Directions: Choose one of the Patterns of Organization from the list to answer the questions.

Definition	Example	Time Order/Sequence	Simple List
Classification	Compare/Contrast	Cause and Effect	

1. What are the patterns of organization for paragraph 1?

_____

2. What are the patterns of organization for paragraph 2?

_____

3. What is the signal word that indicates the pattern for paragraph 2?

_____

4. What is one pattern of organization for paragraph 4?

_____

5. What are the signal words for that pattern?

_____

6. What is the second pattern in paragraph 4?

_____

7. What are the signal words for that pattern?

_____

8–10. Discuss behaviors you have seen in the workplace or at school where people were just "tuning things out." Discuss how those behaviors could be considered rude by some people. _____

_____

_____

_____

_____

_____

MASTER THE LESSON

Patterns of Organization

Directions: Read the passage and answer the questions that follow.

Make Time for Reading

1   "I just don't have the time" is frequently the excuse used by someone who has failed to get through the latest novel he or she intended to read. But you *do* have the time, if you make reading a priority.

2   If you're really serious about finally getting back into the habit of reading—and it *is* a habit that becomes easier if you do it regularly—(then) go back to the system most of us used in school. Either set a specific amount of time to read each day, which can be as little as fifteen minutes, or set a specific number of pages. Your involvement in the book will grow as you make the commitment. Each day, your excitement about this new time you've given yourself will increase. In turn, this excitement will reinforce the habit.

3   Now that you've made the commitment to reading more, you need something to read. When selecting a book, you can suit your mood. Decide whether you want the fun of a mystery, the challenge of a more literary work, or the education offered in a nonfiction book. Now it's time to dive into that book. Good readers say they give every book a fair chance, but they don't force themselves to finish a book. There are too many great books to read. Reading shouldn't feel like work.

4   To help you make more time for reading, take reading material with you everywhere. You can get a lot of pages in while waiting at the dentist's or sitting in the car waiting until your child finishes hockey practice. If you're going out for the day, use a tote bag to take along reading for the train or if you have to wait for an appointment. One client refuses to buy a pocket-book unless it's large enough to hold a paperback book or a magazine, and she never leaves home without something to read. "If I'm meeting a friend for lunch, I don't mind waiting five to ten minutes if I have something to read," she says.

5   As you read more and more each day, you'll begin to explore different sources of reading materials. Use your library. Most libraries permit you to reserve and renew books online. Borrowing books takes the sting out of buying them, and the deadline of finishing before the due date provides a goal. Also, consider audiobooks—you can buy them, borrow them from the library, or download digital book files to your MP3 player. By being able to listen to books in the car or anyplace else, you will greatly expand the amount of time you can devote to reading.

6   It is also helpful to keep current reading materials in the room where they're likely to be read, neatly stored in baskets or containers.

7   Many people read more than one book at a time. They like the variety of having different books to suit their current mood. If you want to do the same, be sure one is a paperback so that you have one book that is portable.

Source: Eisenberg, Ronnie with Kate Kelly. (2007). *Organize Your Life: Free Yourself from Clutter and Find More Personal Time.* Hoboken, NJ: Wiley, pp. 150–151.

Directions: Choose one of the patterns of organization from the list to answer the questions.

Definition	Example	Time Order/Sequence	Simple List
Classification	Compare/Contrast	Cause and Effect	

1. What is the pattern of organization for paragraph 2?

   _____

2. What are the signal words that indicate the pattern for paragraph 2?

   _____

3. What is the pattern of organization for paragraph 3?

   _____

4. What are the signal words that indicate the pattern for paragraph 3?

   _____

5. What is one pattern of organization for paragraph 5?

   _____

6. What are the signal words for that pattern in paragraph 5?

   _____

7–10. What things are you interested in learning more about? Discuss how you can make time for reading more about those things you value.

   _____

   _____

   _____

   _____

   _____

   _____

LEARNING STYLE ACTIVITIES

*L*ook, *L*isten, *W*rite, *D*o

How to Live: Follow Your Heart, Risk Be Damned

Ben Stein Says Happiness Comes to Those Who Pursue Careers That Define Their Passions—Ask His Shrink

(CBS) *As the college class of 2010 heads out into the world, take a moment to hear the advice of our* **contributor Ben Stein***:*

1   It is graduation time for you young people. That means time to make some decisions and take some action about your lives. I would like to offer you some deep thoughts at this season.

2   A few days ago, I asked my shrink, a super-smart guy, how he would generally divide up the people who were happy in life from those who were not.

3   He answered like a shot.

4   The unhappy ones, he said, are people who let their parents or their family talk them into doing something for a career that wasn't really them. They are people who wanted to be writers or performers, and decided instead to take the cautious route and go to accountancy school or law school or dental school.

5   Now, he said, they are well into their middle age and they make a decent living, but they just don't like what they do.

6   What they do, you might say, is not them. It is not who they are or who they wanted to be. It's too late for most of them to try to change, and they haven't built up a lifetime of experience and contacts in the field they want to be in.

7   So, he said, "they just come in to my office and complain."

8   "And what about the happy ones?" I asked him. "What did they do?"

9   My shrink answered that, again, like a shot.

10   "They made a decision to live," he said, and those were his exact words.

11   They decided to do what their hearts told them to do, to do what was in them to do. They took risks and they took chances, and they tried a lot of different things until they got to where they wanted to be.

12   This very often means working incredibly hard and living on the edge. But it gets you to where you can look back on your life and say it wasn't wasted.

13   I left the doctor's office with my brain on fire. His advice is spectacular.

14   Unless you are born rich—or even if you are—you have to earn your keep, that is for sure. But to decide to live—that makes a lot of difference in this difficult world.

15   That's it. Choose to live a life you want to live, not one that's safe or what someone else thinks you should do.

16   Decide to live.

Source: How to Live: Follow Your Heart, Risk Be Damned. Retrieved from http://www
.cbsnews.com/stories/2010/06/13/sunday/main6577542.shtml

*L*OOK   Watch Ben Stein give the speech on the Web site. As you watch the video, think of your own heartfelt desires about what you want in life. What advice can you take from this article to apply to your own life? Draw, paint, photograph, or create a collage of your dreams.

*L*ISTEN   Listen to Ben Stein give the audio speech on the Web site. As you listen to his speech, think of your own heartfelt desires about what you want out of life. What advice can you take from this article to apply to your own life? Tell a friend, loved one, or classmate your dreams. Hearing yourself say them may make them more real.

*W*RITE   When you read the article, think of your own heartfelt desires about what you want in life. What advice can you take from this article to apply to your own life? Jot down your own notes as you read. Write a paragraph, short story, or poem about your own dreams in life.

*D*o   What passions do you have that you want to pursue? When you read the article, think of your own heartfelt desires about what you want in life. What advice can you take from this article to apply to your own life? Are you currently pursuing them? What do you imagine your life to be? Describe it in vivid detail.

Reading Practice

The next section of the chapter will help refine your skills in determining the pattern of organization while you read a variety of materials. All five of the readings address topics related to life and job skills.

The first reading is "11 Warning Signs Your Interview Is in Trouble," from an Internet Web site, msn.careerbuilder.com.

The second reading, "Cyber Considerations," comes from the textbook *The Community College Experience.*

The third reading, "Eyeing the Mountaintop," is from literature, *Of Beetles & Angels: A Boy's Remarkable Journey from a Refugee Camp to Harvard.*

The fourth reading is from an article titled "Best of America," from *Reader's Digest* magazine. The selection features three inspiring people who use their job skills to help the world.

The final reading is visual images of *body language* and interpretations of the messages our body language sends.

Internet **READING 1**

11 Warning Signs Your Interview Is in Trouble

1   During driver's education courses, you learn what each road sign signifies. The two arrows converging means you need to merge. A squiggly arrow means the road winds. "Left Lane Ends" means, well, the left lane ends.

2   Sometimes you don't even need the signs to know what to expect. If you see a flurry of red brake lights, you know traffic is not moving. In an ice storm, if the car in front of you is skidding from side to side, you can bet that the road is slippery.

3   Job hunts come with their own warning signs, but they're not typically as blunt as the bright yellow and orange signs posted on the side of the road. Instead, you're more likely to get context clues, like the brake lights. The interview process is full of uncertainty for a job seeker, and much of the power is in the interviewer's hands. Sometimes you don't know if the interview is going well. Other times you're so nervous you don't recognize the signs that this company isn't right for you.

4   Therefore it behooves you to recognize the warning signs that your job interview is in trouble. Here are 11 warning signs to watch for when interviewing for a job:

1. You're pretty sure you know how to get to the interview site, but you're not positive.

Before you can even look for warning signs of a bad interview, you need to get there first. Lisa Fedrizzi-Hutchins is a human resources/compliance administrator who was heading to a job interview earlier this year. She trusted her GPS unit, but realized the directions were incorrect once she was en route. Fortunately she called the company and asked some clarifying questions so that she could arrive at the interview on time.

2. You're talking more than the interviewer is.

Job seekers shouldn't dominate more than 40 percent of the conversation, says John M. McKee, founder and CEO of Business Success.

"Because many job seekers are anxious to show that they are the best candidate for a job, they often dominate the conversation with things like never-ending answers or run-on sentences," he explains. "The interview time may end before they've had adequate time to deal with all the questions the interviewer had prepared."

3. The interviewer's eyes are on the clock, not you.

As a managing partner at Winter, Wyman and Co., Mark Gleckman knows the importance of an interviewer's body language.

"During an interview, be an active observer," Gleckman advises. "Watch your interviewer's body language—is she glancing at her watch or noticing who is walking by? These could be signs that the interview may not progress to the next phase." He suggests asking the interviewer if you've provided all of the information she was hoping for or if you can offer anything else to get the most out of the interview.

4. **The interviewer decides to take a phone call mid-interview.**
   An interviewer should treat you with the same respect he or she expects. Jennifer Mounce, executive coach and interview adviser for Coach Effect, has heard her share of bad interview stories. One manager stopped an interview to take a 20-minute phone call without warning the interviewee, who was told to stay in the room until it was over. When the call was over, the interviewer resumed with the questions, but his mind was obviously elsewhere.

   "Candidates must ask themselves if they want to work for a person who can't give them their full attention for a short period of time or who doesn't have the communication and/or social skills necessary to put the candidate at ease, apologize or explain the necessity of the disruption," Mounce says.

5. **The interview feels like a test of endurance.**
   Mounce also warns of employers who hold marathon interviews that last seven hours. Applicants are not asked if they'd like a restroom break, snack or glass of water. Mounce advises you to think about what the job would be like if the interview is this bad.

6. **No one wants to work here.**
   An insightful question that many job seekers fail to ask is why the position is available. Or, to frame it so that you sound focused on your future with the company, ask where the employee formerly in the position is today. JR Rodrigues, co-founder of JRBM Software, cautions job seekers to watch for companies with a revolving door.

   "[If] the hiring manager complains to the interviewee about having had his last three hires quit after only a short term of employment, you should wonder about what is causing such turnover and whether this job is for you," he says.

7. **You're participating in a questionnaire, not an interview.**
   Kris Alban, director of strategic partnerships for iGrad, keeps a list of questions in front of him when conducting an interview.

   "During a good interview, I will go off-page as certain responses provoke additional questions or I may ask the interviewee to expand on something they said," Alban says. "If you notice your interviewer just running down their list of questions, then you know that you need to engage them more.

I definitely become more engaged when the interviewee accompanies their answer with a story that anchors it."

ENGLISH 2.0

Go off-page means: stray away from the planned interview

Running down means: reading through a list without much interest

Anchors means: gives it a reference point.

---

8. **You get snippy with the administrative assistant.**
   The interview begins the moment you are on the premises, so don't save your best behavior for the meeting room. Monique A. Honaman, CEO of ISHR Group and a former HR manager, stresses the importance of good manners.
   "I can't tell you how many times I have heard of job seekers being dismissive to certain individuals, and I know hiring managers often ask the receptionist to provide input on the candidates as well as those more heavily involved in the job interview process," Honaman says. "It's not just about having the skills and abilities to do the job; the personality and respect elements are critical, too."

9. **You spend 10 minutes complaining about your last boss.**
   Honaman also cautions against going negative during an interview. "Job seekers must never talk negatively about a former co-worker or former boss, even if it seems like this negativity is being encouraged," she warns. "Take the high road. It's an incredibly small world out there and it's amazing who knows who."

10. **The company is in financial trouble.**
    "[If] there is a loud argument in the office of the company you are interviewing at stemming from a creditor who has not received payment for his product or services that were purchased by the company, you need to consider whether this company will be able to pay you," Rodrigues says.

11. **The employer doesn't keep his or her word.**
    Rodrigues also warns against employers who tell you one thing but do otherwise. Blatant lies are obvious warning signs, but other subtle ones also hint at trouble. If you were given a timetable during the interview but you haven't

heard anything since, Rodrigues says you might have fallen off of the interviewer's radar and need to work your way back into his or her view.

Anthony Balderrama is a writer and blogger for CareerBuilder.com and its job blog, The Work Buzz. He researches and writes about job search strategy, career management, hiring trends and workplace issues. Follow him on Twitter at twitter.com/abalderrama.

Source: "11 Warning Signs That Your Interview Is in Trouble" by Anthony Balderrama, from http://www.careerbuilder.com. Copyright © by CareerBuilder, LLC. Reprinted with permission. **careerbuilder**
http://www.careerbuilder.com

Vocabulary

Use word parts to determine the meaning of **provoke**.

1. Forward

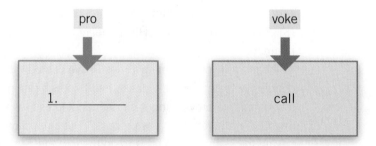

pro   voke

1. _____   call

2. Using the word part clues what is the meaning of **provoke**? _____

_____

Use context clues to find the meaning of **provoke**.

"During a good interview, I will go off-page as certain responses **provoke** additional questions or I may ask the interviewee to expand on something they said," Alban says. "If you notice your interviewer just running down their list of questions, then you know that you need to engage them more. I definitely become more engaged when the interviewee accompanies their answer with a story that anchors it."

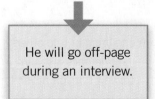

He will go off-page during an interview.

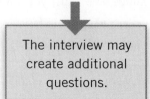

The interview may create additional questions.

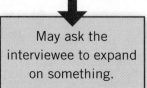

May ask the interviewee to expand on something.

3. Based on the clues, what is the meaning of **_provoke_**? _____

_____

Use word parts to find the meaning of **_creditor._**

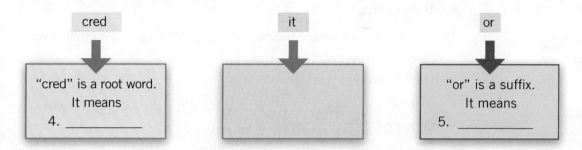

cred | it | or

"cred" is a root word.
It means
4. _____

"or" is a suffix.
It means
5. _____

Use context clues to find the meaning of **_creditor._**

"[If] there is a loud argument in the office of the company you are interviewing at stemming from a **_creditor_** who has not received payment for his product or services that were purchased by the company, you need to consider whether this company will be able to pay you," Rodrigues says.

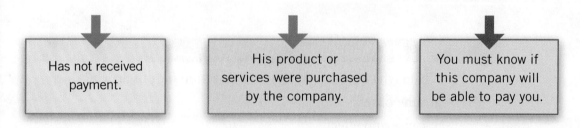

Has not received payment.

His product or services were purchased by the company.

You must know if this company will be able to pay you.

6. Based on the clues, what is the meaning of **_creditor_**? _____

_____

Main Idea

7–8. What is the central idea of the whole article?

_____

_____

_____

Supporting Details

Directions: Using the details in the article, circle **True** if the statement is correct or **False** if the statement is incorrect.

9. True or False:

   If the hiring manager complains that several people quit recently you should be concerned.

10. True or False:

    If the interviewer is frequently looking at the clock during the interview that is a good sign that they care about you.

11. If the interviewer takes a phone call mid-interview what might that mean?

    _____

    _____

    _____

    _____

Patterns of Organization

12. What is the overall pattern of organization for this article?
    a. time order
    b. cause and effect
    c. definition
    d. simple listing

13–15. What advice would you give to someone about to have an interview, based on this article?

    _____

    _____

    _____

    _____

    _____

READING 2

Cyber Considerations

The Internet has made it much easier to find and apply for jobs, communicate with potential employers, and network to improve your contacts and connections. However, it can be a potential hazard if it is not used appropriately and professionally. Most people are aware that posting messages, information, and photos can be risky—even dangerous—to your professional "health," but they may not be aware how much potential employers look for—and find—before they interview candidates online to see what kinds of information and images are out there. In some career fields, the more a candidate exposes (literally and figuratively) himself, the less likely he will get the job.

What can you do to protect yourself? Deleting your accounts is your best defense, but you can also change your account settings to private. Remember that material posted on the Internet is never completely deleted. In addition, be aware that if you have a large network of "friends," people who want to find out about you may still be able to do so. It is best not to post or put into writing anything that you think may be questionable to a potential employer, and if you have posted anything, delete it if you feel it may jeopardize your ability to get the job you want.

Source: "Cyber Considerations" from *The Community College Experience, Brief Edition,* 3rd Edition by Amy Baldwin. Copyright © 2012 by Amy Baldwin. Printed and Electronically reproduced by permission of Pearson Education, Inc., Upper Saddle River, New Jersey.

List a pattern of organization	Write the sentence(s) that show the pattern.
1.	3.
2.	4.

Directions: Use SQ3R to read the textbook selection on the next page.

Survey	Skim over the material. Read the title, subtitle, subheadings, first and last paragraphs, pictures, charts, and graphics. Note italics and bold print.
Question	Ask yourself questions before you read. What do you want to know? Turn headings and subheadings into questions and/or read questions if provided.
Read	Read the material in manageable chunks. This may be one or two paragraphs at a time or the material under one subheading.
Recite	Recite the answer to each question in your own words. This is a good time to write notes as you read each section. Repeat the question-read-recite cycle.
Review	Look over your notes at the end of the chapter, article, or material. Review what you learned and write a summary in your own words.

Use SQ3R to read the next textbook selection.

S—Survey

What are you going to be focusing on when you read this article?

_____

_____

NETWORKING

Diane Darling, in her book The Networking Survival Guide (2003), defines networking as "sharing of knowledge and contacts; getting the help you need when you need it from those from whom you need it ...; [and] building relationships before you need them" (p. 16). Now, even more than ever, networking is an essential part of staying connected with others, especially because social networking sites on the Internet have made it so easy (and addictive) for us to keep up with each other.

Networking Online

One of the largest trends in networking is using online websites such as LinkedIn and Facebook to create networks of friends, family, and special-interest groups. The possibilities seem endless as to how you can use the Internet to connect with others who have special interests and activities or problems to solve. With this said, if you decide to join a network that focuses on an interest of yours, such as autobody repair, be sure to investigate who runs the group, what kinds of information are shared, and how active the group is. Some networks will be more active than others, which will make it easier to connect with people and get involved; networks or groups that are less active won't help you if you are using them to get to know others as potential contacts in the future. Still others may not be legitimate. Because creating networks of your own is so easy, you may want to consider creating an interest group if you cannot find one that relates to the kind of job you want. Networking sites such as Facebook and LinkedIn allow you to set up groups that can be used for professional, educational, or social purposes.

Networking Face to Face

Another way to get to know others is to network with them face to face. Finding active groups who share similar interests may be easier than you think. Look to clubs on campus that share your interests. Even if they are not career related, such as drama club, you will meet people who may be future contacts for jobs. You can also get involved with your community through volunteer programs or civic groups such as your city's chamber of commerce. They may sponsor community-building, fundraising, and social events that allow you to meet other people in career fields that you are interested in. Additionally, involvement in such groups can provide you with more experience to record on your resume. The more people you get to know, the more likely you will be able to use those contacts when you need them—in finding a career or in anything else.

TECH TACTICS

Using Technology to Get Ahead

Numerous resources on the Internet can help you prepare for stepping out into the workforce. Video sites such as YouTube provide examples of interviewing techniques (and probably many examples of what not to do) that you can practice on your own; resume writing sites offer examples of winning resumes, and networking sites, especially the ones designed for professionally networking, can connect you with other people in your career field or your community.

Source: "Cyber Considerations" from *The Community College Experience, Brief Edition,* 3rd Edition by Amy Baldwin. Copyright © 2012 by Amy Baldwin. Printed and Electronically reproduced by permission of Pearson Education, Inc., Upper Saddle River, New Jersey.

Q—Questions (Turn the headings into questions and write them in the spaces provided)

R—Read (Read one section at a time)

R—Recite (Answer your questions as you read and write them in your own words in the spaces provided)

1. _____

_____

_____

A. _____

_____

2. _____

_____

_____

A. _____

_____

3. _____

_____

_____

A. _____

_____

4. _____

_____

_____

A. _____

_____

R—Review (Write a summary of the central idea)

_____

_____

_____

_____

Patterns of Organization

List 2 patterns of organization used in this reading? Give signal words of each pattern you list.

_____

_____

_____

_____

Literature **READING 3**

About the Author

Mawi Asgedom fled war-torn Ethiopia at age three. For the next three years he lived with his family in a Sudanese refugee camp and eventually immigrated to the United States at age seven. Growing up, he overcame language, cultural, and financial challenges and earned a full-tuition scholarship to Harvard University.

Mawi majored in American history and went on to win many honors at Harvard. His classmates elected him to be one of eight class marshals, and he delivered the commencement address at his graduation in 1999.

Now twenty-five years old, Mawi is a highly sought-after speaker of students, community groups, and businesses. He lives in Chicago, where he enjoys playing basketball, hanging out with his family, and listening to his favorite group, Ben Harper and the Innocent Criminals. Mawi maintains a Web site at www.mawispeaks.com.

Eyeing the Mountaintop

1   While schoolwork **consumed** most of my energy, I still loved basketball. I was thrilled when I made the freshman team.

2   But being on the team had its own challenges.

3   Often, especially on Saturdays, I couldn't get a ride to practice. So I would run the three miles. On the coldest days, I showed up unable to dribble because

my hands had become icicles. And on a few crazy days, I ran to practice, ran all throughout practice, then ran back home.

4   After the season ended, I decided to focus completely on schoolwork. I hadn't planned on joining the track team.

5   But one day after school, my basketball coach, Coach Kroger, saw me getting on the bus. It's funny how one word of encouragement can change your life.

6   "What are you doing going home, Mawi? You should be on the track team—you were always way up there in the wind sprints."

7   Several weeks later, I ran my first meet. By the end of the season, I was among the fastest freshmen in our conference.

8   I wanted good running shoes, but spending fifty dollars on a new pair was out of the question. So I wore a **raggedy** pair that my mom had **rustled up.** My track coach, Jim Martin, noticed almost immediately.

9   For each of the next four years, he paid for my training shoes and racing spikes. Sometimes he even took me shopping for school clothes—without telling anyone.

10   Even with such support from my coach, I made only **marginal** progress during my sophomore and junior years. So at the end of my junior year, I made myself a promise: That summer, I would run at least six days and lift weights every other day.

11   I did it, working during the day and training at night.

12   Again, my hard work paid big **dividends**. In cross-country, where four schools in our conference were ranked among the state's top twenty, I earned all-conference honors.

13   **Fueled** by my improvement during the cross-county season, I kept training throughout the **brutal** Illinois winter. I ran almost four hundred outdoor miles between November and January and lifted weights in my room every other day. Before I went to sleep each night, I recorded my mileage and weight training at the front of my journal.

14   The discipline brought results. In track, I ran the *anchor leg* on our all-state 4 x 800-meter relay team. We won our conference championship and competed in the state finals.

15   Looking back, I'm always thankful that Coach Kroger stopped me alongside that bus my freshman year.

Source: Asgedom, Mawi. (2002). *Of Beetles & Angels: A Boy's Remarkable Journey from a Refugee Camp to Harvard.* New York: Little, Brown, and Company, pp. 114–115.

Anchor leg—the last state of the competition

Vocabulary

Directions: Circle the letter of the best definition for the underlined word as it is used in the sentence. Use the context clues in the surrounding paragraph and/or the word parts to help you discover the meaning of the unknown word.

1. **consumed** (see paragraph 1)
   - a. used
   - b. made
   - c. burned
   - d. lost

2. **raggedy** (see paragraph 8)
   - a. new
   - b. old
   - c. stolen
   - d. borrowed

3. **rustled up** (see paragraph 8)
   - a. found
   - b. crackled
   - c. stolen
   - d. crunched

4. **marginal** (see paragraph 10)
   - a. on the side
   - b. crucial
   - c. minor
   - d. courageous

5. **dividends** (see paragraph 12)
   - a. money
   - b. results
   - c. honors
   - d. regrets

6. **fueled** (see paragraph 13)
   - a. heated
   - b. run
   - c. recorded
   - d. motivated

7. **brutal** (see paragraph 13)
   - a. harsh
   - b. mean
   - c. mild
   - d. easy

Main Idea Questions

8. What is the main idea in paragraph 13?
   - a. I recorded my mileage and weight training at the front of my journal.

b. I kept training throughout the brutal Illinois winter.

c. I ran almost four hundred outdoor miles between November and January.

d. I lifted weights in my room every other day.

Supporting Details

9–11. Circle the three supporting details in paragraph 13.

    a. I recorded my mileage and weight training at the front of my journal.

    b. I kept training throughout the brutal Illinois winter.

    c. I ran almost four hundred outdoor miles between November and January.

    d. I lifted weights in my room every other day.

12. What promise did the author make to himself in paragraph 10?

_____

_____

13. Why did he make that promise?

_____

_____

14. In paragraph 14, the author states, "The discipline brought results," in reference to high school sports. What details support this idea?

_____

_____

_____

Pattern of Organization

15. What are the organizational patterns used in this passage? List the patterns and the signal words that signal the patterns.

Organizational Pattern   **Signal Words**

_____   _____

_____   _____

_____   _____

Magazine/Periodical   **READING 4**

The following passages are part of an article in *Reader's Digest,* published July 2009. All three are about people who have used their job skills and life skills to help others and improve the world.

Best of America

What makes America great? From "freedom" to "cheese fries" and "Rocky Mountains" to "miniskirts," you had plenty to say on the subject. We have our picks, too, of the people, places, and ideas that typify the strength and spirit, the *goodness,* across our nation. On the following pages, you'll find fabulous foodstuffs, master craftsmen, inspiring individuals, and even a banker who *gives away* money. Meander around America with us as we celebrate 75 reasons to love our country.

Best Green Speed Demon

"Life is short. Race hard. Live green." Leilani Münter's motto sets her apart from the race-car pack, as does her champion status and distinction as one of her sport's few women. "You can care about the earth and love fast cars too," she says.

Source: "Best Green Speed Demon" from *Reader's Digest,* July 2009. Copyright © 2009 by The Reader's Digest Association, Inc. Reprinted with permission from Reader's Digest.

Münter, 33, who's both a stock-car and open-wheel driver, has made it her mission to "green" big-time auto racing—which, at 100 million strong, may have the most enthusiastic fan base on the planet. Her goals: renewable biofuels and recycled tires for the cars and recycling programs at the tracks. For doubters, she has a message: "Never underestimate a vegetarian hippie chick with a race car."

Not at 200 mph, certainly.

Münter raced horses as a kid in Minnesota. "I've gone from one horsepower to 800," she jokes. She studied biology at the University of California, San Diego, where after class she'd drift down to an old stock-car track and a friendly team owner who encouraged her to drive.

She began her racing career in 2001 and has racked up 28 top-ten finishes, Before every contest, **she buys an acre of rain forest** ($100 from the World Land Trust) to compensate for the 22 gallons of fuel she uses per race. She has also climbed a 252-foot windmill in Abilene; Texas, to push for alternative energies and spoken to the Cleantech conference in Washington, D.C.

If she wins her points on biofuels and recycling, she says, she'll pursue another dream: to speed around the track in an electric car, currently not allowed.

Crazy? "The people who are crazy enough to think they can change the world," she says, "are the ones who end up doing it."

1. What is the central idea of the *Best Green Speed Demon* article?

_____

_____

_____

2. In the *Best Green Speed Demon* article, the main pattern of organization is _____

_____

_____

3. What is the pattern of organization in this sentence?

> If she wins her points on biofuels and recycling she says, (then) she'll pursue another dream: to speed around the track in an electric car, currently not allowed.

_____

"If my grandfather knew how I had served my country, he would be filled with pride and love." —*Jerry Grodin*

Best Call to Duty

Why would a 52-year-old husband and father of three trade a private cardiology practice in Dallas for an Army medic tent in the Middle East? Jerry Grodin's family and friends were puzzled.

But for Grodin, it was always in the cards. He'd wanted to enlist since he was a boy, inspired by his grandfather, a Jewish immigrant from Poland who took in soldiers during World War II, and his father, who fought in that war. "I grew up believing that there is no purer citizen than the citizen soldier," Grodin says, "You have to do something bigger than yourself."

Medical school had kept him out of Vietnam, as had his young children during the Gulf War. Then came 9/11. "I thought, If I don't do this now, I'm never going to do it," says Grodin. In Iraq, over three tours of duty, he treated mass casualties as bombs exploded nearby—**saving limbs, hearts, and lives in 36-hour stints.**

Back home since January, he knows his father and grandfather were right. "The people I served with," Grodin says, "made me a better person."

6 WORDS IN PRAISE OF AMERICA (PART 1)

We asked our readers to give us the Reader's Digest Version of why they love the U.S.A. Some of our favorites:

- Pilgrims went West; donned swimsuits, shades. Sean Elder, Brooklyn, New York
- Miniskirts, high heels, and flowing hair. Heather McKim, Three Springs, Pennsylvania
- Boundaries are limitless; brains, more so. Christine Zibas, Rockford, Illinois
- Calamity strikes; like magnets, we bond. Virginia Mitchell, Johnson City, Tennessee
- I am living the American Dream! Tammy Norton, Bonaire, Georgia
- Freedom, opportunity, safety, and cheese fries. Stacy Melendez, Wichita Falls, Texas ∎

Use word parts to find the meaning of *cardiology*.

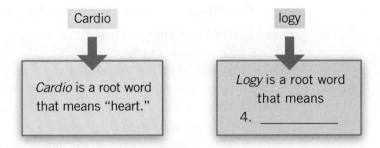

Cardio

Cardio is a root word that means "heart."

logy

Logy is a root word that means
4. _____

Use context clues to find the meaning of *cardiology*.

Why would a 52-year-old husband and father of three trade a private *cardiology* practice in Dallas for an Army medic tent in the Middle East? . . . In Iraq, over three years of duty, he treated mass casualties as bombs exploded nearby—saving limbs, hearts, and lives in 36-hour stints.

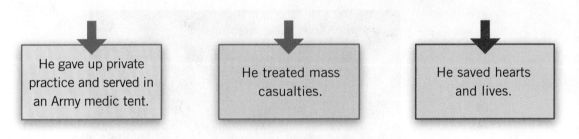

He gave up private practice and served in an Army medic tent.

He treated mass casualties.

He saved hearts and lives.

5. Based on the clues, what is the meaning of *cardiology*? _____

_____

6. What is the central idea of the *Best Call to Duty* article?

_____

_____

_____

Best Farmers' Friend

Three questions for Willie Nelson, singer, songwriter, and cofounder of Farm Aid, which has raised $33 million since 1985 to support independent farms. Nelson will headline the 22nd annual Farm Aid concert this fall.

- *If you could correct one misconception about family farmers, what would it be?*

  That they all live in the Midwest. Farmers are everywhere—urban, rural, and suburban—and they all need us to buy the food they grow, or they won't survive.

- *What was your reaction when you heard that the new White House chef, Sam Kass, is a big fan of using locally grown food?*

"Family farmers are a national resource. They're great Americans and true heroes." —*Willie Nelson*

I think it's wonderful that the Obamas are serving fresh, local farm food. But I'm looking beyond the White House. I'm looking for this administration to help ensure that everyone has access to fresh food—and that we have family farmers on the land to grow that food for us.

- *What can the average person do to support family farms?*

  Find farmers in your community and buy from them directly so there's no middleman. Take your kids to a farm so they won't think food comes out of a box. Tell your town's supermarkets and restaurants you want to eat food that's grown nearby, and let your local school know you want your kids to eat family-farm food. Tell your politicians too. We all need to work together.

Use word parts to find the meaning of ***misconception*** from paragraph 4.

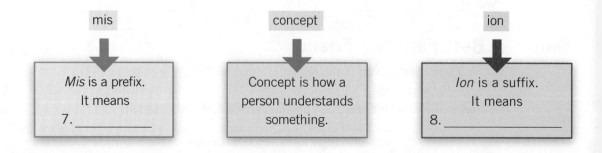

mis	concept	ion
Mis is a prefix. It means 7. _____	Concept is how a person understands something.	*Ion* is a suffix. It means 8. _____

Use context clues to find the meaning of ***misconception.***

> If you could correct one ***misconception*** about family farmers what would it be? "That they all live in the Midwest. Farmers are everywhere—urban, rural, and suburban, and they all need us to buy the food they grow or they won't survive."

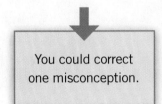

You could correct one misconception.

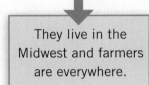

They live in the Midwest and farmers are everywhere.

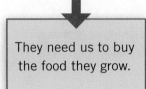

They need us to buy the food they grow.

9. Based on the word parts and context clues, what is the meaning of ***misconception***?

_____

10. Look in the dictionary or www.dictionary.com for the meaning of ***misconception*** as used in the reading.

_____

11. What is the main idea of the *Best Farmers' Friend* article?

_____

_____

_____

List five things you can do to support family farms according to the article:

12. _____

13. _____

14. _____

_____

15. _____

16. _____

17–20. Which person inspired you the most? Discuss the reasons why.

_____

_____

_____

_____

_____

Visual Images **READING 5**

Each of the following pictures represents body language that signals different patterns of attitude. Study the pictures and answer the questions that follow.

Body Language

This cluster can be summed up in one word—negative. The folder is used as a barrier and the arms and legs are folded due to nervousness or defensiveness. His coat is buttoned and his sunglasses hide any eye or pupil signals. Considering that people form 90 percent of their opinion of someone in the first four minutes, it's unlikely that this man will ever get to first base with another person.

1. Describe a time you have seen someone with one or more of the body language patterns shown above. What physical clues let you know the person is negative? Use one or more patterns of organization and signal words in your description.

_____

_____

_____

_____

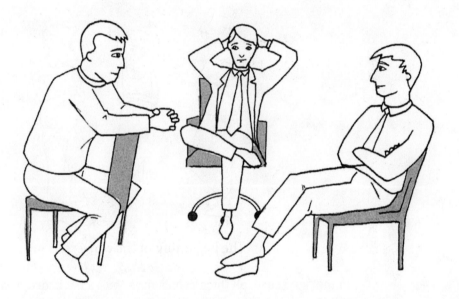

The man on the left is straddling his chair in an attempt to take control of the discussion or to dominate the man on the right. He is also pointing his body directly at the man on the right. He has clenched fingers and his feet are locked together under his chair, showing a frustrated attitude, which means that he's probably having difficulty getting his point across. The man in the center feels superior to the other two because of the Catapult gesture he is using. He also had the Figure Four leg position, indicating that he could be competitive or argumentative. He has a high-status chair that swivels, leans back, and has wheels and armrests. The man on the right is seated on a low-status chair that had fixed legs and no accessories. His arms and legs are tightly crossed (defensive) and his head is down (hostile), body pointing away (disinterest), indicating that he doesn't like what he hears.

2. Describe a time you have seen people with some of the body language behaviors shown above. Use one or more patterns of organization and signal words in your description.

_____

_____

_____

_____

The following three scenes demonstrate typical defense, aggression, and courtship clusters.

The beginning of the conversation

In the first scene, all three people have their arms folded, two have their legs crossed (defensive), and all have their bodies oriented away from each other, all indicating that they may have just met for the first time. The man on the right appears interested in the woman as he has his right foot twisted around to point at her and he is giving her a sideways glance, combined with raised eyebrows (interest) and a smile; he is leaning toward her with the upper part of his body. She is closed off to both men at this point.

3. Have you seen people interact like those in the picture above? Describe what you observed. Use one or more patterns of organization and signal words in your description.

_____

_____

_____

_____

Five minutes later

The woman has now uncrossed her legs and is standing in the Attention Position, while the man on the left has uncrossed his legs and is pointing one foot at her (interest) and leaning toward her. He is using the Thumbs-in-Belt gesture, which is either intended as a competitive display toward the other man, in which case the attitude is aggression, or is directed toward the woman, making it a sexual display. He is also standing straighter to make himself appear bigger. The man on the right seems intimidated by the other man, as seen by his now more erect stance, his crossed arms, and the fact that he is giving the other man a sideways glance combined with eyebrows down (disapproval) and his smile has gone.

4. Have you seen people interact like those in the picture above? Use one or more patterns of organization and signal words in your description.

_____

_____

_____

_____

Fifteen minutes later

The attitudes and emotions of these people are now clearly shown by their body language. The man on the left has kept his Thumbs-in-Belt, Foot-Forward Position and has turned his body more toward the woman, making it a complete courtship display. His thumbs are also gripping his belt much tighter to make the gesture more noticeable and his body has become even more erect. The woman is responding to this courtship display with her own, showing that she is interested in being involved with him. She has uncrossed her arms, turned her body toward him, and is pointing one foot at him. Her courtship gestures include hair touching, exposed wrists, chest forward to show cleavage, and positive facial expression, and she is blowing her cigarette smoke upward (confidence). The man on the right is unhappy about being excluded and is using the Hands-on-Hips gesture (aggressive readiness) and standing Crotch Display to show his displeasure.

In summary, the man on the left has won the woman's attentions and the other man should take a hike in the Himalayas.

Source: Pease, Allan and Barbara Pease. (2004). *The Definitive Book of Body Language.* New York: Bantam, pp. 367, 368, 374–376.

5. Have you seen people interact like those in the picture above? What is the final outcome of the interaction? Use one or more patterns of organization and signal words in your description.

_____

_____

_____

_____

_____

8 Facts and Opinions

LEARNING OUTCOMES

LO1 Determine how to identify facts and opinions.

LO2 Separate facts from opinions in persuasive text.

THEME – Staying Current

SPOTLIGHT ON LEARNING STYLES ✎ WRITE

Reading what others write is a great way to stay current. With Internet news, newspapers, magazines and other written information, there is more than enough to keep me informed about what is going on. The more I read about a subject, though, the more conflicting information I discover. I am constantly trying to figure out what to believe. This is especially true on the Internet. Anyone can create a Web site or change Wikipedia. So this means I have to be really careful about what I read, and I often compare multiple sources of written information before I make decisions. This takes more time, but if it is important enough to research, then it is worth my time to find accurate information.

Facts and opinions are both used to support an author's point or main idea. In this chapter you will learn to:

- distinguish the difference between a fact and an opinion.
- use facts and opinions while exploring numerous ways of staying current with topics and issues in the world.

How to Identify Facts and Opinions

How do I know if what I read is a **fact**? A *fact* is information that can be proven or verified through evidence.

> **LO1**
> Determine how to identify facts and opinions.

Here are some examples of facts:

- By the end of 2000, Google had indexed one billion Web pages.
- Steve Jobs launched Apple's iTunes application in January 2001.
- Within seven years, iPod owners had purchased and downloaded five billion songs.
- That same January, Jimmy Wales and Larry Sanger launched Wikipedia.

Source: Auletta, Ken. (2009). *Googled: The End of the World as We Know It.* New York: Penguin, pp. 65–66.

These facts can be checked for accuracy through researching other materials and sources.

How do I know if what I am reading is an **opinion**? An opinion cannot be proven and is someone's belief or perspective. Opinions may use judgmental words such as *easy, difficult, cheap, expensive, beautiful, ugly, adequate, inadequate,* etc. Opinions may suggest one solution to a complex issue or present the issue from one side or perspective. *Note:* This does not mean the opinion is necessarily bad or good, but that it is a personal view rather than a fact.

Here are some examples of opinions:

- The Internet was *growing and changing at warp speed*.
- January 2001 brought two innovations that *profoundly disrupted* the *existing order*.
- Wikipedia and iTunes were reminders, *as if any were needed*, that we had *entered the dawn of a new digital democracy* that granted more power to individuals.

Source: Auletta, Ken (2009). *Googled: The End of the World as We Know It.* New York: Penguin, pp. 65–66.

Note the words in *italics*. These indicate opinions and cannot be proven.

Essays often use a mixture of facts and opinions. The writer chooses which facts to use to support her opinion. You might form or alter your own opinion based on which facts you read. As a reader, you will learn to decide for yourself what you believe as you become more skilled at separating the facts from the opinions.

- *Already reeling* from piracy, the <u>big four music companies</u> *felt compelled* to <u>allow individual songs</u> to be <u>sold at a price Apple chose</u> (<u>ninety-nine cents</u>), *inevitably undermining* the sale of entire CDs, the centerpiece of their business model.

In the above example, the opinions are in italics. The facts are underlined. The facts can be proven.

EXAMPLE

Directions: Read the statements and write **F** for a fact and **O** for an opinion. If the statement contains both a fact and an opinion, write **F/O** and identify each one.

_____ **1.** It is easy to get information online.

_____ **2.** Checking news sources every day is one way to stay current.

_____ **3.** Students can use library databases to find better information than on the Internet.

Statement 1 is **O** or opinion because *easy* is a judgment. One person may believe it is easy, but another may find it difficult to find information online. Also, the information a person is seeking may affect how easy or difficult it is to get information online. Statement 2 is **F** or a fact. Checking news sources every day is one of the ways a person can stay current. Statement 3 is **F/O** because the sentence contains both a fact and an opinion. The word *better* is a judgment; therefore, the second part of the sentence is opinion. Whether or not students can use the library database can be verified, making the first part of the sentence a fact.

PRACTICE THE NEW SKILL

Directions: Read the statements and write **F** for a fact and **O** for an opinion. If the statement contains both a fact and an opinion write **F/O** and identify each one.

PRACTICE 1

_____ Brin and Page foresee Google users having vast *repositories* of fresh information, some of it public and some private, which is not currently available on the Internet.

_____ This *encompasses* motion pictures, television, and radio programs; still images and text; phone calls and other voice communications; educational materials; and data from space.

_____

Repositories—storehouse, storage area
Encompasses—includes

_____ The pair is also involved in the hunt for clean, renewable energy sources to power Google and broaden economic growth.

Source: Vise, David A. and Mark Malseed. (2005). *The Google Story.* New York: Bantam Dell, p. 282.

PRACTICE 2

_____ The *Net Generation* knows to be skeptical whenever they're online.

_____ When *baby boomers* were young, a picture was a picture; it documented reality.

_____ "Trust but verify" would be an apt motto for today's youth.

Source: Tapscott, Don. (2009). *Grown Up Digital: How the Net Generation is Changing Your World.* New York: McGraw-Hill, p. 80.

PRACTICE 3

_____ When you purchase something that already exists, you're saving natural resources and all the energy used to mine or harvest them, to ship them to a manufacturing facility, to transform those raw resources into finished goods, then to transport those finished goods to warehouses and retail stores.

Net Generation—people born between 1977 and 1997; this generation has grown up digital, also called the *Millennials or Generation Y*, 81.1 million children or 27 percent of the U.S. population.

Baby boomers—people born 1946–1964, TV generation, 77.2 million children or 23 percent of the U.S. population.

_____ So, what do I mean by *recycled clothing*? I mean preowned clothes and also clothing made from recycled materials.

_____ You can find preowned clothing—and shoes—in all sorts of stores and in all sorts of styles. Thrift shops, flea markets, and swap meets are great sources of inexpensive clothing that isn't ready for a landfill—it's ready for a new life in *your* closet.

_____ When you buy recycled clothing and shoes and purses, you're keeping all of these items out of landfills *and* you're reducing energy use and the use of natural resources.

Source: Begley, Ed Jr. (2008). *Living Like Ed: A Guide to the Eco-friendly Life.* New York: Clarkson Potter/Publishers, pp. 202–203.

Your Facts and Opinions

One way to help you see the difference between facts and opinions is to write your own. Think about the topic of the BP oil spill in the Gulf of Mexico. Consider things you've read, watched, heard, or experienced.

PRACTICE

Directions: Write three facts about the BP oil spill in the Gulf of Mexico. (Hint: the facts do not have to come from a governmental report, but you must be able to verify what you call a fact.)

- _____
- _____
- _____

Directions: Write three opinions about the BP oil spill in the Gulf of Mexico. (Hint: words like *should* or *shouldn't, difficult, easy, expensive, horrible,* etc. may be used for opinions.)

- _____
- _____
- _____

In the exercise above, which was easier to write? Why?

_____

_____

_____

How to Separate Facts from Opinions in Persuasive Text

When an author is trying to persuade the reader to take some action or adopt a certain perspective on an issue, there are various techniques that might be used. One technique is to select only

> **LO2**
> Separate facts from opinions in persuasive text.

facts that support your point of view and ignore the opposing facts. You may notice that you are only getting "one side of the story." For example, years ago I was teaching a college reading class and asked my students to read a popular news magazine article about gun control. We noticed the "news report" only included the problems with losing freedom and rights. Several students were hunters, and they initially saw no problem with the article. But, after closer examination, we detected a one-sided perspective with only a pro-freedom argument from the National Rifle Association. The other side of the issue was not presented in the "news" article.

When the author uses words that indicate judgment or value, an opinion is generally being offered. It is important to notice these words because your interpretation may vary from what the author or speaker intended.

For example, just after I graduated from college and moved to Indianapolis, my husband's new coworker recommended that we try a "great seafood restaurant." When my husband asked if it was expensive, the coworker said, "No, it's pretty cheap." We took his recommendation and went to dinner to the seafood buffet that Friday night. When we received our bill, the price for two people (with water to drink) was more than the cash we had between us; it was much more than what we considered "cheap." Since we did not have our first paychecks yet and we had no credit cards, we had to go out to the car to look for change on the floor and between the seats! We found enough to pay the bill that night, but then had to eat a package of bologna and loaf of bread the rest of the week until we received our paychecks! I learned that my perspective of *expensive* and *cheap* was very different from that of this man, who worked at the aerospace firm. I also learned to be careful when people use judgment or value words rather than specific facts.

Some value or judgment **"Words to Watch"** indicating opinions include:

large	a little	long	light
small	a lot	short	heavy
expensive	weak	beautiful	easy
cheap	strong	ugly	difficult

What other value or judgment words can you add to this list?

_____   _____   _____   _____

_____   _____   _____   _____

_____   _____   _____   _____

Also beware of authors who use terms such as *all, most* or *none.* Carefully assess whether "all" people or "most" scientists agree. Sometimes authors use these types of terms to exaggerate the severity of an issue in order to persuade the reader.

Consider the author's use of facts and opinions, and do not be afraid to question the information. A good reader will:

- watch to see if the author is supporting his claim with reasonable and credible information
- consider changing his or her position on an important issue only after the facts and opinions are clear and reliable

EXAMPLE ───────────────────────────────────────

Directions: Read the following paragraph. Then, list the opinions and facts.

Pay as You Throw

The amazing truth is that, depending on where you live, 75 to 90 percent of your waste can be recycled. Things that can't be collected through curbside recycling—such as electronics, paints, and batteries—may still be recyclable at a local drop-off center.

Recycling is a special responsibility here in America, where we produce more than a *third* of the world's garbage: 4.5 pounds of trash per person every day. More than half of it ends up in landfills, where it emits more methane—a greenhouse gas—than any other source. Eventually, those landfills leak toxic materials into the surrounding soil and water.

Luckily, there's a new trend known as pay-as-you-throw (PAYT). PAYT programs charge residents a fee (between $1 and $2) for each bag or can of waste. So garbage collection gets treated like electricity, gas, and other utilities—you pay for what you use. It's a great incentive to recycle more, compost more, and buy items with less packaging—and save money.

Source: Bach, David with Hillary Rosner. (2008). *Go Green, Live Rich: 50 Simple Ways to Save the Earth and Get Rich Trying.* New York: Broadway Books, p. 92.

Opinions:

- The amazing truth
- may still be
- is a special responsibility
- Luckily, there's a new trend
- a great incentive to recycle more, compost more, and buy items with less packaging—and save money

Facts:

- 75 to 90 percent of your waste can be recycled
- Things that can't be collected through curbside recycling—such as electronics, paints, and batteries
- we produce more than a *third* of the world's garbage: 4.5 pounds of trash per person every day

- More than half of it ends up in landfills, where it emits more methane—a greenhouse gas—than any other source
- landfills leak toxic materials into the surrounding soil and water
- PAYT programs charge residents a fee (between $1 and $2) for each bag or can of waste
- garbage collection gets treated like electricity, gas, and other utilities—you pay for what you use

PRACTICE THE NEW SKILL

Directions: Read the following passages. Then, list the opinions and the facts.

PRACTICE 1

Today, we're bombarded with more information, more data, more decisions, and more options than ever before. The benefits of these things are obvious; the detriments to our society may not be. Our wireless world is good for business and helps families far-flung stay in touch, but being connected 24/7 via BlackBerrys and the Internet isn't always healthy. It makes us feel we need to be in touch and plugged in at all times, leaving us feeling anxious when we actually have to turn off our electronic devices. The other downside to technology is that it has conditioned us to want everything in seconds, and when that doesn't happen we feel stressed. Admit it, when your computer takes minutes rather than seconds to download a file you get irritated, and when your supermarket's express line is slow, your heart rate quickens.

Source: McGraw, Phillip. (2008). *Real Life: Preparing for the 7 Most Challenging Days of Your Life*. New York: Free Press, p. 46.

ENGLISH 2.0

Bombarded means: you feel overwhelmed with the things you have to deal with
Families far-flung means: family members who live far apart from each other
Be in touch and plugged in means: check frequently and communicate with others using electronic media such as Internet and cell phones

FACTS	OPINIONS

PRACTICE 2

The world has been Googled. We don't search for information, we "Google" it. Type a question in the Google search box, as do more than 70 percent of all searchers worldwide, and in about a half second answers appear. Want to find an episode of *Charlie Rose* you missed, or a funny video made by some guy of his three-year-old daughter's brilliant ninety-second synopsis of *Star Wars: Episode IV*? Google's YouTube, with ninety million unique visitors in March 2009—two–thirds of all Web video traffic—has it.

Source: Auletta, Ken. (2009). *Googled: The End of the World as We Know It*. New York: Penguin Press, preface.

FACTS	OPINIONS

PRACTICE 3

When it comes to the current culture of eating, we're accustomed to getting what we want when we want it. This can mean blackberries in the Northeast in January, or a prime rib meal in six minutes courtesy of our microwaves. But convenience has a price. It takes an enormous amount of fossil fuel to package, ship, and store out-of-season fruit for consumers. A litany of chemicals is used to preserve frozen convenience meals, none of which enhance the product's health benefits. Add to this our dependence on fast food, and you're talking about a culture whose eating habits leave a lot to be desired. Shifting to a more eco-friendly diet, buying food locally, and eating in season not only can drastically change the way we look and feel personally, but also can change the way we look and feel about food in the context of environmental responsibility.

Source: Coronato, Helen. (2008). *Eco-friendly Families: Guide Your Family to Greener Living with Activities that Engage and Inspire . . . from Toddlers to Teens.* New York: Alpha, pp. 133–134.

ENGLISH 2.0

Litany of chemicals means: a long list of chemicals

Leave a lot to be desired means: are not very good

Eco-friendly diet means: diet which is better for the environment; "eco" is an abbreviation for "ecology," which means study of the environment

FACTS	OPINIONS

REVIEW *WHAT YOU LEARNED*

Facts and Opinions

Compared to California produce, Australian oranges brought to the United States yield 44 times more particulate matter and 6 times more global warming impact; Thai rice has 22 times more particulates and 3 times more impact; tomatoes from the Netherlands bring 2 times more particulates and 500 times more impact; and wine from France pours out 29 times more particulate matter and 5 times more global warming impact.

Produce isn't the only foodstuff making the rounds. According to the *New York Times,* weird things like waffles and bottled water cross oceans, from one industrialized nation to another, churning up a vortex of carbon emissions in their transport. Without fuel taxes on shippers, these goods arrive at irresistibly cheap prices, even more affordable than local items, though efforts are being made in Europe to change this. Few people realize, too, that some organic foods sold everywhere from Wal-Mart to Whole Foods Markets are born and raised in China, where enforceable standards are questionable, water and air quality can be hazardous, and the distance is literally halfway across the globe. Without country of origin labeling, it's hard to tell where your food comes from, even if it's sold as organic.

Source: Heyhoe, Kate. (2009). *Cooking Green: Reducing Your Carbon Footprint in the Kitchen—the New Green Basics Way.* Cambridge, MA: Da Capo Press, pp. 112–113.

Directions: Complete the chart with facts and opinions using the article above.

FACTS	OPINIONS

<table>
<tr><td></td><td></td></tr>
<tr><td></td><td></td></tr>
</table>

REVIEW WHAT YOU LEARNED

More from Google

Google Alerts: find new stuff as it's written

Google Alerts offers a free and reliable way to keep track of a particular topic, story or person on the Web. Simply enter your search terms and whenever they appear in a new or updated webpage, you'll receive an email with a link to the page. Other similar services include TracerLock.

Google Alerts www.google.com/alerts
TracerLock www.tracerlock.com

Google Answers

If, even after you've honed your Web search skills, you still can't locate an answer to that burning question, you could always turn to someone else for help. First, try posting a question to a relevant online forum or try AllExperts—where volunteers advise people on their areas of expertise for free. Still no luck? You could try Google's pay-to-use Answers service. For between $2 and $200, an "expert" researcher will do the hard work for you and present you with a detailed response.

AllExperts www.allexperts.com

Google Answers answers.google.com

Source: Buckley, Peter and Duncan Clark. (2007). *Rough Guide to the Internet.*
New York: Penguin Group, pp. 100–101.

Directions: Complete the chart with facts and opinions using the article above.

FACTS	OPINIONS

RSS feeds

Choose your own news

One of the greatest things to happen to the Web in recent years has been the massive growth of RSS—short for Really Simple Syndication. RSS allows you to view "feeds" or "newsfeeds" from blogs, news services and other websites. Each feed consists of headlines of new or updated articles, along with the full text or a summary or extract. If you see something that you'd like to read, click on the headline to view the full story.

One benefit of RSS is that it saves you regularly visiting your favourite sites to check for new content: if something's been added or changed, you'll always know about it. But the real beauty of the system is that you can use a tool called an **aggregator** or **feed reader** to combine the feeds from all your favourite sites. It's almost like having your own personalized magazine or newspaper.

Source: Buckley, Peter and Duncan Clark. (2007). *Rough Guide to the Internet.* New York, NY: Penguin Group, p. 102.

Directions: Complete the chart with facts and opinions using the article above.

FACTS	OPINIONS

Fact vs. Opinion

Sorting Your Inbox Can Be a Huge Chore

1   The creation of the Internet is having a greater effect on communications than anything else in history.

2   We can instantly send e-mails to people in China and Australia. We can read today's newspapers in Moscow, if we can understand Russian. The whole world is at our fingertips.

3   When the Internet was just getting started, some people believed it would lead to a Great Age of Communication. But it hasn't happened.

4   What we have right now is the Great Age of Miscommunication.

5   The good and bad thing about the Internet is that it's unfiltered.

6   The result is, we get a lot of e-mails every day making all kinds of accusations and claims and it's up to us to sort out truth from fiction.

7   Basically, if it's something we want to believe, we say, "Yeah! That's the truth." If we don't like it, we hit "delete."

8   I've decided to start sending out my own e-mails making various claims.

9   Here's the kind of e-mail I'm going to send: "You need to pass this on to all your friends because they need to know about it. Studies have now proved absolutely that men who do housework are 50 times more likely to develop severe fatigue syndrome than husbands who sit in reclining chairs watching football games all weekend."

10   I might put my wife on that e-mail list.

11   Or how about this: "I know you're not going to believe this and I didn't when I first read it either. But it's absolutely true. Scientific studies have proven that eating Fannie Mae caramel turtles three times a day will add five years to your life."

12   Why doesn't anyone ever send me an e-mail like that?

13   Here's another one I think I'll send out: "I always suspected that this was going to happen, but now I know for certain that it's true. Newly found 16th century writings reveal that more than 400 years ago Nostradamus prophesized that a pack of cubs in an area now known as Chicago would be unhappy for 200 consecutive years!"

14   Of course, it's silly to think we can get accurate information from e-mails. I pay no attention to them.

15   I get all my information from talk radio.

Source: Norberg, John. (September 27, 2009.) Sorting Your Inbox Can Be a Huge Chore.
My Life. *Journal & Courier*, D1.

Directions: Complete the chart with facts and opinions using the article above.

FACTS	OPINIONS

Fact vs. Opinion

Nike Uses Old Magazines For New Shoes

1   Print media isn't dead; it's at least getting new life as shoes—of all things—thanks to Nike.

2   The Premium Print Pack, made from magazines, is part of a long line of recycling initiatives from Nike.

3   The Nike Premium Print Pack, which features The Blazer, Air Rift and Flash Macro woman's styles, uses strips of recycled magazines to create a unique design on each shoe.

4   Besides looking downright awesome, the shoes are treated so that they remain water-resistant and durable.

5   This isn't the Nike's first foray into recycling efforts. Nike has been recovering old athletic shoes for decades. The Reuse-a-Shoe program, started in the early 1990s, collects and processes shoes into Nike Grind, which is then used to create parts of playgrounds as well as other Nike products.

6   Nike has recycled 24 million pairs of shoes thus far and lets you bring up to 10 athletic shoes, even if they're not Nike brand, to any Nike retail store for collection.

7   The recycled-magazine shoes debuted in limited quantities on January 1 in European and Asian markets, and may eventually become available in the U.S. So, even though you may never get your hands on them, kudos to Nike for embracing innovation, slick design and more importantly, recycling.

Source: Dobransky, Megan. *Nike Uses Old Magazines for New Shoes.* Published on January 5th, 2011. Retrieved from http://earth911.com/news/2011/01/05/ nike-uses-old-magazines-for-new-shoes/

Directions: Complete the chart with facts and opinions from the reading above.

FACTS	OPINIONS

LEARNING STYLE ACTIVITIES

*L*OOK, *L*ISTEN, *W*RITE, *D*O

Form a small group with your classmates and complete one of the Learning Style activities below. Remember, you may choose to use your preferred learning style or you may work outside of your "comfort zone" to help you develop one of the other styles. As you work with your group, think about how you will present the results to the class.

👁 *L*OOK   Read the article. Search the Internet or periodicals or use your camera to find images of examples discussed in the article. Create a poster or PowerPoint presentation with the most interesting information.

🔊 *L*ISTEN   Read the article out loud. Pause at each subheading and then put what you hear into your own words. Talk to someone who is a member of one of the religions mentioned in the article. Ask the person their perceptions. Prepare a speech with the most interesting information to share with your class.

✎ *W*RITE   Read the article. Take notes and create a formal or informal outline with the most important information. Write a summary of the useful information. Or write a letter to a person from a religion different from your own. In the letter, address your concern for their issues of terrorism as discussed in the article.

✋ *D*O   Read the article. Find someone from one of the religions mentioned in the article. Talk to the person and ask them about their experiences. Report your findings to the class.

Religious Terrorism

A Short Primer on Religion and Terrorism

The world's great religions all have both peaceful and violent messages from which believers can choose. Religious terrorists and violent extremists share the decision to interpret religion to justify violence, whether they are Buddhist, Christian, Hindu, Jewish, Muslim, or Sikh.

Buddhism and Terrorism

Buddhism is a religion or approach to an enlightened life based on the teachings of the Buddha Siddhartha Gautama twenty-five centuries ago in northern India. The edict not to kill or inflict pain on others is integral to Buddhist thought. Periodically, however, Buddhist monks have encouraged violence or initiated it. The primary example in the 20th and 21st century is in Sri Lanka, where Sinhala Buddhist groups have committed and encouraged violence against local Christians and Tamils. The leader of Aum Shinrikyo, a Japanese cult that committed a lethal sarin gas attack in the mid-1990s, drew on Buddhist as well as Hindu ideas to justify his beliefs.

Christianity and Terrorism

Christianity is a monotheistic religion centered on the teachings of Jesus of Nazareth, whose resurrection, as understood by Christians, provided salvation for all mankind. Christianity's teachings, like those of other religions, contain messages of love and peace, and those that can be used to justify violence. The 15th century Spanish inquisition is sometimes considered an early form of state terrorism. These Church-sanctioned tribunals aimed to root out Jews and Muslims who had not converted to Catholicism, often through severe torture. Today in the United States, reconstruction theology and the Christian Identity movement have provided justification for attacks on abortion providers.

Hinduism and Terrorism

Hinduism, the world's third largest religion after Christianity and Islam, and the oldest, takes many forms in practice among its adherents. Hinduism valorizes non-violence as a virtue, but advocates war when it is necessary in the face of injustice. A fellow Hindu assassinated Mohandas Gandhi, whose non-violent resistance helped bring about Indian independence, in 1948. Violence between Hindus and Muslims in India has been endemic since then. However, the role of nationalism is inextricable from Hindu violence in this context.

Islam and Terrorism

Adherents of Islam describe themselves as believing in the same Abrahamic God as Jews and Christians, whose instructions to humankind were perfected when delivered to the last prophet, Muhammad. Like those of Judaism and Christianity, Islam's texts offer both peaceful and warring messages. Many consider the 11th century "hashishiyin," to be Islam's first terrorists. These members of a Shiite sect assassinated their Saljuq enemies. In the late 20th century, groups motivated by religious and nationalist goals committed attacks, such as the assassination of Egyptian president Anwar Sadat, and suicide bombings in Israel. In the early 21st century, al-Qaeda "internationalized" jihad to attack targets in Europe and the United States.

Judaism and Terrorism

Judaism began around 2000 BCE when, according to Jews, God established a special covenant with Abraham. The monotheistic religion focuses on the importance of action as an expression of belief. Judaism's central tenets involve a respect for life's sanctity, but like other religions, its texts can be used to justify violence. Some consider the Sicarii, who used murder by dagger to protest Roman rule in first century Judea, to be the first Jewish terrorists. In the 1940s, Zionist militants such as Lehi (known also as the Stern Gang) carried out terrorist attacks against the British in Palestine. In the late 20th century, militant messianic Zionists use religious claims to the historical land of Israel to justify acts of violence.

Source: Zalman, Amy Ph.D., from about.com Guide http://terrorism.about .com/od/politicalislamterrorism/tp/Religious-terrorism.htm

Reading Practice

The following readings are related to the theme of staying current and come from a variety of sources: the Internet, textbooks, literature, magazines, and visual images. They were chosen not only to help you improve your ability to distinguish facts from opinions but also to continue to build your other reading skills of learning vocabulary, locating main ideas and supporting details, and understanding implied main ideas and organizational patterns. The diverse readings were also selected to give you the opportunity to think about and comprehend ideas that are important in our society today.

The first reading is "U.S. Army Dips a Toe in Wind Power Waters" from *ScientificAmerican.com*.

The second reading is "Gay and Lesbian Couples" from the textbook *Society: The Basics,* by John Macionis.

The third reading is from a piece of literature titled "Don't Eat Anything Your Great Grandmother Wouldn't Recognize as Food" from *In Defense of Food: An Eater's Manifesto* by Michael Pollan.

The fourth reading is a newspaper editorial called "Don't Blame Ronald for Kids' Weight."

The fifth reading is a visual image related to a farmer's market.

READING 1

U.S. Army Dips a Toe in Wind Power Waters

1   The U.S. Army has just flipped the switch on its first wind power project, a single wind turbine at the Tooele Army Depot in Utah. That might sound like small potatoes but it's a giant step forward for the U.S. military, which has been cautious about wind power primarily due to concerns over radar interference. The installation took more than five years to come to fruition, starting with an approval process in 2005.

2   Though the military has been *reticent* about wind power, it has been surging into a clean energy future on other fronts. For the past several years it has been moving rapidly to convert its operations to other forms of renewable energy such as solar and **geothermal.** That comes along with an aggressive push for energy conservation and biofuels, too, as well reducing the use of toxic chemicals and preserving habitats on Department of Defense lands.

TOOELE ARMY DEPOT, WIND POWER, AND SOLAR POWER

3   Tooele provides a pretty good illustration of the variety of future-oriented energy tactics that the military is pursuing at its many facilities. The single wind power turbine alone is expected to generate 1.5 megawatts annually, saving more than $200,000 in current electricity costs. Tooele is also installing passive solar heating walls on 11 buildings, and these perforated metal sheets are expected to save about $100,000 annually in heating costs. Meanwhile, last year the base won an award for a water conservation program that reduced usage by almost 100 million gallons annually.

ENERGY INDEPENDENCE FOR THE U.S. MILITARY

4   With the solar and wind installations, along with other conservation efforts, Tooele is already within shouting distance of 7.5% reliance on renewable energy, a federal goal that kicks in two years from now in 2013. The depot's energy manager isn't stopping there. He envisions more turbines, geothermal power, and other measures to make the base completely energy independent and self sustaining. As for drill baby drill, that's nowhere in the picture.

Source: Casey, Tina. (July 18, 2010). U.S. Army Dips a Toe in Wind Power Waters. *Scientific American.* Retrieved from http://www.scientificamerican.com/article.cfm?id=us-army-dips-a-toe-in-wind-power-wa-2010-07

Reticent–silent

Vocabulary

Use word parts to determine the meaning of the word *geothermal*.

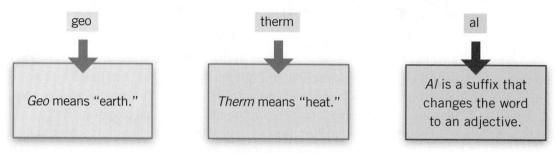

geo

therm

al

Geo means "earth."

Therm means "heat."

Al is a suffix that changes the word to an adjective.

Using the word parts, *geothermal* means _____

_____

Directions: Complete the chart with facts and opinions from the reading above.

FACTS	OPINIONS

What is the author's central idea?

_____

_____

_____

What details provide support?

_____

_____

_____

_____

Gay and Lesbian Couples

1   In 1989, Denmark became the first country to permit registered partnerships with the benefits of marriage for same-sex couples. Since then, more than fifteen countries, including Norway (1993), Sweden (1994), Iceland (1996), Finland (2001), the United Kingdom (2004), and Australia (2008) have followed suit. However, only seven countries have extended marriage—in name as well as in practice—to same-sex couples: the Netherlands (2001), Belgium (2003), Canada (2005), Spain (2005), South Africa (2006), Norway (2008), and Sweden (2009).

2   In the United States, Massachusetts became the first state to legalize same-sex marriage in 2004. As of 2010, Iowa, Vermont, Connecticut, New Hampshire, and the District of Columbia have also changed their laws to allow same-sex marriage.

New Jersey, California, Oregon, and Nevada permit same-sex civil unions or domestic partnerships with nearly all the rights of marriage.

3   Back in 1996, Congress passed a law defining marriage as joining one man and one woman. Since then, a total of thirty states have amended their constitutions to permit marriage only between one man and one woman. Nonetheless, the trend in public opinion is toward greater acceptance of same-sex marriage. Currently, more than one-third of U.S. adults support gay marriage, and over half support civil unions providing the rights enjoyed by married couples (Newport, 2005; NORC, 2009: 1712; Pew Research Center, 2009).

4   Most gay couples with children in the United States are raising the offspring of previous heterosexual unions; others have adopted children. But many gay parents are quiet about their sexual orientation, not wanting to draw unwelcome attention to their children or to themselves. In several widely publicized cases, courts have removed children from the custody of homosexual couples, citing the "best interests" of the children.

5   Gay parenting challenges many traditional ideas. But it also shows that many gay couples value family life as highly as heterosexuals do.

Source: Macionis, John J. (2011). From "Chapter 13: Family and Religion, Alternative Families," *Society: The Basics,* 11th edition. Upper Saddle River, NJ: Pearson, p. 383.

Questions

Directions: Write **F** if the sentence is a fact, **O** if it is an opinion, or **F/O** if the sentence contains both fact and opinion.

_____ **1.** In 1989, Denmark became the first country to permit registered partnerships with the benefits of marriage for same-sex couples.

_____ **2.** New Jersey, California, Oregon, and Nevada permit same-sex civil unions or domestic partnerships with nearly all the rights of marriage.

_____ **3.** Since then, a total of thirty states have amended their constitutions to permit marriage only between one man and one woman.

_____ **4.** Nonetheless, the trend in public opinion is toward greater acceptance of same-sex marriage.

_____ **5.** Currently, more than one-third of U.S. adults support gay marriage, and over half support civil unions providing the rights enjoyed by married couples (Newport, 2005; NORC, 2009: 1712; Pew Research Center, 2009).

_____ **6.** Most gay couples with children in the United States are raising the offspring of previous heterosexual unions; others have adopted children.

_____ **7.** But many gay parents are quiet about their sexual orientation, not wanting to draw unwelcome attention to their children or to themselves.

_____ **8.** In several widely publicized cases, courts have removed children from the custody of homosexual couples, citing the "best interests" of the children.

_____ **9.** Gay parenting challenges many traditional ideas.

_____ **10.** But it also shows that many gay couples value family life as highly as heterosexuals do.

11. Use examples from the reading to support your view of whether or not the author has a balance of facts and opinions.

_____

_____

_____

_____

_____

12. What is your opinion on the issue? Support your opinion with reasons.

_____

_____

_____

_____

_____

13. What sources of information can you use to confirm the author's information and support your own view point?

_____

_____

_____

_____

_____

Literature

READING 3

In Defense of Food: An Eater's Manifesto

Don't Eat Anything Your Great Grandmother Wouldn't Recognize as Food

Why your great grandmother? Because at this point your mother and possibly even your grandmother is as confused as the rest of us; to be safe we need to go back at least a couple generations, to a time before the advent of most modern foods. So depending on your age (and your grandmother), you may need to go back to your great- or even great-great grandmother. Some nutritionists recommend going back even further. John Yudkin, a British nutritionist whose early alarms about the dangers of refined carbohydrates were overlooked in the 1960s and 1970s, once advised, "Just don't eat anything your Neolithic ancestors wouldn't have recognized and you'll be ok."

What would shopping this way mean in the supermarket? Well, imagine your great grandmother at your side as you roll down the aisles. You're standing together in front of the dairy case. She picks up a package of Go-Gurt Portable Yogurt tubes—and has no idea what this could possibly be. Is it a food or a toothpaste? And how, exactly, do you introduce it into your body? You could tell her it's just yogurt in a squirtable form, yet if she read the ingredients label she would have every reason to doubt that that was in fact the case. Sure, there's some yogurt in there, but there are also a dozen other things that aren't remotely yogurtlike, ingredients she would probably fail to recognize as foods of any kind, including high-fructose corn syrup, modified corn starch, kosher gelatin, carrageenan, tricalcium phosphate, natural and artificial flavors, vitamins, and so forth. (And there's a whole other list of ingredients for the "berry bubblegum bash" flavoring, containing everything but berries or bubblegum.) How did yogurt, which in your great grandmother's day consisted simply of milk inoculated with a bacterial culture, ever get to be so complicated? Is a product like Go-Gurt Portable Yogurt still a whole food? A food of any kind? Or is it just a food product?

There are in fact hundreds of foodish products in the supermarket that your ancestors simply wouldn't recognize as food: breakfast cereal bars transected by bright white veins representing, but in reality having nothing to do with, milk; "protein waters" and "nondairy creamer"; cheeselike foodstuffs equally innocent of any bovine contribution; cakelike cylinders (with creamlike fillings) called Twinkies that never grow stale. *Don't eat anything incapable of rotting* is another personal policy you might consider adopting.

There are many reasons to avoid eating such complicated food products beyond the various chemical additives and corn and soy derivatives they contain. One of the problems with the products of food science is that, as Joan Gussow has pointed out, they lie to your body; their artificial colors and flavors and synthetic sweeteners and novel fats confound the senses we rely on to assess new foods and prepare our bodies to deal with them. Foods that lie leave us with little choices but to eat by the numbers, consulting labels rather than our senses.

It's true that foods have long been processed in order to preserve them, as when we pickle or ferment or smoke, but industrial processing aims to do much more than extend shelf life. Today foods are processed in ways specifically designed to sell us more food by pushing our evolutionary buttons—our inborn preferences for sweetness and fat and salt. These qualities are difficult to find in nature but cheap and easy for the food scientist to deploy, with the result that processing induces us to consume much more of these ecological rarities than is good for us. "Tastes great, less filling~" could be the motto for most processed foods, which are far more energy dense than most whole foods: They contain much less water, fiber, and micronutrients, and generally much more sugar and fat, making them at the same time, to coin a marketing slogan, "More fattening, less nutritious!"

The great grandma rule will help keep many of these products out of your cart. But not all of them. Because thanks to the FDAs willingness, post-1973, to let food makers freely alter the identity of "traditional foods that everyone knows" without having to call them imitations, your great grandmother could easily be fooled into thinking that that loaf of bread or wedge of cheese is in fact a loaf of bread or a wedge of cheese.

Source: Pollan, Michael (2008). In Defense of Food: An Eater's Manifesto. The Penguin Press: NY; p. 148-150

Questions

List 5 words you see in this reading that either use prefixes or root words or are new to you.

1. _____

2. _____

3. _____

4. _____

5. _____

Look up the word in the dictionary or www.dictionary.com and write the meaning.

6. _____

_____

7. _____

_____

8. _____

_____

9. _____

_____

10. _____

_____

What is the central Idea the writer, Michael Pollan, is trying to share about eating right?

_____

_____

_____

_____

List 3 major supporting details Pollan uses to support his central idea.

_____

_____

_____

_____

Complete the chart with the facts and opinions from the reading.

FACTS	OPINIONS

Do you agree or disagree with Pollan's statement "Don't eat anything your great grandmother wouldn't recognize as food."?

_____

_____

_____

Support your answer with at least three reasons. Write your answer in a well-developed paragraph.

_____

_____

_____

_____

_____

Using the information in the reading above, what specific things might you question or investigate in the foods you usually consume?

_____

_____

_____

_____

Magazine/Periodical **READING 4**

Directions: Use SQ3R to read the selection below.

Survey	Skim over the material. Read the title, subtitle, subheadings, first and last paragraphs, pictures, charts, and graphics. Note italics and bold print.
Question	Ask yourself questions before you read. What do you want to know? Turn headings and subheadings into questions and/or read questions if provided.
Read	Read the material in manageable chunks. This may be one or two paragraphs at a time or the material under one subheading.
Recite	Recite the answer to each question in your own words. This is a good time to write notes as you read each section. Repeat the question-read-recite cycle.
Review	Look over your notes at the end of the chapter, article, or material. Review what you learned and write a summary in your own words.

What are you going to be focusing on when you read this article?

_____

_____

Q—**Questions** (Turn the headings into questions or write your own questions.)

R—**Read** (Read one section at a time.)

Don't Blame Ronald for Kids' Weight

1   Here's the funhouse mirror version of explaining why there are too many overweight kids in America: It's all the clown's fault.

2   Last week, Corporate Accountability International called for McDonald's Corp. to force its 48-year-old corporate mascot into early retirement. According to the group, it's Ronald McDonald's magnetism that drives children to the roadside fast-food emporiums.

3   Funny, the last time we looked it was the adult in the driver's seat who was steering the SUV into Mickey D's drive-through to order lunch for those little passengers buckled into the car seats.

4   Those same parents are the ones who crack open their wallets to pay for super-sized fries, quarter pounders (with cheese, please) and containers of sweet tea that are the size of a cheerleader's megaphone.

5   While we would admit that McDonald's has done a fine job over the years of exploiting television to market directly to children, with ads featuring Ronald, Mayor McCheese and that fugitive from justice, the Hamburglar, somebody in those TV households could have changed the channel or turned off the set. Of course, that would be if someone in that household was accountable, responsible and paying attention to the kids.

6   We have always been a little leery of clowns, ever more so after reading Steven King's "It," but we are coming to Ronald's defense on this specious assertion that he has plumped up America's kids, merely by existing.

7   Why stop at Ronald? Why not Wendy, the pig-tailed lass who beckons millions to the burger emporium bearing her name? Why not Jack from Jack in the Box? Why not Popeye, whose Louisiana fried chicken makes our cholesterol go north just thinking about it?

8   Ronald McDonald is no more responsible for the epidemic of childhood obesity than the Vermont Syrup lady is for driving up the rates of Type II diabetes.

9   There are plenty of reasons why kids are bigger than ever. Slashed school budgets that have eliminated recess and physical education classes have more to do with unfit overweight kids than a pitchman in a yellow jumpsuit.

10   Inattentive parents and grandparents, who themselves may be overweight, have contributed to the rise in obesity. They've provided the poor examples to their children by ignoring the all-too-familiar warnings about a diet loaded with fat and sugar.

11   McDonald's has been offering lower-calorie, lower-fat alternatives on its menu board for years, but the only people we see ordering the grilled chicken sandwich and side salads are the already skinny ones.

12   McDonald's recently added a fruit-and-oatmeal combo to its breakfast menu. It's there for the taking. And no one behind the counter, clownish or otherwise, is ordering customers at gunpoint to go for the bacon-and-cheese biscuit and hash browns.

13   It's a fact: One of three citizens of this state is obese.

14   A clown didn't make those Hoosiers tubby.

15   Poor choices did.

Source: Editorial. (May 23, 2011). *Journal & Courier*, Lafayette, IN.

(Q) What are your SQ3R questions from surveying the article?

_____

_____

_____

_____

_____

(R) What are your answers to your questions after reading?

_____

_____

_____

_____

(R) Write a summary of the article in your own words.

_____

_____

_____

_____

_____

Complete the chart with the facts and opinions from the reading.

FACTS	OPINIONS

What details does the writer use to support the central idea? (*Hint:* First complete the facts and opinions chart)

_____

_____

_____

What is the central idea the writer is trying to share?

_____

_____

_____

Visual Image   READING 5

Directions: Examine the photograph and answer the questions.

1. What is the main idea of this photograph? _____

_____

_____

_____

2. What facts does the photo show? _____

_____

_____

_____

_____

3. What opinions does the photo show? _____

_____

_____

_____

_____

4. What emotions might the photo evoke in the readers? _____

_____

_____

_____

_____

_____

9 Inferences

THEME – What Are My Dreams?

380

SPOTLIGHT ON LEARNING STYLES 👁 Look 🔊 Listen ✏️ Write 👆 Do

When I was a young girl, I liked to play "school." I was always the teacher. Sometimes I convinced the kids in the neighborhood to pay me a nickel to attend my "breezeway school" with old desks and chairs, and carefully prepared lessons and activities matching their learning needs. In later years, I enjoyed "teaching" and "tutoring" any chance I could get, whether it was with nieces and nephews, kids I babysat, or children in school. But when I was thinking about choosing my career, adults in my life told me things like "Whatever you do, don't go into teaching." "They don't get paid anything." "You're too smart to be a teacher." . . . and things like that. So I took their advice and pursued a career in health, and then in business. I graduated with a degree in management and went to work for a utility company and an airline, in auditing and accounting positions. My teaching dream was in the back of my mind, but it seemed less possible the more I acquired car payments, a mortgage, and a lifestyle that kept costing a little more to maintain than my pay raises supported. Then one day, my boss said they needed a volunteer for Junior Achievement, a program to teach economics to 7th graders. I jumped at the chance. When I started teaching, I noticed the students looked really bored with the lesson in the manual—the supply and demand curves. So I asked them about the restaurants in their town. Within minutes I heard the students asking questions, and saw them making connections to their experiences with Dairy Queen and Pizza Hut. Then we drew our own supply and demand curves and they got it! I was hooked! Helping students use all of their learning styles in ways they could learn was so much fun! That simple volunteer opportunity reignited my dream to be a teacher. Going to the classroom was the best part of my week and I looked forward to it every day. I knew then that I needed to teach. I decided to do the work and make the sacrifice of going back to school to achieve my dreams. I love helping students make sense of the things in their lives and I am blessed that my passion and joy are now my career. Every day, I get to help others turn their dreams into reality, to learn about things that matter to them, and to change their lives. How cool is that?

How to Find Inferences (What can you see between the lines?)

Making an inference or drawing a conclusion is a skill you have been using all of your life, but you may not have known that was the name of what you were doing. How do

LO1
Find inferences.

you know when you are making an inference? Every day you encounter situations where you do not have all of the information or facts, yet you must make decisions or choose what actions you will take based on what you do know. In these instances you may rely on your own judgment or experiences to fill in the missing information.

Imagine this scenario: You come home from school and see a clock flashing 12:00 (and it is not 12:00). What would you guess happened? Check the answer that most likely explains the situation.

_____ **1.** The cat unplugged the radio.

_____ **2.** The electricity turned off temporarily while you were gone.

_____ **3.** Someone came into your house and reset the clock.

My guess would be 2: the electricity turned off temporarily while you were gone. Answers 1 and 3 would not be inferences because they are not likely causes, and there is no evidence to suggest it. Answer 1 is only likely if you have an extraordinary cat that pulls electrical cords out and puts them back into sockets. Answer 3 is also unlikely since resetting a clock would then display a specific time rather than a flashing 12:00. So, even though you do not know for sure that the electricity turned off, you can draw that conclusion using your experiences and knowledge of digital clocks, and you can safely eliminate the other two choices. This is *making an inference* based on the information given.

Making an inference when you read may also be called *reading between the lines.*

- When you think about the situation presented, every detail may not be explained.
- It is then up to you, the reader or listener, to figure out the missing information.
- Think of making inferences as if you are a detective or investigator.
- The best inferences will be based on some reasons, hints, or clues.
- Inferences are not random guesses, but rather judgment calls made from the existing evidence.

As you read and work through the material in this chapter, you will develop your ability to find inferences in written text. The theme is "What Are My Dreams?" So, as you work through this chapter, you will gain reading skills to bring you closer to your dreams. You will also read about people who have set goals and achieved their dreams.

EXAMPLE

Directions: Read the passage below and write the author's inference in your own words.

> *"I know of no more encouraging fact than the unquestionable ability of man to elevate his life by conscious endeavor."*
>
> —*Henry David Thoreau*

_____

_____

Thoreau is implying that a person can make his or her life better by working at it. He is encouraged by knowing that it is a person's choice and there is no doubt that people have this ability to choose a better life if they are willing to work at it.

PRACTICE THE NEW SKILL

Directions: Read the passages below and write the inference for each in your own words.

1.   The only way around is through.

—Robert Frost

_____

_____

2.   The gem cannot be polished without friction, nor man perfected without trial.

—Chinese proverb

_____

_____

3. Everyone who got where he is, had to begin where he was.

—Robert Louis Stevenson

_____

_____

How to Separate Valid from Invalid Inferences (Can the inference be supported?)

A valid inference is one that is supported by information in the passage. An invalid inference has no support in the passage. Think of it this way: If you were a detective, you would need some reason to follow your hunch—or in other words, it would need to be based on something. So as you read a passage, look to the clues in the text to draw your conclusions. Remember, to be valid, an inference must be supported by something. If you are in doubt, try to underline the support for your inferences.

> **LO2**
> Separate valid from invalid inferences.

EXAMPLE

Directions: Read the passage below and write **V** for valid inferences and **I** for invalid inferences.

As Oprah tried to distance herself more and more from Trash TV, she found different ways to make her show part of the solution, rather than part of the problem. Sometimes the smallest things gave Oprah big ideas. That was the case with her Angel Network, which invites viewers to help improve the lives of others. The idea sprouted when Oprah heard about a little girl named Norah who started collecting pennies for charity from friends and neighbors and wound up with thousands of dollars. If a child could collect that much money, Oprah thought, how much could her audience put in what she was calling "the world's largest piggy bank"? Asking viewers for their spare change, she hoped to provide scholarships for fifty needy students, one from every state in the union.

Source: Cooper, Ilene (2007). *Up Close: Oprah Winfrey.* New York: Viking, pp. 143–146.

_____ Oprah saved millions of pennies to help Norah.

_____ Oprah asked viewers to donate their spare change to help needy students.

——————— Every state in the union gave money to the scholarships.

——————— Oprah hoped to provide a scholarship to one needy student from every state.

——————— Viewers of Trash TV donated money to the Angel Network.

Three of the statements are valid (V) inferences: Oprah asked viewers to donate their spare change to help needy students; she hoped every state in the union would give money to the scholarships; Oprah hoped to provide a scholarship to one needy student from every state.

Oprah saved millions of pennies to help Norah is invalid because the article states Oprah asked viewers to donate spare change but she personally did not save her pennies.

Viewers of Trash TV donated money to the Angel Network is invalid because "Oprah tried to distance herself more and more from Trash TV."

PRACTICE THE NEW SKILL

Directions: Write **V** for valid inferences and **I** for invalid inferences about the following passages.

1.   This was not the first time Oprah had been involved in providing scholarships to those in need. Back in 1987, Oprah had decided to fulfill

a promise she had made to her father, Vernon, to finally finish up the senior project she had left undone at Tennessee State University when she moved to Baltimore. After she completed the requirements, the university asked her to give the commencement address when she received her diploma along with the rest of the graduating class. In her speech, Oprah announced that she was endowing ten scholarships to the school in honor of her father, who had always encouraged her to pursue an education, telling her it was the keystone to a successful future.

_____ Oprah had not finished her senior project when she left Tennessee State University.

_____ Oprah respected and honored her father, Vernon.

_____ Vernon thought making money was more important than an education.

_____ Oprah graduated from college much later in life than a traditional student.

_____ Oprah received a scholarship to college.

2.   The response to the world's largest piggy bank was overwhelming. Even First Lady Hillary Clinton came on Oprah's show with a piggy bank her own family had been dropping coins into. In ten months, more than one million dollars was collected, and each of the fifty students was provided with a $25,000 scholarship. At the same time, Oprah was using the Angel Network to build homes with Habitat for Humanity for those in need. Two hundred homes were built all over the country from Anchorage, Alaska, to Dallas, Texas.

_____ The Angel Network helped fund Hillary Clinton's education.

_____ Habitat for Humanity was overwhelmed by the Angel Network.

_____ The Angel Network collected money to build homes for Habitat for Humanity.

_____ Hillary Clinton's family saved $25,000 in pennies.

_____ The First Lady donated money to the Angel Network that her family collected.

Source: Cooper, Ilene. (2007). *Up Close: Oprah Winfrey.* New York: Viking, pp. 143–146.

3.   What about a passion for baking cookies? Mrs. Fields seems to have managed that one. How about a passion for watching movies? Roger Ebert figured that one out.

You don't have the skills? Do you know any famous musicians with terrible singing voices (we don't want to insult anyone, but we're sure you can think of as many as we can). Ever heard any stories about CEOs who were once mail room clerks? Did you know that Albert Einstein flunked most of his courses in school? How about Abraham Lincoln? He lost his mother, lost election after election, lost his money, failed at business, and if you were just looking at the things that didn't work out, appeared to be a failure most of his life until he was elected president of the United States.

You're too old? Do you know that most millionaires are made after the age of fifty-five? While he cooked chicken for years, it wasn't until Colonel Sanders was sixty-two that he started Kentucky Fried Chicken. . .

No matter what limiting belief you hold, there is evidence in the world to the contrary. Even if there is no one who has ever done what you are passionate about doing, there is abundant evidence of people who have been successful doing what others thought was impossible.

You are powerful beyond your imagination. You have created your life, and the good news is, if you don't like it you can change it. Remember this mantra:

Your life is created first in your mind then in the world.

Source: Attwood, Janet Bray and Chris Attwood. (2007). *The Passion Test: The Effortless Path to Discovering Your Destiny.* New York: Hudson Street Press, pp. 187–189.

_____ Roger Ebert was passionate about baking cookies.

_____ Albert Einstein was not a very good student.

_____ Abraham Lincoln rarely failed in his life.

_____ Colonel Sanders became a millionaire cooking chicken at age 55.

_____ You are powerful to change your life if you don't like it.

REVIEW WHAT YOU LEARNED

Directions: Write your inference for each of the quotations below.

Finish each day and be done with it. You have done what you could. Some blunders and absurdities no doubt crept in; forget them as soon as you can. Tomorrow is a new day; begin it well and serenely and with too high a spirit to be encumbered with your old nonsense.

—Ralph Waldo Emerson

_____

_____

_____

Great things are not done by impulse, but by a series of small things brought together.

—Vincent Van Gogh

_____

_____

_____

Success is not final, failure is not fatal; it is the courage to continue that counts.

—Winston Churchill

_____

_____

_____

Success seems to be connected with action. Successful men keep moving. They make mistakes, but they don't quit.

—Conrad Hilton

_____

_____

_____

I feel that the greatest reward for doing is the opportunity to do more.

—Jonas Salk

_____

_____

_____

/ *REVIEW* WHAT YOU LEARNED /

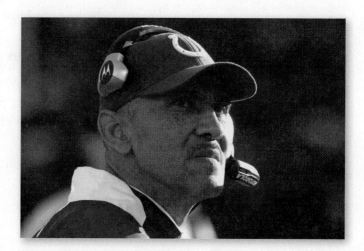

What Does It Take to Be a Modern-Day Hero?

"I really wanted to show people you can win all kinds of ways . . . For your faith to be more important than your job, for your family to be important than that job . . . we all know that's the way it should be . . . I'm not afraid to say it."—Tony Dungy

People of all ages crave heroes. But it's rare to find someone in the media spotlight like Tony Dungy—whose life and work reflect positive, value-driven *precepts*.

In Coach Dungy, many have found a role model. Sports fans admire the way he intensely pursues success without sacrificing the well-being of his team members. Parents point to his example when teaching their children about the importance of hard work, persistence, and graciousness whether they win or lose. Even his fiercest competitors acknowledge that Coach Dungy is a class act who knows how to get the job done and who keeps his priorities intact while he's doing it.

To all these people and more, Tony Dungy is a real-life hero—one who teaches us about the importance of quiet strength, fierce determination, and a humble heart.

Source: Dungy, Tony with Nathan Whitaker. (2007). *Quiet Strength A Memoir: The Principles, Practices, & Priorities of a Winning Life.* Carol Stream, IL: Tyndale House Publishers, inside cover.

Precepts—principles, guidelines

Directions: Write **V** for valid inferences and **I** for invalid inferences based on the reading.

_____ Tony Dungy believes your faith is more important than your job.

_____ Coach Dungy's team members crave real-life heroes.

_____ Coach Dungy puts his team and children first.

_____ The importance of hard work, persistence, and graciousness are values parents teach to their children using Tony Dungy's example.

_____ Coach Dungy is focused on one way of winning.

Inference

Best Trailblazer

"I've been blind since 2004," says Trevor Thomas, 40, "I'd just graduated from law school, and I contracted a rare disease called atypical central serous chorioretinopathy.

"I had to learn to live as a blind guy, using tools like a cane and a talking computer program. Trying to figure out what to do with the rest of my life, I started hiking the trails near my home in Charlotte, North Carolina. **I got the idea to hike the Appalachian Trail,** and that gave me a goal.

> *"I proved to myself that although my world had changed, it wasn't becoming smaller."*
> —*Trevor Thomas*

"I trained for more than a year, hiking 20 miles a day. My sister drove me to the trailhead in Springer Mountain, Georgia, on April 6, 2008, to meet a hiking friend. When he didn't show up, I went on alone with a high-tech walking stick and a 50-pound pack holding a sleeping bag, cooking gear, a first aid kit, water, and food.

"A bunch of strangers helped me along the way. I met a 22-year-old student, Noah Clark, at a lean-to and started talking about the trail ahead. He handed me his trail book, and I said, 'I can't read that. I'm blind.' He hiked 400 miles with me after that.

"I trekked 8 to 25 miles a day, depending on the terrain, through blizzards, extreme heat, and flooding from Hurricane Kyle. I fell thousands of times. I stopped counting at maybe 3,000. I had multiple hairline fractures in my foot, four broken ribs, and a chipped hip. On October 8, I climbed 5,268 feet to the summit of Mount Katahdin in Maine. I'd made it.

"Now I'm training to hike the Pacific Crest Trail, 2,650 miles from Mexico to Canada. I'm happy on the trail—it's where I feel most alive."

Good News File

• Number of Americans who inquired about becoming a Big Brother/Big Sister during Mentor Month in January (a record): **32,000**

Source: "Best Trailblazer" and "Good News File" from Reader's Digest, July 2009. Copyright © 2009 by The Reader's Digest Association, Inc. Reprinted with permission from Reader's Digest.

- Kinds of organic vegetables First Lady Michelle Obama and two dozen Washington D.C., schoolchildren planted in the new White House kitchen garden: **55**
- Percentage increase in Teach for America applications for the 2009–10 school year: **40**
- Percentage of Americans who have a library card (the highest ever): **68**
- Percentage increase in registration at the Points of Light Institute, a nonprofit that connects people with volunteer opportunities, since January: **60**
- Number of Facebook fans for Captain Chesley Sullenberger after his miraculous Hudson River plane landing despite his insistence that he was not a hero: **625,292**
- Percentage of U.S. high schools offering community-service credits (a record): **86**
- Number of sandbags filled by residents of Fargo, North Dakota, to protect the city during record flooding in March: **3.5 million**
- Percentage of Americans who say the country's best days are ahead: **56**

Directions: Write **V** if the statement about the reading above is valid and **I** if the statement is invalid.

_____ 1. Trevor Thomas had to adjust to becoming blind.

_____ 2. Hiking the trails near his home helped Thomas figure out what to do.

_____ 3. Hiking the Appalachian Trail was too big of a goal for a blind person.

_____   **4.** Thomas did not need to train for the hike since he was so motivated by his goal.

_____   **5.** Thomas was very determined and courageous.

_____   **6.** Thomas' injuries caused him to lose faith.

_____   **7.** Noah Clark felt sorry for Thomas and decided to walk beside him.

_____   **8.** Besides hiking trails, Thomas also climbs mountains.

_____   **9.** According to the "Good News File," more people are helping others.

_____   **10.** Fewer high schools are becoming community service-oriented.

MASTER THE LESSON

Inference

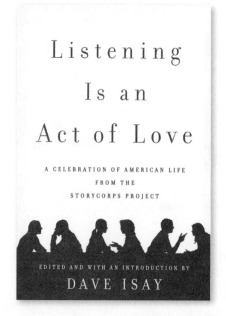

Listening

Is an

Act of Love

A CELEBRATION OF AMERICAN LIFE
FROM THE
STORYCORPS PROJECT

EDITED AND WITH AN INTRODUCTION BY
DAVE ISAY

Following are excerpts from an interview with Dr. Monica Mayer, 45 by her cousin and patient, Spencer Wilkinson Jr., 39, recorded in New Town, North Dakota.

Spencer Wilkinson, Jr.: What made you choose to pursue a career in medicine?

Dr. Monica Mayer: My father was a full-blood German, and my mother was full-blood Indian, and it was pretty tough in the sixties growing up half-breed, so to speak. My father didn't have any sons, so he raised us like little boys. And I must have been in about seventh grade, and I wasn't doing well in school. In fact, I was maybe getting Cs, and I'm the oldest of three girls.

So my dad packed us up in his pickup truck and took us out to his old homestead land, which is about eighteen miles north of New Town, in the middle of nowhere. Well, New Town's kind of in the middle of nowhere, but, I mean, this is *really* in the middle of nowhere. And he packed us some lunches and some water. He dropped us off out there at seven or eight in the morning and said he wanted all the rocks picked up and put in the northwest corner in one big pile and that he'd come back that night to pick us up, and it had better be done.

So there we were, working hard all day, and then he comes back. And we're dirty, stinky, sweaty, sore muscles, crying. My dad pulls up, and he gets out of the pickup. And we must have been a sight to see. I looked at him and I said, since I was the oldest—my two younger sisters are hiding behind me—"Dad, we don't think this is fair we have to work this hard." And I remember him saying, "Is that right? Well, do you think I like working hard like this every day?" "No." He said, "You know, your mother said you girls don't like school and you're not doing very well. So I talked to Momma, and we decided that you're going to come out here and work like this so your hind ends will get used to how life's going to be when you get older." So I said, "Well if we got good grades, do we have to come out here and work this hard?" And he said, "No. That's the deal."

Well, he didn't have to bust my head twice up against a brick wall. My two younger sisters and I were laughing about that, because they remember that particular day exactly the way I remembered it. One day of hard labor changed everything.

July 29, 2005

Today, Monica Mayer practices family medicine on the Fort Berthold reservation in New Town, North Dakota. Her sister Holly is the Director of Public Health Nurses on the reservation, and her sister Renee is Tribal Social Services Director.

Source: Isay, Dave, Editor. (2007). *Listening Is an Act of Love: A Celebration of American Life from the Storycorps Project*. New York: Penguin, pp. 57–58.

ENGLISH 2.0

Hind ends will get used to means: your bodies will know hard labor, you will know what hard work will be like in your life

He didn't have to bust my head twice up against a brick wall means: they understood what their father meant without being told a second time

---

Directions: Write **V** for valid inferences and **I** for invalid inferences about the reading.

1. _____ Dr. Mayer was an honors student.

2. _____ Her parents were very strict.

3. _____ Her father dropped off the girls in the country to punish them.

4. _____ The girls enjoyed their day in the country.

5. _____ Her father thought the girls would learn a lesson by working hard all day.

6. _____ The parents knew the girls did not want to work hard in school.

7. _____ The parents thought the girls would prefer the physical labor of picking up rocks to school work.

8. _____ The parents had different cultural backgrounds.

9–10. What lesson can you infer the girls learned? _____.

_____

_____

LEARNING STYLE ACTIVITIES

*L*ook, *L*isten, *W*rite, *D*o

What Is Failure?

Every successful person is someone who failed,
yet never regarded himself as a failure.

In an interview years ago, David Brinkley asked advice columnist Ann Landers what question she most frequently received from readers. Her answer: "What's wrong with me?"

Landers' response reveals a lot about human nature. Many people wrestle with feelings of failure, the most damaging being doubtful thoughts about themselves. At the heart of those doubts and feelings is one central question: Am I a failure? And that's a problem because I believe it's nearly impossible for any person to believe he is a failure and succeed at the same time. Instead, you have to meet failure with the right attitude and determine to fail forward.

It seems that advice columnists (such as the late Ann Landers) and humor writers recognize that keeping a good attitude about yourself is important in overcoming adversity and mistakes. The late Erma Bombeck, who wrote a widely syndicated weekly humor column until a few weeks before her death in 1996, had a firm grasp on what it meant to persevere and fail forward without taking failure too personally.

From Newspaper Copy Girl to *Time* Magazine Cover Girl

1   Erma Bombeck traveled a road that was filled with adversity, starting with her career. She was drawn to journalism early in life. Her first job was as a copy girl at the *Dayton Journal-Herald* when she was a teenager. But when she went off to college at Ohio University, a guidance counselor advised her, "Forget about writing." She refused. Later she transferred to the University of Dayton and in 1949 graduated with a degree in English. Soon afterward she began working as a writer—for the obituary column and the women's page.

2   That year adversity carried over into her personal life. When she got married, one of her deepest desires was to become a mother. But much to her dismay, her doctors told her she was incapable of having children. Did she give up and consider herself a failure? No, she and her husband explored the possibility of adoption, and then they adopted a daughter.

3   Two years later, a surprised Erma became pregnant. But even that brought her more difficulties. In four years she experienced four pregnancies, but only two of the babies survived.

4   In 1964 Erma was able to convince the editor of a small neighborhood newspaper, the *Kettering-Oakwood Times,* to let her write a weekly humor column. Despite the pitiful $3 per article she was paid, she kept writing. And that opened a door for her. The next year she was offered the opportunity to write a three-times-a-week column for her old employer, the *Dayton Journal-Herald.* By 1967 her column was syndicated and carried by more than nine hundred newspapers.

5   For slightly more than thirty years Erma wrote her humor column. During that time she published fifteen books, was recognized as one of the twenty-five most influential women in America, appeared frequently on the television show *Good Morning America*, was featured on the cover of *Time* magazine, received innumerable honors (such as the American Cancer Society's Medal of Honor), and was awarded fifteen honorary degrees.

More than Her Share of Problems

6   But during that span of time, Erma Bombeck also experienced incredible troubles and trials, including breast cancer, a mastectomy, and kidney failure. And she wasn't shy about sharing her perspective on her life experiences:

7   I speak at college commencements, and I tell everyone I'm up there and they're down there, not because of my successes, but my failures. Then I proceed to spin all of them off—a comedy record album that sold two copies in Beirut . . . a sitcom that lasted about as long as a donut in our house . . . a Broadway play that never saw Broadway . . . book signings where I attracted two people: one who wanted directions to the restroom and the other who wanted to buy the desk.

8   What you have to tell yourself is, "I'm not a failure. I failed at doing something." There's a big difference . . . Personally and career-wise, it's been a corduroy road. I've buried babies, lost parents, had cancer, and worried over kids. The trick is to put it all in perspective . . . and that's what I do for a living.

9   That winning attitude kept Erma Bombeck down to earth. (She liked to refer to herself as "a former homeroom mother and obituary writer.") It also

kept her going—and writing—through the disappointments, the pain, the surgeries, and the daily kidney dialysis until her death at age sixty-nine.

Source: Maxwell, John C. (2003). *Attitude 101: What Every Leader Needs to Know.* Nashville, TN: Thomas Nelson Publishers, pp. 71–74.

Complete one of the following Learning Style activities. Remember, you may choose to use your preferred learning style or you may work outside of your "comfort zone" to develop one of the other styles. As you work with your group, think about how you will present the results to the class.

👁 *L*OOK   As you read the passage, create your own magazine cover. Imagine how your life will be once you reach your dreams. Include the title of the magazine and several specific details about your life.

🔊 *L*ISTEN   As you read the passage, create your own talk show interview where you are the guest. It should be based on how your life will be once you reach your dreams. Write questions and answers in a conversation/interview form. If you prefer, you may act out the interview with a classmate.

✏ *W*RITE   As you read the passage, think about your own life several years from now once you reach your dreams. Write a portion of your autobiography (pretending it is the future) where you describe in detail the obstacles you have overcome to make you such a successful person.

👆 *D*o   As you read the passage, think about your own experiences with failure and success. Imagine yourself several years from now as the person who has achieved their dreams. Create a skit, a video, or build a model of your dream life. Include details that show how your character was built.

Reading Practice

The following readings are related to the theme "What Are My Dreams?" and come from a variety of sources: the Internet, textbooks, literature, magazines, and visual images. They were chosen not only to help you improve your ability to make inferences but also to continue to build your other reading skills of learning vocabulary, locating main ideas and supporting details, understanding implied main ideas, recognizing patterns of organization, and distinguishing facts from opinions.

The first reading is from the Internet Web site about Sandra Cisneros from *Gale: Free Resources: Hispanic Heritage: Biographies.*

The second reading is the section "Achievement" from the textbook *Psychology: An Introduction* by Charles G. Morris and Albert A. Maisto.

The third reading is a section from literature titled "*The Little Engine That Could:* I Think I Can" from *The Book That Changed My Life: 71 Remarkable Writers Celebrate the Books That Matter Most to Them.*

The fourth reading, "Motivational Achievement Quotes Lead to Greatness," is from About.com Guide.

The fifth reading is a visual of *The Essence of Achievement.*

Internet

READING 1

Directions: Practice the SQ3R strategy as you read the article below.

First, let's go over the five steps of SQ3R and then practice using them.

Survey	Skim over the material. Read the title, subtitle, subheadings, first and last paragraphs, pictures, charts, and graphics. Note italics and bold print.
Question	Ask yourself questions before you read. What do you want to know? Turn headings and subheadings into questions and/or read questions if provided.
Read	Read the material in manageable chunks. This may be one or two paragraphs at a time or the material under one subheading.
Recite	Recite the answer to each question in your own words. This is a good time to write notes as you read each section. Repeat the question-read-recite cycle.
Review	Look over your notes at the end of the chapter, article, or material. Review what you learned and write a summary in your own words.

S—Survey

What are you going to be focusing on when you read this article?

_____

_____

Sandra Cisneros

Born 1954
Poet, Writer

1   "It was not until this moment when I separated myself, when I considered myself truly distinct, that my writing acquired a voice."

2   In her poetry and stories, Mexican American author Sandra Cisneros writes about Mexican and Mexican American women who find strength to rise above the poor conditions of their lives. These types of characters have not been presented so clearly in writing before. Cisneros is determined to introduce them to American readers, and so far her efforts have been successful. A reviewer for the *Washington Post Book World* described Cisneros as "a writer of power and eloquence and great lyrical beauty."

3   Cisneros' ability to write about these strong characters comes from her childhood experiences. Born in Chicago, Illinois, in 1954, she grew up in poverty. As the only girl in a family of seven children, Cisneros spent a lot of time by herself. Because her family moved often, she was not able to form lasting friendships. "The moving back and forth, the new school, were very upsetting to me as a child," she explained to Jim Sagel in *Publishers Weekly.* "They caused me to be very introverted and shy. I do not remember making friends easily." Instead, Cisneros became a quiet, careful observer of the people and events around her, and recorded her feelings through secret writings at home.

SHYNESS MASKS HER TALENT

4   Because she was too shy to volunteer or speak up in class, Cisneros often received poor grades while attending Catholic schools in Chicago. Her Mexican American mother and her Mexican father, however, both knew the importance of education. Her mother made sure all the children in the family had library cards, and her father made sure they all studied so they wouldn't have to work as hard for a living as he did. "My father's hands are thick and yellow," Cisneros wrote in *Glamour* magazine, "stubbed by a history of hammer and nails and twine and coils and springs. 'Use this' my father said, tapping his head, 'not this' showing us those hands."

5   Although Cisneros learned to study hard, she was still too shy to share her creative writings at school. She felt many of her early teachers were not interested in her experiences. Finally, in the tenth grade, Cisneros was encouraged by one of her teachers to read her works to the class. She was also encouraged to work on the school's literary magazine and eventually became its editor.

DREAMS OF BEING A WRITER

6   After high school, Cisneros attended Loyola University in Chicago to study English. Her father thought she might find a good husband if she went to college. What Cisneros discovered instead was the desire to be a writer. After graduating from college, encouraged by another teacher who recognized her writing talent, Cisneros enrolled in the poetry section of the Iowa Writer's Workshop, a highly respected graduate school for aspiring writers.

7   Cisneros's old fears about sharing her writings with others soon came back. Many of Cisneros's classmates had come from more privileged backgrounds than she had, and she felt she could not compete with them. As she explained in an interview in *Authors and Artists for Young Adults,* "It didn't take me long to learn—after a few days of being there—that nobody cared to hear what I had to say and no one listened to me even when I did speak. I became very frightened and terrified that first year."

REALIZES THE IMPORTANCE OF HER HERITAGE

8   She soon realized, however, that her experiences as a Mexican American and as a woman were very different, but just as important as anything her classmates wrote about. "It was not until this moment when I separated myself, when I considered myself truly distinct, that my writing acquired a voice," she explained to Sagel. Out of this insight came her first book, *The House on Mango Street.*

9   Published in 1984, the book is composed of a series of connected short passages or stories told by Esperanza Cordero, a Mexican American girl growing up in a Chicago barrio. Much like Cisneros when she was young, Esperanza wants to leave

her poor neighborhood to seek a better life for herself. As Esperanza tells her stories, readers come to understand how people live their lives in her neighborhood. Although Esperanza gains enough strength by the end of the book to leave her house on Mango Street, she is reminded by one of the other characters that she must never forget who she is and where she came from: "You will always be Esperanza. You will always be Mango Street. You can't erase what you know. You can't forget who you are."

THE HOUSE ON MANGO STREET

10   *The House on Mango Street* was a successful book. Many schools, from junior high schools through colleges, have used it in their classes. The book's success, however, didn't provide an easy life for Cisneros. After graduating from Iowa with a masters degree in creative writing, she worked as a part-time teacher. In 1986, she moved to Texas after receiving a fellowship (a financial award) to help her finish writing *My Wicked, Wicked Ways,* a book of poetry. After this volume was published in 1987, Cisneros's money ran out, and she could not find a job. She wanted to stay in Texas and even tried to start a private writing program. She passed out fliers in supermarkets to get interested people to join, but the program failed. Sad and broke, Cisneros had to leave Texas to take a teaching job at California State University in Chico, California.

SIGNS MAJOR PUBLISHING CONTRACT

11   While in California, Cisneros received another grant of money to help her write a book of fiction. This new award from the National Endowment for the Arts revitalized Cisneros and inspired her to write *Women Hollering Creek and Other Stories.* Random House offered to publish the book in 1991, making Cisneros the first Chicana (Mexican American woman) to receive a major publishing contract for a work about Chicanas. The book, a series of short stories about strong Mexican American women living along the Texas-Mexico border, received praise from critics across the nation.

12   In 1994 another large publishing company issued *Loose Woman,* Cisneros's second collection of poetry. The main theme behind many of the poems in the book was love and its many powerful forms. A reviewer for *Publishers Weekly* wrote that the book again presents "a powerful, fiercely independent woman of Mexican heritage, though this time the innocence has long been lost." And at the beginning of 1995, Random House issued a Spanish-language translation of *The House on Mango Street, La casa en Mango Street.* Cisneros also published a children's picture book in 1994, *Hairs/Pelitos,* which presents diversity, individuality, and family bonds to readers ages 4-8.

13   The writer was in the news in Texas for two years over the color of her house. Cisneros lives in a historic district of San Antonio, so when she painted her house a very brilliant purple in 1997, the city board objected. For two years the dispute

went on, until the paint faded to a shade of lavender, which the city deemed "historically appropriate."

14 Cisneros feels it is important for people of all races in America to understand the lives of Mexican Americans, especially Mexican American women. And Cisneros feels it is her duty to write about them. As she stated in *Authors and Artists for Young Adults,* "I feel very honored to give them a form in my writings and to be able to have this material to write about is a blessing."

Source: Gale: Free Resources: Hispanic Heritage: Biographies: Retrieved from http://www.gale.cengage.com/free_resources/chh/bio/cisneros_s.htm

Use the passage above to fill in the SQ3R questions and answers.

Q—Question (Turn the headings into questions and write them in the spaces provided.)

R—Read (Read one section at a time.)

R—Recite (Answer your questions as you read and write them in your own words in the spaces provided.)

Subheading 1. Shyness Masks Her Talent

Question: _____

_____?

Recite: _____

_____

Subheading 2. Dreams of Being a Writer

Question: _____

_____?

Recite: _____

_____

Subheading 3. Realizes the Importance of Her Heritage

Question: _____

_____?

Recite: _____

_____

*Subheading 4. **The House on Mango Street***

Question: _____

_____?

Recite: _____

_____

Subheading 5. **Signs Major Publishing Contract**

Question: _____

_____?

Recite: _____

_____

R—Review (Review your notes and write a summary in your own words.)

_____

_____

_____

_____

_____

Inference Questions

1. Can you infer that Sandra Cisneros' family supported her in becoming a writer? Why or why not? _____

_____

_____

2. What can you infer influenced Sandra Cisneros' first book, *The House on Mango Street*? _____

_____

_____

Achievement

1   Climbing Mount Everest, sending rockets into space, making the dean's list, rising to the top of a giant corporation—all these actions may have mixed underlying motives. But in all of them there is a desire to excel, "to overcome obstacles, to exercise power, to strive to do something difficult as well and as quickly as possible" (Murray, 1938, pp. 80–81). It is this desire for achievement for its own sake that leads psychologists to suggest there is a separate **achievement motive**. *[Achievement motive—The need to excel, to overcome obstacles.]*

2   Using a self-report questionnaire called the Work and Family Orientation (WOFO) scale to study achievement motivation, some researchers discovered three separate but interrelated aspects of achievement-oriented behavior: *work orientation,* the desire to work hard and do a good job; *mastery,* the preference for difficult or challenging feats, with an emphasis on improving one's past performance; and *competitiveness,* the enjoyment of pitting one's skills against those of other people (Helmreich & Spence, 1978).

3   How do individual differences in the three aspects of achievement motivation relate to people's attainment of goals? Surprisingly, having a high degree of competitiveness may actually interfere with achievement. In one study, students' grade-point averages (GPAs) were compared to their WOFO scores. As you might expect, students who scored low in work, mastery, and competitiveness had lower GPAs. But students who scored high in all three areas did not have the highest GPAs. It turned out that the students with the highest grades were those who had high work and mastery scores but low competitiveness scores. The counterproductive effects of competitiveness curbs achievement in other groups of people as well, including business people, elementary-school students, and scientists. What accounts for this phenomenon? No one knows for sure, but some researchers speculate that highly competitive people alienate the very people who would otherwise help them achieve their goals; others suggest that preoccupation with winning distracts them from taking the actions necessary to attain their goals.

4   From psychological tests and personal histories, psychologists have developed a profile of people with a high level of achievement motivation. These people are fast learners. They *relish* the opportunity to develop new strategies for unique and challenging tasks, whereas people with a low need for achievement rarely deviate from methods that worked for them in the past. Driven less by the desire for fame or fortune than by the need to live up to a high, self-imposed standard

---

Relish—enjoy, appreciate, like

of performance (Carr, Borkowski, & Maxwell, 1991), people with a high level of achievement motivation are self-confident, willingly take on responsibility, and do not readily bow to outside social pressures. Although they are energetic and allow few things to stand in the way of their goals, they are also apt to be tense and to suffer from stress-related ailments, such as headaches. They may also feel like imposters even—or especially—when they achieve their goals.

Vocabulary

Use word parts to determine the meaning of the word ***interrelated***.

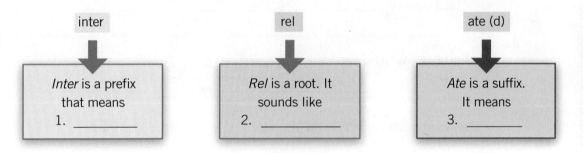

inter	rel	ate (d)
Inter is a prefix that means 1. _____	*Rel* is a root. It sounds like 2. _____	*Ate* is a suffix. It means 3. _____

Use context clues to find the meaning of ***interrelated***.

Using a self-report questionnaire called the Work and Family Orientation (WOFO) scale to study achievement motivation, some researchers discovered three separate but ***interrelated*** aspects of achievement-oriented behavior: *work orientation,* the desire to work hard and do a good job; *mastery,* the preference for difficult or challenging feats, with an emphasis on improving one's past performance; and *competitiveness,* the enjoyment of pitting one's skills against those of other people (Helmreich & Spence, 1978).

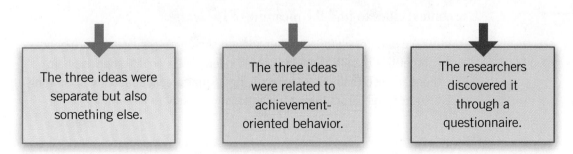

The three ideas were separate but also something else.	The three ideas were related to achievement-oriented behavior.	The researchers discovered it through a questionnaire.

4. Based on the clues, what is the meaning of ***interrelated?*** _____

_____

5. Using the dictionary, what is the meaning of ***interrelated?*** _____

_____

Directions: Using the context clues from the textbook passage, write the meaning of the following words.

6. Achievement motive _____

_____

7. Work orientation _____

_____

8. Mastery _____

_____

9. Competitiveness _____

_____

Use word parts to determine the meaning of the word ***speculate.***

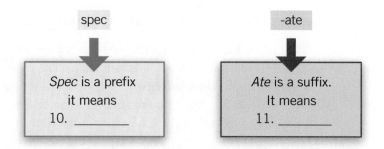

spec	-ate
Spec is a prefix it means 10. _____	*Ate* is a suffix. It means 11. _____

Use context clues to find the meaning of ***speculate.***

No one knows for sure, but some researchers ***speculate*** that highly competitive people alienate the very people who would otherwise help them achieve their goals; others suggest that preoccupation with winning distracts them from taking the actions necessary to attain their goals.

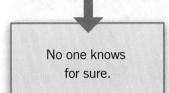

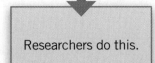

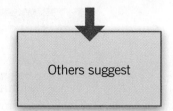

| No one knows for sure. | Researchers do this. | Others suggest |

12. Based on the clues, what is the meaning of *speculate*? _____

_____

13. Using the dictionary, what is the meaning of *speculate*? _____

_____

Use context clues to find the meaning of ***deviate.*** (*Hint:* The prefix *de* means "down" or "away from.")

> They relish the opportunity to develop new strategies for unique and challenging tasks, whereas people with a low need for achievement rarely ***deviate*** from methods that worked for them in the past.

| People with a high need for achievement develop new strategies for unique tasks. | Whereas people with a low need for achievement do something else. | They use methods that worked for them in the past. |

14. Based on the clues, what is the meaning of ***deviate***? _____

_____

15. Using the dictionary, what is the meaning of ***deviate***? _____

_____

Main Idea

16. What is main idea of paragraph 1?

    a. Climbing Mount Everest, sending rockets into space, making the dean's list and rising to the top of a corporation show a person is successful.

    b. But in all of them there is a desire to excel, "to overcome obstacles, to exercise power, to strive to do something difficult as well and as quickly as possible."

    c. It is this desire for achievement for its own sake that leads psychologists to suggest there is a separate achievement motive.

Supporting Details

What are the three aspects of achievement-oriented behavior?

17. _____
_____
_____
_____

18. _____
_____
_____
_____

19. _____
_____
_____
_____

20. True or False: Highly competitive people are most successful.

_____

_____

Patterns of Organization

21. Paragraphs 3 and 4 are organized primarily by which pattern of organization?

    a. cause and effect   **c.** compare and contrast

    b. definition   **d.** time order

Fact and Opinions

22. Is this passage developed mostly through facts or opinions?

_____

Inferences

23. What type of person could you infer would have the most stress: a person with high achievement motivation or one with low achievement motivation? _____

_____

_____

24–25. Describe someone you know who mostly shows high achievement motivation or low achievement motivation. Discuss ways the passage's description of this person compare to the person you know.

_____

_____

_____

_____

_____

The Little Engine That Could: I Think I Can

1   "Let's read a book." When I was a little boy, that's what my mother used to say to me at bedtime. She read my favorite ones—like *Mike Mulligan and His Steam Shovel* and *Where the Wild Things Are*—over and over, but the one we read most often was *The Little Engine That Could.* I can still remember the glossy feel of its pages and the colorful illustrations of trains, animals, toys, and candy.

2   Mostly, however, I remember the lessons my mother taught me from the story. One lesson was about humility. At the outset of the book, a train carrying toys to children breaks down. A shiny passenger train and a big locomotive each pass by the stranded toys that are pleading for deliverance. Although able—both trains feel too important to help. This arrogance ultimately hurts the children.

3   Service, my mother taught, has the opposite effect. It can replace a child's tears with a smile. My mother knew this from experience. She was a single mom. I was her only child. She worked hard, but money was tight. If not for the help of others, we would sometimes have gone without basics like groceries, clothing, and even housing. Maybe that's why she and I were so drawn to *The Little Engine That Could.* He came to the rescue.

4   Mother started calling me her Little Engine That Could. "Look at this little train and look at what he can do," she would say. "You're my little boy and you're like this little engine."

5   Even when I became a teen, my mother would remind me of the Little Engine's motto whenever I began to doubt my abilities: *I think I can.* Over time,

this phrase—short and simple—changed my life in a dramatic way. When I decided to become an author I had no writing experience. None. I had never written for a magazine or newspaper. I had not studied journalism in college. In fact, I had never even taken a writing course. I was a lot like the Little Engine that had no sense of the mountain's height when he promised to take the toys up over the top. I didn't know enough about publishing to know that starting out with a book is a very tall order. I just thought I could write one. And I did.

6   My confidence to try new things and be unafraid of failure began with a simple children's book. Besides the importance of humility, service, and self-confidence, *The Little Engine That Could* taught me the priceless value of taking time to read with children. Unbeknownst to me, my mother saved most of my favorite children's books, storing them in boxes. When I became a parent, she wrapped them up and gave them to me as a gift so that I could read them to my own children.

7   I am now the father of four. In the tradition of my mother, my wife and I read individually to them every night. As a result, they love books too. There is no greater tool for bonding with children than books. There is no greater instrument for teaching lessons for life. Now my children reach for books before they reach for the remote control. No doubt one day they will read to their children, a family tradition that started with *The Little Engine That Could.*

Jeff Benedict is an award-wining investigative journalist, a bestselling author of six books, and an attorney. He has been a contributing writer for *Sports Illustrated*, the *Los Angeles Times*, and the *Hartford Courant*. He is also a frequent television news commentator and an essayist whose work has appeared in *The New York Times*, *The Chronicle of Higher Education*, and ESPN's online magazine.

Source: Coady, Roxanne and Joy Johannessen, Eds. (2006). *The Book That Changed My Life: 71 Remarkable Writers Celebrate the Books That Matter Most to Them*. New York: Penguin, pp. 20–22.

Vocabulary

Use context clues to find the meaning of ***arrogance.***

Mostly, however, I remember the lessons my mother taught me from the story. One lesson was about humility. At the outset of the book, a train carrying toys to children breaks down. A shiny passenger train and a big locomotive each pass by the stranded toys that are pleading for deliverance. Although able—both trains feel too important to help. This arrogance ultimately hurts the children.

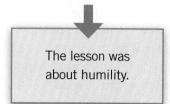

The lesson was about humility.

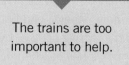

The trains are too important to help.

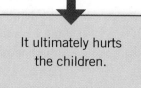

It ultimately hurts the children.

1. Based on the clues, what is the meaning of ***arrogance***? _____

_____

2. Using the dictionary, what is the meaning of ***arrogance***? _____

_____

Main Idea

3. What is main idea of paragraph 5?

   a. The phrase, *I think I can*, changed the writer's life—it made him say yes to writing a book, even though he had no professional writing experience.

   b. As a teenager, the writer was not confident he could write.

   c. As an adult, the writer accomplished many great things.

   d. The writer's mother read to him every night and helped him build his confidence.

Supporting Details

How did the writer's mother know service could replace a child's tears with a smile?

4. _____

_____

5. _____

_____

6. _____

Patterns of Organization

7. Paragraph 7 is organized primarily through what pattern of organization?

a. cause and effect   c. compare and contrast

b. definition   d. time order

Fact and Opinions

8. Is this passage developed mostly through facts or opinions? _____

_____

Inferences

9–11. Why does the writer infer it is important to read to children? _____

_____

_____

12–15. From the reading, what can you infer is the most important lesson from the children's book, _The Little Engine that Could_, especially the phrase, "I think I can"? _____

_____

_____

_____

Motivational Achievement Quotes Lead to Greatness

If you believe that you are born for greater things, it is time you followed your true calling. Greatness is achieved only when you rise above the ordinary. Hard work, sincerity, and passion can make your dream to achieve greatness come true. Find your inspiration. Motivational quotes such as these will light up your road to greatness.

Wilma Rudolph
My mother taught me very early to believe I could achieve any accomplishment I wanted to. The first was to walk without braces.

Dag Hammarskjöld
Never measure the height of a mountain, until you have reached the top. Then you will see how low it was.

John Wooden
Never mistake activity for achievement.

Ernest Hemingway
Never mistake motion for action.

General George Smith Patton, Jr.
Never tell people how to do things. Tell them what to do and they will surprise you with their ingenuity.

William Blake
No bird soars too high if he soars with his own wings.

Denis Waitley
No man or woman is an island. To exist just for yourself is meaningless. You can achieve the most satisfaction when you feel related to some greater purpose in life, something greater than yourself.

Thomas Carlyle
Nothing builds self-esteem and self-confidence like accomplishment.

Charles De Gaulle
Nothing great will ever be achieved without great men, and men are great only if they are determined to be so.

Source: Simran Khurana, about.com Guide
http://quotations.about.com/cs/inspirationquotes/a/Achievements11.htm

Questions

For each of the 9 quotes above, write the inference you believe the writer is implying and give a specific example of each meaning from your own life.

Wilma Rudolph

_____

_____

_____

_____

Dag Hammarskjöld

_____

_____

_____

_____

John Wooden

_____

_____

_____

_____

Ernest Hemingway

_____

_____

_____

_____

General George Smith Patton, Jr.

_____

_____

_____

_____

William Blake

_____

_____

_____

_____

Denis Waitley

_____

_____

_____

_____

Thomas Carlyle

_____

_____

_____

_____

Charles De Gaulle

_____

_____

_____

_____

Visual Image **READING 5**

Directions: Look closely at the picture. Then answer the questions below.

1. What details do you notice in the picture?

_____

_____

_____

2. What do the red arrow and boxes remind you of?

_____

_____

_____

3. What do you notice about the people on the red arrow?

_____

_____

_____

4. What can you infer about the people in the image?

_____

_____

_____

5. Write a caption for this image.

_____

_____

_____

Text Credits

Chapter 1

Hansen, Randall S. "Choosing a College Major: How to Chart Your Ideal Path" from *Quintessential Careers*, May 22, 2010. Copyright © 2010 by Randall S. Hansen. Reprinted with permission.

Kirberger, Kimberley. "College Talk" from *Chicken Soup for the College Soul*, Edited by Jack Canfield, Mark Victor Hansen, Kimberly Kirberger, and Dan Clark. Copyright © by John T. Canfield and Hansen & Hansen LLC. Reprinted with the permission of The Permissions Company, Inc., on behalf of Health Communications, Inc. www.hcibooks.com.

Rockler-Galden, Naomi. "High School Versus College Life: A Freshman Year Guide to Different Student Academic Expectations" from Suite101.com, April 23, 2007. Copyright © 2007 by Naomi Rockler-Galden. Reprinted with permission of the author.

Chapter 2

Dictionary.com. Definitions of "predict," "subscription," "sympathize," "incredible," "solace," and "antidepressant" from Dictionary.com and *The Random House Webster's Unabridged Dictionary*. Copyright © Random House, Inc.

Gulley, Philip. "Exercise and Other Dirty Words" from *Porch Talk*. Copyright © 2007 by Philip Gulley. Reprinted by permission of HarperCollins Publishers.

Jegtvig, Shereen. "How to Lose Weight" from ABOUT.COM. Copyright © Shereen Jegtvig (http://GUIDESITE .about.com). Reprinted by permission of About, Inc. which can be found online at www.about.com. All rights reserved.

Mishori, Dr. Ranit. "How Safe Are Cellphones?" from PARADE Magazine, March 21, 2010. Copyright © 2010 by Dr. Ranit Mishori. Reprinted with permission. All rights reserved.

Neergaard, Lauran. "Your Own Brain Can Sabotage Success" from JOURNAL & COURIER, January 4, 2011, p. A4. Copyright © 2011 by The Associated Press. Reprinted with permission of The YGS Group.

Waehner, Paige. "Change Your Exercise Vocabulary." Copyright © 2011 by Paige Waehner (http://exercise.about .com). Used with permission of About, Inc. which can be found online at www.about.com. All rights reserved.

Chapter 3

Carlson, Richard, Ph.D. Excerpt from *Don't Sweat the Small Stuff for Teens*. Copyright © 2000 by Richard Carlson, Ph.D. Reprinted by permission of Hyperion. All rights reserved.

Dictionary.com. Definition of "comprehension" from Dictionary.com and *The Random House Webster's Unabridged Dictionary*. Copyright © Random House, Inc.

Ferrucci, Piero. Excerpt from "Preface" from *The Power of Kindness*, Foreword by the Dalai Lama, Translated by Vivian Reid Ferrucci. Copyright © 2006 by Piero Ferrucci. Translation copyright 2006 by Vivian Reid Ferrucci. Used by permission of Jeremy P. Tarcher, an imprint of Penguin Group (USA) Inc.

McGraw, Dr. Phil. *Escaping the Anger Prison*, www.drphil.com. Copyright © 2009 Peteski Productions, Inc. Reprinted by permission.

Moore, Natalie Y. "Rule of Thumbs: Love in the Age of Texting" from *The Washington Post*, September 16, 2007. Copyright © 2007 by Natalie Y. Moore. Reprinted with permission of the author.

Pease, Alan and Pease, Barbara. Excerpts and illustrations from *The Definitive Book of Body Language*. Copyright © 2004 by Alan Pease. Used by permission of Bantam Books, a division of Random House, Inc.

Chapter 4

Chapter 5

Casey, Tina. "U.S. Army Dips a Toe In Wind Power Waters" from CLEANTECHNIA, July 18, 2010. Copyright © 2010 by Important Media. Reprinted with permission.

Dobransky, Megan. "Nike Uses Old Magazines for New Shoes" from EARTH911.com, January 5, 2011. Copyright © 2011 by Megan Dobransky. Reprinted with permission. www.earth911.org

"Don't Blame Ronald for Kids' Weight" from JOURNAL & COURIER, May 23, 2011. Copyright © 2011 by The Associated Press. Reprinted with permission of The YGS Group.

Norberg, John. "Sorting Your Inbox Can Be a Huge Chore" from JOURNAL & COURIER, September 27, 2009, D1. Copyright © 2009 by The Associated Press. Reprinted with permission of The YGS Group.

Pollan, Michael. "Eat Food: Food Defined" from *In Defense of Food*. Copyright © 2008 by Michael Pollan. Used by permission of The Penguin Press, a division of the Penguin Group (USA) Inc.

Zalman, Amy, Ph.D. "Religious Terrorism" from ABOUT.COM. Copyright © Amy Zalman (http://GUIDESITE .about.com). Reprinted by permission of About, Inc. which can be found online at www.about.com. All rights reserved.

Chapter 9

Benedict, Jeff. "The Little Engine That Could" from *The Book That Changed My Life*, Edited by Roxanne J. Coady and Joy Johannessen. Copyright © 2006 by Roxanne J. Coady. Used by permission of Gotham Books, an imprint of the Penguin Group (USA) Inc.

Bombeck, Erma. Excerpt by Erma Bombeck. Copyright © by Erma Bombeck Estate. Reprinted by permission of The Aaron Priest Literary Agency.

"Cisneros Bio" from http://www.gale.com. Copyright © 1984 by Gale, a part of Cengage Learning, Inc. Reproduced by permission. www.cengage.com/permissions

Cooper, Ilene. Excerpt from *Up Close: Oprah Winfrey*. Copyright © 2007 by Ilene Cooper. Used by permission of Penguin Group (USA) Inc. www.penguin.com

Dungy, Tony with Nathan Whitaker. "What Does It Take To Be a Modern-Day Hero?" from *Quiet Strength A Memoir: The Principles, Practices, & Priorities of a Winning Life*. Copyright © 2007 by Tony Dungy. Reprinted with permission of Tyndale House Publishers, Inc. All rights reserved.

Khurana, Simran. "Motivational Achievement Quotes" from ABOUT.COM. Copyright © Simran Khurana (http:// GUIDESITE.about.com). Reprinted by permission of About, Inc. which can be found online at www.about.com. All rights reserved.

Maxwell, John C. *Attitude 101: What Every Leader Needs to Know*. Copyright © 2003 Thomas Nelson Inc. Reprinted by permission of Thomas Nelson Inc. Nashville, Tennessee. All rights reserved.

Wilkinson, Spencer Jr. "Dr. Monica Mayer" by Spencer Wilkinson Jr., from *Listening Is an Act of Love* by David Isay. Copyright © 2007 by Sound Portraits Productions, Inc. Used by permission of The Penguin Press, a division of Penguin Group (USA) Inc.

Photo Credits

Index